LAY IT
on the LINE

LAY IT
on the LINE

A BACKSTAGE PASS
TO ROCK STAR ADVENTURE,
CONFLICT AND TRIUMPH

Rik Emmett

Published by ECW Press
665 Gerrard Street East
Toronto, Ontario, Canada M4M 1Y2
416-694-3348 / info@ecwpress.com

Editor for the press: Michael Holmes
Copy editor: Crissy Calhoun
Cover design: Jessica Albert
Cover photograph by John Rowlands

To the best of his abilities, the author has related experiences, places, people, and organizations from his memories of them. In order to protect the privacy of others, he has, in some instances, changed the names of certain people and details of events and places.

LIBRARY AND ARCHIVES CANADA CATALOGUING
IN PUBLICATION

Title: Lay it on the line : a backstage pass to rock star adventure, conflict and Triumph / Rik Emmett

Names: Emmett, Rik, author.

Identifiers: Canadiana (print) 20230228623 | Canadiana (ebook) 2023022976X

ISBN 978-1-77041-628-4 (softcover)
ISBN 978-1-77852-182-9 (ePub)
ISBN 978-1-77852-183-6 (PDF)
ISBN 978-1-77852-184-3 (Kindle)

Subjects: LCSH: Emmett, Rik. | LCSH: Rock musicians—Canada—Biography. | LCSH: Guitarists—Canada—Biography. | LCSH: Triumph (Musical group)

Classification: LCC ML419.E54 A3 2023 | DDC 782.42166092—dc23

This book is funded in part by the Government of Canada. *Ce livre est financé en partie par le gouvernement du Canada.* We acknowledge the support of the Canada Council for the Arts. *Nous remercions le Conseil des arts du Canada de son soutien.* We acknowledge the funding support of the Ontario Arts Council (OAC), an agency of the Government of Ontario. We also acknowledge the support of the Government of Ontario through the Ontario Book Publishing Tax Credit, and through Ontario Creates.

PRINTED AND BOUND IN CANADA   PRINTING: FRIESENS   5 4 3 2 1

MIX
Paper from
responsible sources
FSC® C016245

*Like all of my creative work throughout my whole
professional life, this book is dedicated to Jeannette Ann.*

It's also dedicated to:

*Family and friends, who loved me with toleration,
indulgence, and encouragement.*

*Fans, who aided and abetted decades of
my crimes and misdemeanours.*

*Artists, especially songwriters and guitarists,
who inspired and motivated me.*

*Collegial faculty peers and countless students, who
rewarded me with engaging honesty and sincere work
ethic. You all kept reminding me: Student for Life.*

*And finally, to strangers who make it through
this book and, in the end, grant that the time and
energy it took to write it all down was worth the time
and energy it took for them to read it.
Thanks. I'll take it.*

CONTENTS

INTRODUCTION

I try to find the kind of truth that only time will tell.
It's a higher education but I'm learnin' all my lessons well.

— "BANG ON," 1992

L ay it on the line. But what's *it*?
Creativity was, and still is, *it* for me. It's the singular explanation, the hook upon which I hang my hat, the focused reason for it all. Creativity is my way — my compass, my journey, and my means of transport. That's the truth, and I really did bet my life on it, over and over again.

It is also *play*. The play's the thing: one man, in his time, plays many parts. That's also my truth, in a Shakespearean nutshell, and I put it out there and bet my life on it.

So, this is *it* — memoir, autobiography, anecdotes, stories within the story, insights, and perspectives on my many roles.

Life is a mysterious gift of the physical, intellectual, and spiritual — a parade of sensation and emotion that delivers confrontations with the beasts of human nature. My life has always had quite the psychological gumbo, parboiling away. The spotlight became an addiction that fed my self-worth, and it wasn't until I retired that I finally outgrew it. Yet here I am writing a memoir — trading one kind of spotlight for another.

Allow me to issue the standard disclaimer: our minds play stupid human tricks with our recollections. We transpose, integrate, edit, and create composites. I tried my best here to give it to you straight, but time makes us all unreliable witnesses. Mea culpa.

I was never in it for the sex and drugs . . . ah, but the *rock and roll*. I was *definitely* in it for the play of it all, for the love of music. Whenever that became obscured or got trumped, I began to lose interest — then chafe. Being a rock star was simply a gig, a character to inhabit. But what a gig it was: a catalytic door-opener leading to other adventures. These are the stories I've chosen to tell.

This is *it*.

IT'S ONLY ROCK AND ROLL, BUT I LIVED IT

I will not be a puppet — I cannot play it safe
I give myself away with a blind and simple faith.

— "ORDINARY MAN," 1981

S ome things only a rock star can tell you. I know how it feels to be
in the bowels of another arena, night after night, walking from the
limo past the massive tractor-trailers at the loading bay into the cavernous
building — a monument to the rich and powerful network of corporate
real estate and franchise majority shareholders, in business with media
chains and distribution companies — past the lesser rungs, the overseers
of parking lots and concession stands, down to the union workers and
working-class stagehands, ushers, and vendors. Tonight I'm part of the
draw, the ticket. Tomorrow it's the NBA, then the NHL, then a Disney on
Ice show, then a rap star or a country act. And so it goes. If your luck holds,
maybe you'll return every eighteen months for the four or five glory years
of your career. Marquee acts — our era's jongleurs and court jesters —
come and go, while the real estate stays in the nobility's hands generating

the wealth that is power. The system is designed to deliver fresh goods: as a performer, you're simply a commodity on their stock exchange.

This is how a gig feels: the sound makes lights dance, and the lights in turn make the music swell and glow and burn in a dreamworld of shadows and fire. Spectacular theatrical pyrotechnics — smoke and mirrors — create an intensity on an epic scale. It's colossal and you get to be heroic. *But only for ninety minutes.* The other twenty-two and a half hours are all about life support for The Show. Deviate from the itinerary at your own peril, at the risk of failing that aforementioned network of the rich and powerful, or your partners in this band business, or the guys on the buses and trucks, or the fans in the seats, who bring *their* expectations to bear.

The game dictates that the carnival of bang will move on, leaving you behind as demographics shift and profits drop. Rock stars eventually arrive at this knowledge: the whimpering disappointment of general disinterest. (But let's not get ahead of ourselves.)

There were true joys in being a rock star. My success as a musician came in stages. At first, it enabled me to afford to move out of my parents' house and in with my girl, Jeannette; then get married, buy a house, and start a family; then *more* kids. Success as an artist meant being able to provide a better life for my parents, my brother and his family, as well as college educations for my children. All of it added up to a great deal of happiness and pride. Even though I often failed to prioritize them on my calendar, family always outranked my own pursuits as a musician, writer, or minor-league celebrity. But success also breeds friction between career choices and creative fulfillment. Worse — between career and family needs.

The success I had as a commercial artist allowed me, later in my life, to make classical guitar and jazz records. I'm a west end Toronto boy who has jammed with George Benson, Steve Morse, Steve Vai, Alex Lifeson, Liona Boyd, Ed Bickert, Ted Nugent, Sammy Hagar, Sal Salvador, Bruce Cockburn, Ian Thomas, Randy Bachman, Nathan East, and Jerry Jeff Walker. I got to make indie albums with Dave Dunlop, Michael Shotton, Pavlo, and Oscar Lopez. I never would have been invited to become a college professor (a gig I truly enjoyed) if not for my success in rock music. It certainly wasn't *only* about my musicianship, which is realistic, not falsely modest, because in my case, it's impossible to separate the musician from the career. There were lots of choices made for commercial success, not musicianship. Later, that reversed, and I made decisions purely for the sake of artistic fulfillment. It balanced out okay in the end. And my creative life goes on.

The pursuit of creative writing — songs, columns, essays, course curricula, lesson plans, prose, poetry — expanded my inner life and my vision of the universe. It wasn't always wonderful and happy, but that's life: sometimes it's messy, painful, and complicated. Writing has helped me cope with some of that, and it's brought me perspectives I never would have had as just a musician. Writing this memoir was in a way like a cathartic unburdening in a confessional.

On balance, the joys far outweigh the sorrows. It's only rock and roll, but I lived it.

Anyone and everyone who's had a career in the music biz has a unique story to tell, because no two careers are the same. The music business chose me, as much as I chased it. It's the only life I know, and I can't pretend that some things didn't happen, and I haven't forgotten lessons learned from the experience. That school of hard knocks made me somewhat cynical. Still — romantically, but just as realistically — I thank my lucky stars that I got to live a life where creative play was my work; I never had to routinely punch a time clock or drive in rush hour. A different kind of work ethic imprinted on me.

Part of the gig here is to offer some insight into an artist's process. You choose a performer's life and the show must go on: folks don't pay to see you be less than great. They want 100 percent but prefer 110: they love to see the pain, physical and mental, as you encounter your boundaries, your limits. Drama engenders drama queens. But it also wears down the troupers until they're running on fumes. Or drugs. Or therapy. Or all of the above.

Maybe you'll choose to be in a band, because that's such a cool thing — a private little club that everyone wishes they could be a part of, or witness as a fly on the wall. For me, the all-time coolest club *ever* was the Beatles. Their collective roller-coaster ride lasted all of thirteen years.

Hey — *I* was also in a band for thirteen years. And I couldn't take it anymore either. I wanted more control and autonomy of my own life, for the sake of my marriage, family, and mental health. I had artistic differences with Mike Levine and Gil Moore even *before* I agreed to join them. We all knew it, addressed it, and accepted it. Arguably, it was part of the chemistry, the push and pull, that gave our band a dramatic charisma as we gained public notoriety. As the young ambitions of our all-for-one, one-for-all, Three Musketeers idealism eventually gave way to individualized lifestyle choices, we were forced to confront the very nature of our beasts. And how does one deal with beastly human nature?

Over a lifetime of constant dealings with business associates — agents, managers, colleagues, the folks who populate showbiz — I kept negotiating with my own career ambitions. When I got to my mid-sixties and couldn't handle the stress anymore, any ambition that might lead to anxiety, conflict, or tension was no longer worth it.

I was finally learning how to say no.

Hindsight tells other tales: how I would burn up all my fuel chasing my aspirations, crash, and then, in show-must-go-on fashion, get up and back in the race. But the race causes damage, wear and tear. Life got heartbreakingly hard. There was a price that my wife and children paid. I'll lay *that* on the line in these pages.

In my optimism, I never anticipated how shallow and dumbed down our culture would widely become. During the COVID-19 pandemic, our world grew too fearful, too pessimistic, too unimaginative. I get disheartened by the unenlightened yokes of all stripes of fundamentalist religions, which generate so much regression, and by the people who seek and hold power yet fail to embrace the creative potential of liberal arts and sciences. Despite the grind of ignorance, I still have a (tiny) glowing ray of optimism that eventually reason will carry the flow of our human history; that war, disease, poverty, famine, and ecological destruction will be overcome and managed by a more universal global vision. I can't explain that rationally. I look back in amazement at my own naïveté and the sheer dumb luck that arose out of my "blind and simple faith." I can't believe I still have some of it — but I do.

Miraculously, I still retain a flicker of hope that my creative work can counter my disillusion.

At the core of showbiz, we're just out to give people a good time, provide recreation. But my work in this life also remains a search for personal balance. I'm as much a product of sorrow and disappointment as I am a grateful husband and family man who had a rock star career. Obliged to my cynicism as much as my positivity, I've tried to be as aware of my humility as my ambition. In the end, the way we live our lives reveals the depth of our own questioning and understanding.

Curiously, a rock and roll life led me to that.

Let's see how it all got started.

ORIGIN STORIES

Is it fate or random chance? How can I decide?

— "SOMEBODY'S OUT THERE," 1986

M y family didn't have any extra money, so there were no musical instruments in our modest, rented, middle-class home. My first instrument was a yellow plastic banana harmonica, and around age seven or so I figured out how to play simple tunes like "Oh! Susanna" and "Red River Valley." By 1963, at the age of ten, I'd been singing in church and school choirs as a first soprano for a few years, so to reinforce the emerging musical talent, my granddad rescued a used 1940s catalogue guitar from dusty obscurity in his sister's closet and dropped it off at 94 Abbott Avenue in west Toronto. It had a hula dancer and a few palm trees stencilled on the cracked face, with a braided skinny lanyard rope as its shoulder strap. The action was ridiculously high, with fret ends like razor wire and crusty old steel strings as thick as telephone cable — but that gift set the main catalyst of my life into motion. I started picking melodies out right away. Here's where the plot thickens.

I am what's called cross-dominant: *dextrosinistral*. Not a pure south-paw, not ambidextrous — I do things of fine motor control with my right hand (write, eat with a fork) and gross motor control (feats of strength) with my left hand (chuck a baseball, swing a hammer). Ten people in one hundred are left-handed, but only one in one hundred have cross-dominance. Some might say freak; some might say outlier. Some just said, "Ricky, stop playing road hockey and come in for dinner."

I won eight free guitar lessons in the spring of '64 by answering a skill-testing question pamphlet from the Regency School of Music, located just west of Jane and Bloor Streets, one block from the end of the TTC streetcar loop on the second floor above a Household Finance storefront. When I showed up for those lessons, I was strumming with my left hand, emulating Paul McCartney. (This was just after the historic February 9, 1964, appearance of the Beatles on *The Ed Sullivan Show*, a tipping point for thousands of budding rock stars, including this one.)

Again the plot twists. My guitar teacher was a fellow named Jack Arsenault — by some fluke of the universe, *a leftie who played right-handed*. He turned my guitar around the other way on my lap. I protested the awkwardness, but he said, "Trust me, in a month you'll outpace all your rightie pals, with your strong left hand on the fretboard." He also informed my parents that left-handed guitars were rare and much more expensive. That was the clincher. In any case, Jack was right: my cross-dominant brain wiring made me perfectly suited for the techniques of right-handed guitar playing.

The pure serendipity of a rescue guitar and a cross-dominant teacher set me on a path toward my future. (And if you doubt that cross-dominant tendencies give lefties an advantage playing guitar right-handed, check the bios of Johnny Winter, Duane Allman, Waddy Wachtel, Paul Simon, Ritchie Blackmore, Steve Morse, Elvis Costello, Joe Perry, Mark Knopfler, Gary Moore, Noel Gallagher, Billy Corgan . . .)

My mom had been taking me to our Alhambra United Church choir practices on Thursday nights after dinner since I was seven. I sang in school choirs from grade three (age eight) on. In fact, in the springs of '62 and '63, I sang on stage at the world-famous Massey Hall in Toronto in the Kiwanis city-wide public school choir. I also played violin (poorly, I grant) throughout high school. So, I'm obviously not a self-taught musician, but as a guitarist, despite my early start in Mel Bay grade one with Jack Arsenault, and then a short stint at Humber College in the fall semester of 1972 with private lessons from Peter Harris, I've mostly been a self-starter.

My road toward a career began in basement bands. What I really wanted was to write my own songs and be a Beatle. Some guy reading guitar charts off a music stand behind Lawrence Welk had a cool enough gig, but the Beatles had girls screaming. *That* was a hormonal tsunami.

I was always a total sponge for guitar stuff and didn't exercise too much discriminating taste. I credit *Guitar Player* magazine for much of my guitar education. Once Triumph had risen to widespread recognition, I'd still make the occasional pilgrimage to the home of Peter Harris to jam, talk guitar, and drink some wine — essentially absorbing free lessons from a master. He gave me copies of cassette tapes he'd made of his own private lessons with Joe Pass and Lenny Breau.

I always kept up my subscription to *Guitar Player*. Probably thanks to a combination of willpower and lucky coincidence, I ended up as a feature columnist in that magazine for over a dozen years.

I had a bunch of part-time and/or summer seasonal jobs in my life. In order:

- bicycle delivery boy for a drugstore
- pin boy in a bowling alley
- floor mat vacuum guy in a car wash (that lasted all of one day)
- camp counsellor
- public school teaching assistant (mostly in special ed classes)
- gym-rat "cop" for an after-hours drop-in centre at a high school
- music teacher (both hired for someone else's program and on my own, privately)

While still in high school, I became a jobbing musician, working the occasional one-nighter here and there — playing school and recreation centre dances, then weddings and bars.

I'd always been a jock. I *loved* sports and games and played only one way — competing all out. I wasn't built to take the grind. Serious injuries began when I was fourteen, and for the next three years, the damages compounded to the point that I had to face reality: my body was incapable of sustaining my ambitions to become an elite athlete. Torn ligaments in my right knee at age seventeen led me to a full mental commitment to music in the fall of 1971 at eighteen, because I didn't want to have to *work* for a living. I wanted a life where I could *play*. Modest gig opportunities were coming at me, and I was developing some of my own — indicators to take a calculated leap of faith. In a way, it was as if a life in music was choosing me. A career in showbiz is often an exercise of trying to bang square pegs into round holes; it's so much harder when your pegs don't fit the tiny holes that are too few and far between.

At the end of high school, my drummer friend Chet Paskowski pulled me into a gig three nights a week playing in a kind of country and western bar band (guitar and amp provided). I saved up my money from that gig and bought a sharp second-hand grey pinstripe suit from Chet; a Fender Telecaster guitar and Vibrolux Reverb amp from the Long & McQuade store on Yonge Street in Toronto; paid my dues, got my union card, and started playing Jewish weddings and bar mitzvahs.

Round pegs were fitting into round holes. I was on my way toward . . . something.

Roots: Teachers

I've been very fortunate to learn from some extraordinary teachers, picking up a lot of stuff, even if only by osmosis. Certainly, my parents were both sensitive, compassionate people — especially my mom, who encouraged my artistic streak. My dad was a conservative guy who valued duty, honour, obligation, and responsibility, balancing the home front. He taught me how to throw and catch a baseball in the backyard, the whole *Field of Dreams* thing. I was well-adjusted; my high school pals would joke about how it was *Leave It to Beaver* at my house, starring my straight parents as Ward and June Cleaver. (It was. They were.)

In '61 and '62, my class accelerated through grades three, four, and five in two years with a teacher named Florence Herchmer. On the cusp of retiring, in her sturdy orthopedic black shoes and cat's-eye glasses with a neck chain, she was *phenomenal*, developing my love for reading, art, and creativity as well as my penchant for spelling, grammar, and writing stories. She encouraged singing and putting on skits and plays, and she was the one who selected me for the city-wide choir that sang at Massey Hall.

My beaming music teacher and choir leader in grades seven and eight was Mr. Mayben, followed by my high school music teacher Hans Gasteiger, a violinist and no-nonsense orchestra conductor. I learned invaluable stuff about how to run rehearsals. We both had to cope with the fact that guitar techniques did not translate to a violin's classical bowing and finger vibrato. But I got to play electric guitar for the high school band's *Jesus Christ Superstar* medley, as well as harmonica for Aaron Copland's "Hoedown" one year for the orchestra. (I couldn't play my violin, as my right arm was in a cast from a football injury.)

My high school also had some terrific English teachers: Dorothy Cameron in grade nine, who encouraged my writing, and Margaret McLean in grade eleven, whose straight-arrow, no B.S. insight came with sensitivity. History teachers were always challenging thinkers, providing context and perspective.

Most memorably, my good-hearted grade twelve math teacher Andrew Monk (who was also an assistant football and track coach) called me in privately after class to inform me that I'd flunked and had to go to summer school. But I already had a job lined up as a camp counsellor, as well as teaching some guitar lessons and playing gigs. I floated my intention to pick up the necessary credit via night school at some hazy point in the future. He frowned, gave that a few seconds of consideration, then made me an offer: if I promised never to take the subject of math ever again, for as long as I lived, he'd graciously and quietly give me a passing grade of fifty-one for the credit. We shook hands on it, and ever since, I've gratefully kept his good faith.

In the spring of '72, Peter Harris auditioned and admitted me into the Humber College music program for the fall. His belief went a long way in assuaging my insecurities and doubts. Long after I'd dropped out of the course, he was always an encouraging mentor. (Pivotally, he gave me his copy of *The Inner Game of Music* by Barry Green.) The last time we saw each other, Peter was battling stage four cancer. He'd been a great teacher — not just about how to play, but even more about how to think, how to approach the arts, and how to wrestle with my gifts. He personified dignity and grace, teaching me the last great lesson he could: how to face mortality with class. We toasted that.

During my life, I learned from students I taught, and athletes I coached. I had rewarding collaboration with fellow faculty members, but in particular, I coached baseball alongside some very fine men: in Lorne Park with Frank Giannone and the late Jim Wallace; then, after my son moved to the Mississauga North Tigers, Jack Carrajola, Don Moroney, and Lino Condotta. They were ethical straight arrows — dudes who had *The Right Stuff*. Coaching baseball was one of the great joys of my life, in the decade from 1994 to 2004 (Please see photo section at the end of the book).

The river runs, and you try to let it flow "within you and without you," as George Harrison put it. Students and athletes — always, my wife and children — have been teaching me. Far too often, I feared leaving myself vulnerable, but there's an infinite supply of things to learn, if you'll just open yourself up. That's necessary to move forward, to play.

Influences

My eclecticism was always a source of tension — first in the Triumph days, then with my management, marketing, and agency representation throughout the balance of my career. I couldn't restrict myself to a narrow commercial focus. I was a by-product of my inclinations and my heterogeneous roots from my hometown jobbing gigs. Trial by fire forged my musical DNA.

My influences were varied. As with almost all players my age, the earliest and most influential force was the Beatles. The British Invasion brought me the Yardbirds alumni Eric Clapton, Jeff Beck, and Jimmy Page. Clapton was probably the biggest electric blues influence on me — especially because of *The Beano Album* (with John Mayall and the Bluesbreakers) and then Cream — even more so than Hendrix, though the two were contemporary for me during that era. Clapton's liquid style of melodic, pentatonic phrasing and tone spoke to me more than Jimi's psychedelia.

Later, Jimmy Page's Zeppelin stuff was hugely influential, and Triumph was a Zep cover band in its very early bar band days. It's impossible to overlook Hendrix (who was influencing Clapton, Townshend, and every guitar hero from then on), but in my high school years, the phrasing and style of Ritchie Blackmore became a stronger personal influence. At that time, I also learned the "Handy" solos of Wishbone Ash's Ted Turner and Andy Powell, note for note. By the time high school was winding down, my friends, contemporaries, and I had become huge fans of prog bands: Focus, Gentle Giant, Genesis, King Crimson. My number one was always Yes, with guitarist Steve Howe the heroic role model and biggest influence on seventeen- to twenty-one-year-old Rik Emmett — again, evident in my eclecticism. Those bands created a stylistic mashup that I loved.

Along the way, others influenced me very directly. In my early teenage years, I had a Julian Bream LP of Bach pieces and a Segovia album of Sor and Tarrega studies. (Bream holds the place in my heart for the greatest classical guitar recording: *Julian Bream Plays Granados and Albeniz, Music of Spain Vol. 5*.) By the time I was in college, jazzers Joe Pass, Wes Montgomery, and Kenny Burrell had also won me over. In between, singer-songwriters like Paul Simon, James Taylor, and Jimmy Webb were in my repertoire for campfires and coffeehouse gigs. I'd also worked up a half-assed version by ear of "Malagueña" after watching Roy Clark on *Hee Haw* — which went over well during solo gigs on my nylon string guitar. (I had a factory-second Yairi, purchased at Whaley, Royce & Co. on Yonge Street in the summer of '69 for $150. It's the classical guitar on "Moonchild" from the first Triumph album, and apart from some fretboard wear, it's still a fine instrument in my collection to this day.)

I never took classical guitar lessons. During my one semester of study at Humber, my slapdash self-taught fingerstyle method evolved under Peter Harris's influence; he was an exceptional fingerstyle player in the Lenny Breau style, though I could never hope to reach his level.

My roots were church hymns, Christmas carols, simple folk songs, MOR pop (my mom's radio preferences), rock and roll, and Bob Dylan. As an electrified teen, British blues led me back to its Chicago roots. In my grade nine homeroom class, I had the good fortune to team up with a guitar buddy, Lou Muccilli, and we shared our discoveries and kicked each other's butts. In grade eleven, we hooked up with a bass player in our school named Rik Weiditch (yes, he also spelled his first name that way!) — also a huge stroke of luck, since he had an extensive album collection in his basement hangout room on Indian Road. He turned us on to that *Beano* LP, and Mike Bloomfield with the Paul Butterfield band, amongst dozens of other vinyl gems. We gained an understanding of where the Yardbirds alumni had mined the riffs of Albert, Freddie, and B.B. King, Willie Dixon, Muddy Waters, and John Lee Hooker. Rik W.'s taste became foundational to my own. Blues always takes me right back to my high school days, cutting my teeth in basement bands, with the same kind of roots that gave birth to the Stones, Led Zep, and Jeff Beck. Blues and R & B was strong in the Toronto scene due to its geographic proximity to Chicago and Detroit. Tours would often hit Toronto, with James Cotton or Junior Wells and Buddy Guy. I recall seeing many great blues musicians in my later teenaged years. Honestly, though, I dug the blues simply for the chance to strap on an electric guitar and let 'er rip.

The first gigs I played were with high school basement bands at a church, school, or YMCA dance, where we'd get to keep the door, maybe making $25 in total. For those gigs, three guys from the band would go to the Long & McQuade store at Yonge and Bloor and rent a Traynor Voice Master PA setup — one head, two columns, an Electro-Voice 664 microphone, and a mic stand — then carry it on the subway to our rehearsal space. Either Weiditch's grandfather or my dad would load up their car with the entire band's gear, PA columns sticking out from the trunk, and drive to those rare bookings.

I once played my own high school cafeteria at Bloor Collegiate in a blues band we called Flint, which rehearsed in the basement of the West End YMCA in Toronto (which also held Thursday night open mic coffee houses, where I played). During this era, as previously mentioned, I was jobbing occasionally with drummer Chet Paskowski on weekends in Jon Kirk and the Amberjacks at the Robin Hood Inn out in Pickering. That was an accordion, guitar, and drums trio — all over the place stylistically. I'd sing a Beatles tune or two in the first set. Joanie, the platinum-blonde accordionist, could play a wide range of middle-of-the-road stuff, and then Jon would come up on stage for the second set and do country songs like "Green, Green Grass of Home" and "Tie a Yellow Ribbon." As the big show moment, he'd dance with his wife, Tammy, singing the song of the same name to her. Pure non-union hokum, Chet and I occasionally smoked hash out in the parking lot between sets. I got paid $60 a week in cash; I saved up and joined the union local 149.

After the Amberjacks gig, there wasn't enough jobbing work to satisfy my parents about room and board, and my goal became finding a short-term job that would earn me enough money to attend Humber College's music program in the fall of '72. A family friend knew a supervisor for the Toronto Board of Education, and in January of '72 I became a teaching assistant in the special education classes at Lord Dufferin Public School in Regent Park. I also took on a part-time evening job as a gym rat in my old high school's drop-in centre, essentially as a babysitter who got to practise a lot of basketball foul shots, making sure nothing got stolen, no one got seriously injured, and the place didn't burn down. I also auditioned successfully for the Bill Berle Orchestra, a jobbing act on the Jewish wedding circuit in Toronto. Bill was the music director at the Royal Alexandra Theatre, and his son Paul had a more contemporary bar mitzvah band, so I started getting a bit of weekend work with them as well.

My Humber College music adventure in the fall of '72 lasted all of one semester. Academically disinclined, my theory and harmony grades were terrible. I failed basic keyboard because we'd never had one in our house, and over the eleven weeks of the term, I didn't practise enough. I could play my guitar by ear and read chord charts, but I was (and still am) a horrible sight-reader. Most of all, I was *not* motivated to drag my carcass (with guitar case and gym bag stuffed with books) on the bus up to the north campus of Humber College. The two-and-a-half-hour daily commute was not for me, especially to a program where other guitarists who could sight-read fly droppings were destined for future careers as studio musicians and jobbers.

Why try to force my way into a career based on academics? None of the guitarists in that program could sing or write songs the way I could. My instincts were telling me that it would be a greater mistake if I didn't bet on my own creativity and talent. What some might see as risky seemed logical and natural to me — a choice that suited me best.

Intuition and ego are sometimes selfish and misguided, but I thought I could play the game with the cards already in my hand — laying *that* on the line, as it were.

Starting in January of '73 — back jobbing at weddings and bar mitzvahs, still living in my parents' home, building connections to other musicians who could find me some work with a few lounge singers — I worked on my chops. Chet and I envisioned starting up a Holiday Inn–style show band, and that fall we began auditioning musicians — among them a bass player from Winnipeg named Glenn Stewart. He didn't dig what we were trying to get started, but he pulled me aside and said, "There's another audition happening for a new band backing a singer named Justin Paige, who's making a big career shift into glam rock behind his management and a Capitol Records deal. He already plays a bar circuit from Thunder Bay to Dartmouth. Are you interested in going to that audition with me?" I said, "Hell yeah."

Glenn and I got the gig. It was a showbiz act, and we were backing sidemen, all expected to wear outlandish stage clothes or costumes. The singer, Justin, was the guy with the record deal and his name on the marquee. His management had indeed secured a Capitol Records Canada deal, and they needed a revitalized band behind him to develop his repertoire, learn new songs (written and arranged specifically for the record by Joey Miller, an accomplished musical theatre style writer), tour for a while, then go into the studio. I started in early '74 at $150 a week and stayed with him until November of that year, by which time my pay had risen to a princely $175 a week. (This figure will come into play again later, in the summer of '75.)

I wore Alice Cooper–style makeup and entered a world where management directed discussions about repertoire choices and song arrangements to fit into the idea of image projection (album cover art, photo sessions) — it was all an entry-level tutorial for me on the way the game was played. I wasn't the front man, but I could see how he carried himself as a public commodity versus how he was as a private person, writing me my weekly paycheque, sometimes picking me up at my parents' house in his leased Monte Carlo (with his two Afghan dogs in the backseat, who had hairdos like his). I toured in the equipment van and paid some fascinating dues.

Justin's co-managers ran a successful hair-cutting franchise across the country. (One of them, Frank Angelo, became a founding business partner in MAC Cosmetics.) The act tried to build on the glam success that had arisen out of alternative bar scenes in big cities. There were two background singers, one of whom (Honora Doran, stage-named Rexie) was said to have toured with Dusty Springfield. We learned a bunch of bar band tunes (the band did its own dog's-breakfast set before Justin did his two show sets), and Justin's repertoire included Lou Reed's "Walk on the Wild Side," David Bowie's "Suffragette City," and Billy Joel's "Captain Jack." (Drug references were a big part of the culture.) The best moment of every night belonged to background singer Fran Cheslo; she did a cover of Stevie Wonder's "All in Love Is Fair," always killing it. Glenn Stewart wasn't the right fit and was quickly replaced. They liked me, though, in my stage makeup and costume, black tights and a wire-and-foam-stuffed white glove holding my crotch (Please see photo section at the end of the book). The band could always work, week in and out, because Justin Paige had a track record and reputation in the bar circuit. But I could see that the act's music lacked an artistic depth of character. Despite modest pay raises, I yearned to be in a band featuring prog rock and my own original writing.

I got to play on some recording sessions for the Justin Paige album; the first LP I ever played on came out in the late summer of '74. I was the electric rhythm guitarist on eight cuts of the bed tracks (plus one with an acoustic guitar part), but all overdub solos were handled by Alice Cooper's guitarist at the time, Dick Wagner, who was hired by the producer-engineer, Lee DeCarlo. It was disappointing not to get more of an opportunity to showcase my abilities, but Wagner's well-earned reputation and the politics of producer, management, and arranger (Joey Miller) played out well above my rookie status. I did get to do sessions with the great bassist Prakash John (hot off the Lou Reed *Sally Can't Dance* album sessions), working a few days at the beautiful Manta Sound studios in Toronto. Sadly, the album stiffed.

A green punk of twenty-one was playing six nights a week (with Saturday afternoon matinees) in the bars of Ontario, Quebec, and Nova Scotia, gaining some education and insight both on and off the bandstand. I tried magic mushrooms once, pulling an all-nighter in the dance clubs of Stanley Street. At the end of the week, I drove the gear rental van solo from Café de l'Est in Montreal to the Generator at Yonge and Eglinton in Toronto, rolling down Highway 401 on bald, splitting tires, watching the sunrise in my rear-view mirror — a truly nerve-racking experience. (The tires were so badly shot, I parked the truck at The Generator's loading doors at about seven a.m. and took the subway home to bed.)

In the fall of '74, another high school drummer friend named Denton Young was out of a steady gig and looking to get back into the scene. We cooked up a plan between us, held auditions, and found a great bass player named Chris Brockway (originally from Cornerbrook, Newfoundland) to round out our prog-slash-show-band trio concept. I gave my notice to Justin in October '74, playing out a few weeks of gigs into November.

As '74 became '75, Act III was born in the basement of the Rectory and Parish Hall of St. Anne's Church, where Denton's dad, the Reverend Canon George Young, was the minister. In a basement rehearsal space on Eglinton Avenue, Neill Dixon came and auditioned the band, then he and Steve Propas (of Solid Gold Records and Management) started booking us, and gigs began in the spring of '75. Dixon and Propas had a client list of B lounges all over the province, and Act III played venues like the Manatonna Hotel in Brockville, the Tri-Town Motor Inn in Haileybury, the Plaza Hotel in Cobourg, the Wallaceburg Inn, the Riviera Motor Inn in Windsor, the John Scott Hotel in St. Thomas, Yonge St. Station in Toronto, and the Spruce Villa in Whitby. On a warm spring night in Hull, Quebec, at the Green Door Room of the Chaudière Hotel, Chris Brockway lost his temper with Denton's leadership and quit. Denton and I replaced him with a bassist named Cory Turnbull, but it wasn't the same for me. When Mike Levine and Gil Moore came to scout me playing in Act III at the Hollywood on Queensway Avenue in Etobicoke in the summer of '75 and then offered me the chance to be in Triumph, I reluctantly decided to give my notice to Denton and go for it.

That career move didn't seem risky at the time because I had almost nothing to lose — except my friendship with Denton. Thankfully, he was too kind-hearted to hold it against me for long.

The Five Bands I Was in during Middle and High School

My very first band was with John and Jim Todd (guys I played soccer with), Stan Pus, and Murray Bone during grades eight and nine, in '66–67. We never really had a name, played in the Todds' basement, never got paid for anything, and only did one birthday party gig that I recall.

Next band was in grade ten — The Sunshine Incident — with Lou Muccilli, Peter Mantas, and me on guitars (none of us owned a bass guitar); Charlie Kresnick as our singer; and Bohdan Hluszko on drums (who went on to become the drummer for Prairie Oyster). We played in Charlie's basement on Lansdowne Avenue. We played one gig that I booked for us at a Runnymede United Church dance.

Next band — in grades eleven and twelve — was General Mudd with Lou Muccilli (guitar), Pat McGuire (drums), and Rik Weiditch (bass). We played a few school and church dances, including a Jesse Ketchum Public School Friday night concert down close to Yorkville. We made enough money from the door (25 cents a person) to buy a pizza afterwards. We also rehearsed at a couple of local churches: St. Martin's in the Fields Anglican Church on Glenlake Avenue and Alhambra United Church on Bloor Street, where we also played a dance (where no one danced except me).

In 1970 and '71, the band I was in was called Messiah with Denton Young (drums), Bob Petyhyrysch (keys), Lou Muccilli, and Rik Weiditch. (I was only the singer, no guitar.) We rehearsed in the basement of St. Anne's and did a gig at a York University common-room pub once. I was in a full leg cast from a football injury.

I also played in a blues band in '72 — billed as Flint, the lineup had Chet Paskowski on drums and Rik Weiditch on bass, and we added a sax player named Bruce Gorrie. Rehearsals were held at the West End YMCA, and we might have played a gig there once as well, for the door. We also played a dance at my own old high school, Bloor Collegiate, and got paid real money — probably a few hundred bucks.

FAMILY

Let the light that shines in your eyes shine on me,
let it shine forever . . .
we can build a dream together — now.

— "LET THE LIGHT," 1987

I was born at eleven p.m. on Friday, July 10, 1953, weighing in at seven pounds, twelve ounces at Toronto Western Hospital. The second son of Robert Gordon and Thelma Margaret, my birth was relatively routine, my arrival unexceptional. More than 108 billion members of our modern *Homo sapiens* species have inhabited this planet over fifty thousand years. Still, at times I feel like a freak of nature, and sometimes my life has been flat-out weird. (Maybe that's been true 108 billion times.)

After going through the exercise of bringing together this book, it certainly seems like ambition and good faith led to a lot of fortunate happenstance, flukes, and blind dumb luck. I'll take it. Thank you very much.

Let's begin at the beginnings.

The name *Emmet* can be of Hebrew origin, meaning *truth*. I've also seen a derivation of *Emmett* as German, meaning *powerful*. I suspect the German roots led to the Anglo-Saxon heritage in our family tree. But it bears mentioning that there were a lot of Irish Emmetts, including two brothers of note — one whose head ended up on an English pike for his insurrection, and the other, a lawyer who left for America and eventually became an enslaver and contributor to the American Revolution.

My two brothers have died without male heirs, and unless my son has a son, the surname *Emmett*, from our branch of the family tree, will pass into history.

In the nuclear family, I was something of an outlier, as the only blonde, blue-eyed relative was my paternal grandmother, Marjorie Grace (née Beesley). Born in Staffordshire, England, in 1901, she immigrated to Canada as a little girl with her mom, dad, and two older brothers, living on Lansdowne Avenue, north of Bloor Street in the neighbourhood now known as Wallace Emerson. Marjorie met her future husband, Gordon Neve Emmett, just after the First World War. At that time, Gordon's family resided on Alhambra Avenue, just south of Bloor, on the northern edge of the community now known as Roncesvalles.

My paternal grandfather Gordon (I got my middle name from him, as did my father) was born in Toronto, the youngest of eight siblings, with both teetotaling Presbyterian and Baptist culture in the clan. The Emmett Family Bible and Ancestry.com reveal that my white Anglo-Saxon Protestant privilege started in the servant and farm-labourer lower class of merry old England. Thomas Emmett was a gardener and a widower in Kingston, county of Surrey (Greater London), when he married Elizabeth Stuckey in 1841. Along came son Daniel William Emmett in 1842, and nineteen years later he married an English woman named Eliza Roberts. Nine months later, in August 1862, Daniel and Eliza had a boy named Harry Roberts Emmett, born in Lancashire.

Harry proved to be the real pioneering entrepreneur who fashioned a turning point in the family history. Harry's mother, Eliza, died eight years later. In 1871, his dad, Daniel, remarried Elizabeth Williams, who bore four children.

At twenty, Harry Roberts Emmett was following in his father's footsteps as a labourer when he married Mary Anne Neve in 1883 in Norfolk. Four years later, Harry and Mary and their first two children, Elton and three-month-old Eleanor, left England looking for a better life, immigrating to Canada on March 31, 1887, on the SS *Circassian* out of Liverpool, docking in Halifax on April 11, 1887. Harry was listed as a labourer on the arrival paperwork, and once established in Canada, he became primarily a master carpenter and a self-taught jack-of-all-trades, building houses. He prospered thanks to his Protestant work ethic and expected his children to do the same. He and Mary continued to have children — eight in total.

The runt of the litter, my (paternal) grandfather Gordon altered the last numeral of his 1899 birth certificate year into an *8*, so that he could enlist at age seventeen and follow his older brothers into the Canadian army in the First World War. His meticulous war record documentation shows that he sent $20 of his monthly paycheque home to his mother Mary, back on Alhambra Avenue. Gordon's war adventure was short-lived, because on September 30, 1918, forty-two days before the Germans surrendered, he was poisoned with shell gas, then spent two weeks stretchered at Dannes Camiers, before crossing back over the channel to Eastern General Hospital in Cambridge. Forty-one days later, he went to casualty clearing at Wokingham, then got shipped home for discharge on February 8, 1919.

After the First World War, craving his own fruit and vegetable garden, my great grandfather Harry Roberts sold the family starter home on Alhambra Avenue and bought a big chunk of acreage out on Laurel Avenue north of Bloor Street in Etobicoke, building his own house there. When the Depression hit, Harry and Mary sectioned off two lots and built more houses and gardens, spring-boarding some of their children into a measure of security during trying times. Lower class British labour was now moving on up into the Canadian middle class, as property owners.

Gordon soon followed his brother Elgin into the employ of Canadian Pacific Railway and Express, built up some savings, and married Marjorie Beesley in 1925. Their only child, my father, Robert Gordon, was born on the Ides of March, 1928. At first, the small family lived in a rented flat on Durie Street in west Toronto. My dad went to the local Presbyterian church for Sunday school. The Great Depression motivated a mid-1930s move to a house on one of Harry's sectioned lots on Laurel, where they could have their own garden, preserving cellar, and chicken shack. This is where my dad grew up, from childhood through adolescence and into manhood.

Life for Gordon, Marjorie, and their only child, Bob, was framed and coloured by the deprivations and rationing of the First World War, the Depression, and the Second World War. It was a life of duty and humble obligation, forging my father's character and outlook. He was conservative, stoic, cautious, only reacting when finally forced — never a man of ambitious action.

Grandpa Gordon, even after his war injury, was a lifelong smoker, and his health was never good. He died of a heart attack on November 25, 1965, at the age of sixty-six, when I was twelve years old. I remember my grandpa as a sad, burdened, earnest man, hospitalized for kidney and gall stones to go along with his damaged lungs. His longest enduring duty was to his wife, for the last day that Marjorie ever walked on her own two feet was September 23, 1950, at my parents' wedding. After that, she slowly became a bedridden arthritic invalid, passing away in 1969 after almost a decade in a six-bed ward of the Our Lady of Mercy Catholic chronic care hospital, which sat behind St. Joseph's Hospital on Sunnyside Avenue.

Back in his youth, in the '30s and '40s, my dad loved the open farmland sprawling around Laurel Avenue. He had duties, helping to build the coop, raising chickens, tending vegetable gardens and fruit trees, and working part-time jobs for produce farmers in the community. He had an uncle on the street who was a carpenter like his father, Harry, and another uncle who was a dog breeder, raising champion Newfoundland show dogs that won cups and blue ribbons at the Canadian National Exhibition. Teenaged Bob rode his bike everywhere, played community baseball in the summer as an outfielder for White Way (a grocer sponsor in the local youth league), and was an ice hockey goalie in the winter, rising to Junior B with the Etobicoke Indians. When the Second World War came along, he was still a boy in middle and high school, too young to be a soldier. The influence of his family and the strictures of rationing made indelible impressions on him: you finished everything on your plate, saved rubber bands and tin foil, folded and reused paper bags and wrapping paper, wore hand-me-downs, and nothing ever went to waste.

My dad was a disinterested student who never got his high school diploma. Though it was never openly talked about in our house, I guessed that he'd been held back at some point, then failed some grade eleven subjects and dropped out before grade twelve in order to convert a summer job into a career at Canadian Pacific. He was Clerk #3 in the payroll department, out of the main building downtown at King and Simcoe Streets. This qualified him as a good provider for his high school sweetheart, Thelma. Our family's history grew out of the working-class Protestant work ethic, with my father following his father and uncle into a full-time railroad company career. He worked his way up, humbly and patiently, by keeping his head down at his desk for the next forty-six years.

My mom, Thel, was a high school cheerleader and choir member (an excellent soprano) who kept sincere, innocent, faithful diaries and scrapbooks. She loved reading, listening, and singing along to the radio or spontaneously solo in the kitchen — a natural, frequent occurrence in our home that made me feel happy and secure. She would also sing us a lullaby most nights. My creative ambitions and artistic instincts surely came from and were nurtured by her. Both of my parents were regular churchgoers, as their parents and grandparents had been, but my mom was the most devout. We were taught to pray every night at bedtime, and I'm sure my mom talked to her God every night of her life.

As mentioned, my dad's family was extremely frugal and temperate to the point of teetotalling; the only booze might be a glass of cordial for a Christmas dinner toast. My mom's parents, on the other hand, were smokers and heavy social drinkers. Thelma's dad, Ted, was born Edward Douglas Baxter in Woodbridge, Ontario, in October 1900 to Charles and Amanda, both also Canadian born, making my mom a third-generation Canadian. Ted had plenty of discretionary dough from the family truck-ing business, which he inherited fully when his own dad passed away in 1943. As a butcher, Charles had built up a meat-trucking company to service a network of independent farmers, slaughterhouses, and family butcher shops, so Ted was a middleman with many business associates who required schmoozing. The Baxters threw cocktail parties, always took summer vacations at a resort on Lake Simcoe, had season tickets at Maple Leaf Gardens, and road-tripped to Buffalo for dinners and dancing with other couples. The Emmetts were about investing every little nickel and dime; the Baxters were free-spending partiers.

Life hadn't started out like that for my maternal grandmother, Agnes, however. She was a Spence, the oldest of seven sisters, with her origins on the Lanarkshire side of Scotland. The entire Spence clan, led by father Alfred and mother Margaret, emigrated in 1912. I have very vague childhood memories of "Ma" Spence, my great-grandmother, with her thick Scottish brogue.

Ted and Nessie enjoyed their upper-middle-class lifestyle in the Kingsway, with their two daughters, Thelma and her little sister, Joan, in a trim two-storey house on Grenview Boulevard, which was eventually claimed by the city when the Bloor subway line was extended west. I never knew my grandfather Ted; he died of a heart attack on October 1, 1954, when I was fifteen months old. My nanna affectionately became a granny in go-go boots in the '60s. Still a smoker and drinker, with friends who bought her out of the meat-trucking business and set her up for a life of leisure, she drove a big-finned Buick Electra and had a French poodle named George as her constant companion; she took oil-painting lessons, holidays to Florida and Bermuda, and shot movies on her Super 8 camera. She participated in bowling leagues and drank herself to sleep on many lonely nights in her apartment on Mabelle Avenue in Islington, as my mom prayed for her.

I grew up on a quiet little side street in a middle-class west Toronto neighbourhood now called High Park North, filled with mature trees and houses built in the first few decades of the twentieth century. My parents never owned that semidetached house at 94 Abbott Avenue; they rented it from Nessie, who had inherited it in her husband's estate. (His mother, Amanda, in poor health in a retirement home, passed when I was a baby.)

Though my natural musical, artistic, and creative abilities came from my mom, she had an overabundance of modesty and timidity, combined with her religious spirit. Since childhood she'd suffered from bronchiectasis, and a common cold would keep her bedridden for a week or more with a wicked phlegmy cough. Our house was either joyous with her singing, or under a pall with her coughing coming from the upstairs front bedroom. Although her social outlook was conventional, my mother had intellectual leanings that were more liberal. In sharp contrast, my father distrusted liberality; his stolid imagination went along with his conservative, xenophobic politics.

My dad often said he "couldn't carry a tune in a bucket" (which wasn't true — he had decent pitch singing hymns in church and carols at Christmas). He'd played sports as a teenager, and I'd also seen some pretty good little sketches he'd done as a boy. But he had such a strong case of stoical Canadian WASP severity, that around his sons he avoided anything that might seem to be a frivolous or unmanly activity. He'd given up all recreational pastimes when he started working at the railroad, remaining a loyal company man, working his way up slowly by tenure, until he retired. They gave him a modest mantle clock.

In his middle age, he retreated from religion, distancing himself from my mom. But he was not particularly committed to anything: no hobbies or special interests, no ambition or imagination. Both of my parents were very much products of their generation, culture, and upbringing: born into the Great Depression, children in families scraping by and making do; teenagers during the Second World War with rationing — and their generation's peculiarly naive kind of Frank Capra view of life, dancing to Glenn Miller, listening to the radio with their parents, having a sense of style that was, for all intents and purposes, no different than their own parents' and grandparents'.

As a middle child (with an underachieving older brother), I was wired to try to please my parents. At around seven years old, three different characteristics emerged in me: the first was that I was eager to please all aspects of authority. I call this little Ricky 'The Golden Boy'. He had a drive and ambition, wanting to finish first, be the smartest kid in class, the quickest in the race. Academically, until grade seven, he was top of the class. (Sports, music, and girls were my downfall. By the time I graduated high school, that order had reversed to become girls, music, and lastly sports.)

Hockey, as a general cultural chunk of my Canadian life, got imprinted deep in my DNA. When I see a rain-soaked city street at night, I can still hear the B section of Jerry Toth's orchestration of the Dolores Claman *Hockey Night in Canada* theme song in my head. Before there were the Beatles, there were the Toronto Maple Leafs in the Original Six. I knew every player's name and jersey number, collected cards and coins, played road hockey with tennis balls out on the street, and did play-by-play for our neighbourhood. The Leafs won the Stanley Cup when I was eight, nine, ten, and thirteen. So it's in my blood. Saturday night? How are the Leafs doing?

That's my inner child. He followed artistic instincts, loved to draw, was creative and pretty good at it. I got a lot of positive feedback from everyone about my talent. By the time I was seven, my mom was determined to have me conquer my shyness by having me sing in the church choir, and my teachers had me in the Kiwanis city-wide choir. At my mom's encouragement, I was designated as a leader in Sunday school, Bible class, Wolf Cubs, and then Boy Scouts.

The next personality that emerged was the Jock. I loved sports. I was the fastest sprinter in the school for my age and won the Toronto District School Board's dash event at Christie Pits in grades five and six. I played in a soccer league for the local church and boy's club. My quick twitch muscles also took to baseball in the local youth league.

My parents' old-fashioned values meant my mom worked in the home for her three boys. My awkward older brother needed eyeglasses and braces for his teeth by the age of eight. So, my dad would come home from his day job, take off his suit jacket and roll up his sleeves, eat his dinner, then walk over to a local grocery store and work a second job part-time, bagging groceries, stocking shelves, and pricing inventory, to pay for my brother's braces. The demonstration of selfless duty was not lost on me.

In grade seven in 1964, with the British Invasion really blossoming, I was discovering girls, and they began teaching me many wonderful things. Guitar lessons and a one-pickup Kay electric guitar (no amp, though — I plugged it into our inherited second-hand Nordmende radio) were deemed a manageable expense, as my mom now had a part-time job doing some in-house clerical work. But the '60s hit me like a cultural tsunami. The cocky rebel rock star in me no longer wanted to try to please adults. Like so many of my peers, I was beginning to question authority. My inner Peter Pan was born — and my grades fell off. I fought bitterly with my parents over the length of my hair.

My grandfather died, and it awakened in me a different perception of reality, setting off a chain reaction in my own psychological makeup. I questioned God and religion and decided that church on Sunday was not for me. This caused a *huge* rift with my mom. A part of her always stood by my artistic gifts and talents, and as a frustrated writer all her life, she had vicarious emotions tied up in my creativity. I could see that I was hurting her, and my mom was not above playing both guilt and sympathy cards, as she'd been a victim of her own health since her childhood. She hated my obsession with sports and couldn't understand my wiring to play all out, recklessly. I'd been her golden boy until I hit puberty, and then the '60s started to swing and the generation gap opened up between us.

Eventually, she accepted but never really understood my inclination toward an agnostic, humanist view of life. She did have a more open mind about a generation that was saying "Make Love, Not War," believing that "God Is Love," and so there were some things about hippie culture that aligned with my mom's own religious, spiritual values.

My dad, on the other hand, was quietly very supportive of my sports ambitions. He actually took time off work to come to my high school football games — and was the guy who drove me to the hospital to get casts put on and taken off too. But my father distrusted everything about music, hippies, and the '60s counterculture, booting me out of the house just before I turned eighteen when I refused to cut my hair. I was still a kid in high school, but it was the classic "*my* rules under *my* roof!" So I left. I spent a night or two in the basement of the west end YMCA (I had a set of keys for the place because our band rehearsed there, with a storage closet for our gear), then arranged to sleep on a couch at my friend Alec Borsenko's house on Gladstone Avenue. (His parents, then grandmother, had passed away, leaving him an independent man-child at nineteen.)

My parents saw my playing in rock bands as just a phase, a hobby; my mother wanted me to become a lawyer, minister, or a teacher. My ever-pragmatic dad simply wanted me to bring part of *any* paycheque home and contribute to rent and groceries if I lived with them. Once my gigs started generating more income than I would get in an office or factory, my bewildered father passively accepted dough for room and board, swallowing his negativity about my hair-length, career, and lifestyle choices.

In the summer of '74, both my parents came to see me play in the glam rock band backing Justin Paige at the Backstage Lounge of the Seaway Hotel down on Lakeshore West. (It's now a condo.) They watched me in my provocative stage costume — full Alice Cooper makeup, with that stuffed white leather gloved hand cupping my package over a black leotard. The volume must have terrified them. Justin wore a lot of chains, a garter belt, and thigh high boots (and little else), and the two background singers were wearing chastity belts. The whole show was about counterculture gay behaviour, loaded with references to drugs and booze.

I'm sure my parents were gobsmacked by it all, but the job was full-time, and they were supportive, as I already had a ticket on the rock music career carnival midway. By that time, how they felt had become irrelevant to my own momentum. Only four years later, Triumph would play Maple Leaf Gardens and be on the front page of the entertainment section of the newspaper. In the mid-'80s, I bought them a house in our Mississauga neighbourhood. My father settled into it all, only half-jokingly saying something along the lines of "So this music thing seems to be working out for you, eh?"

The truth is, from *my* perspective, Mom and Dad were passive but slightly negative and fearful, as they were about most things in life, and I'd fought to overcome that, which rendered them pretty much irrelevant. It was much more about my own ambition, independence, and self-motivation — an "I'll show you" cockiness of youth.

———

I had two brothers. Robert Edward was two years older, and Russell Baxter was younger by five. My older brother, Rob, had a hard go through this life. He struggled in school, failing grade two as I accelerated through grades three and four, so by grade five I'd caught up to him. (My mom believed he had been oxygen-deprived through her very long labour in childbirth.) Later, he had an impossible time holding a job, struggled with drugs but mostly alcohol, and burned every bridge in the social welfare system (twice). Never married, he completed his Alcoholics Anonymous twelve steps a few times and always had to take everything one day at a time. His health was in a constant fragile state in his final five or six years, because of decades of abuse. Through it all, he remained a heavily addicted cigarette smoker.

My younger brother, Russell, was an entirely different kind of guy: always a warm, entertaining, and accommodating character, he charmed everyone around him with his never-ending upbeat personality (a lot like my mom, except far more extroverted). He was in car sales in his twenties and thirties (after a short stint with his own theatre company just out of high school). After he married and had a daughter, he ran his own very successful pet-food franchise store in Oakville for many years. I had some deep stuff with Russell Baxter. He's going to recur in this memoir, playing an essential pivotal role.

How I Met My Wife

Jeannette Ann Bernadette Groulx and I went to the same high school, Bloor Collegiate, but we never dated then. She was still in grade eight when I was in grade ten, but she'd seen my photo in a friend's older sister's yearbook, which got me on her radar. (My wife has a personal kind of willpower and belief in her own perception of reality that is quite something to behold.) The next year, I was a football jock and track star: Jeannette was a hippie-looking grade niner. At a high school athletic night, a classmate of Jeannette's pointed her out to me across the gym and said, "See that girl over there? She likes you." I sniffed. I was crushing on girls who only tolerated me; I was a typical teenaged idiot: foolish, confused, clueless, and chasing fantasies. Over the next few years, Jeannette went steady with two very different guys over two different time periods — both of whom I vaguely knew. One night at a friend's house party, she and I were in a room alone together for a moment, and she gave me a look that was unmistakable — eye contact I've never forgotten. No words were spoken; she was someone else's girlfriend, and I wasn't going to attempt a move across that kind of line. (The kicker here? She has no memory of that moment.)

Four years after that — Halloween night, 1974 — I was playing guitar in Justin Paige's band at the Edwin Hotel. It was a dive in Toronto's east end, filled with bikers, drunks, druggies, sex workers — and young people who didn't know any better. I'd given my notice to Justin and was playing out a few weeks until they could groom my replacement. I was in my glam rock stage outfit, wearing makeup, and because it was Halloween, many people were dressed in costumes. Jeannette showed up with another one of my pals, Pat McGuire, who worked at a bakery. His Halloween costume was his work outfit, including the toque blanche, with flour all over him. Jeannette was masquerading as a hooker. Again, she was with my pal, so there was only polite conversation. On November 5, a letter from Jeannette arrived at our house. (I still have this letter in a stash-box of keepsakes.) It was midday: I'm having my breakfast at the kitchen table (musician's hours) while my mom is having her lunch. I open the letter, and it says "I find you attractive, interesting. If this idea is to your liking, we could get together for a coffee, walk in the park, etc. May I suggest that you call me?" I show it to my mom and say, "What do you think about this?" And she says, "Any girl who would write a letter like that is only interested in one thing." And I say, "You think?" and immediately use the kitchen wall phone to call her.

I took her to Second City to see improv comedy on our first date, and I kissed her good night on her front porch steps. It took me about four or five months to get to the point that I could tell her that I loved her — but when I did, she said she already knew. My fate, apparently, had been sealed ever since she spied my photo in a yearbook — a sideline shot at the end-of-season championship football game, face in profile, with my helmet pushed up. It had been snowing a little bit, and there were a few flakes on my shoulder pads. I look like I'm about eleven years old, but in fact I was fourteen.

On the morning of July 3, 1976, I put on a tailor-made white suit, a blue striped tie, a pair of white clogs (yes, wooden soles, white tops), conquered some pre-ceremony nausea, and headed for the altar of St. Anne's Church on Gladstone Avenue, at noon, to marry the woman who would have the likes of me. It turned out to be the smartest, best thing I ever did. We bounced around the west end of Toronto, hitting three small low-budget family receptions, ending the day back at our own tiny little semidetached rental house at 530 Dufferin Street, filled with our own friends, who had been smoking pot, drinking beer, listening to albums, and eating chili from a giant stovetop cauldron — a '70s hippie-style party. Afterwards, exhausted, we drove ourselves downtown in my mom's avocado-green AMC Hornet and passed out in a fancy hotel room at the Windsor Arms, before driving up north for a honeymoon week in Barry's Bay.

We ended up with a *lot* of CorningWare casserole dishes as wedding presents.

Now, it's been forty-seven years: three rented houses, then two homes, renovated six times; Jeannette's broken neck (1980) and life-or-death abdominal surgery (1995), then a successful skirmish with breast cancer in 2015; over a half-dozen cars each; four children, four university educations, four marriages paid for, and four grandchildren so far. We've been on vacations together to England and Wales, did the drive up the California coast from L.A. through Carmel to San Francisco, and vanned it out to the lower Maritime provinces once with the kids, when they were little; as a couple, we've been to Jamaica, St. Thomas, Florida (a few times); spent a week in New York City, a weekend in San Francisco, a river cruise up the Danube and the Rhine — also Vancouver, St. John's, and a Rocky Mountaineer train trip.

I might as well deal with the broken neck story right here and be done with it.

On a wintry stretch of road one morning in 1980, late for her job in the A & R department, Jeannette anticipated her arrival at the Capitol Records building up on American Drive by Pearson Airport by undoing her seatbelt just a few blocks from the office. Suddenly the car hit a patch of black ice and skidded across the centre line of the road, crashing head-on into a truck. Her forehead punched a softball-sized hole in the far-right upper corner of the windshield; she fractured the C2 vertebra in her neck — the hangman's break. When I got to the emergency department, the doctor met me in the hall before I went in to see her. His first words were "She's going to be fine." He went on to explain the stitches closing the cut in her eyebrow and the fact that she had a very large bruise on her shoulder. "That's where the guardian angel was sitting," he said. She spent six weeks on a Stryker frame bed with screws in her temples to stabilize her broken neck, and I visited her every day in the hospital, my life in a holding pattern of smoking dope, eating bad food, shooting snooker, and practising guitar. A few millimetres either way, and she could have been quadriplegic, or dead. Instead she recovered, and we've made forty-three years of history.

Jeannette deserves so much credit for my life, my career, the very existence of my creativity. She was, and still is, the best partner I could ever have had along for the ride. She was steady and calm when I was flailing, solid and practical when I was coming apart. I took her for granted too often, counted on her and leaned on her far too much. She somehow forgave me and miraculously stood by me. It was always my greatest good fortune that when I needed a teacher, a mentor, and my best friend, I only had to look across the dinner table, roll over in bed, or yell up the stairs from the basement studio.

It's a miracle that she was able to go along with the wild fluctuations of my creative ambition, hanging in with me through it all. That's the long and short of it, truly.

I'm agnostic, but love always made supreme sense to me. My favourite anniversary card that I tucked away and saved reads:

> From the moment I saw you, I wanted to meet you. From the moment I met you, I wanted to know you. From the moment I knew you, I was in love with you. From the moment I loved you, I wanted to share my life with you.
>
> And from that moment to this moment, and for all the moments to come, I will love you with all my heart.

The smartest thing I ever did in my whole life was marry Jeannette Ann Bernadette Groulx. The best thing we ever did in our life together was raise four incredible people, who have given me immeasurable pride and joy. I'm truly not worthy but grateful to have had this incredibly diverse, robust life we built together, full of highlights and good fortune — love, luck, laughter, happiness, and the hard work of commitment. Through five decades, we've been two crazy roller-coaster riders hanging on to each other for dear life.

By 2000, Jeannette was our family's more consistent breadwinner, with medical and dental benefits, which allowed me to indulge myself creatively. If she hadn't been such a selfless, hardworking spouse, there's no way I would have been able to sustain any kind of indie music writing and recording career. Whatever successes I may have enjoyed have all been built upon my dependence on her — a dependency that was unfair and one-sided. It's an amazing miracle, really, that she loves me, despite my shortcomings and all-too-human mistakes and faults. She has been far more consistent in that love than I have; she has been able to teach me and support me and raise our children, demonstrating how true character works. I am an artist, after all, and artists don't usually end up being very complete people. (I'm not stating this to excuse myself; it's a regrettable fact.) My wife's integrity comes naturally; a more even keel is her standard resting place. Artists are much too self-centred, emotional, and nutso for that. Too often I'm so far into my own head that I fail to notice it's shoved up my own backside.

I know that most folks will read this book because I had some fame and fortune, maybe wrote some songs they've heard. But the most important thing I can convey in this book is that my career enabled my family life, and that was the best thing we ever did. I got to live my life, constantly aware that family and friends were the best things in it. As the days go by, these remain life's greatest gifts. Hardly earth-shattering, but it's the most fundamental truth I have to offer.

My private life remained so because I kept it relatively manageable. My career never took on the uncontrollable proportions that many bigger rock stars have experienced. I was a minor league celebrity, at best. It would be pretentious and self-delusional to conflate my career with Ozzy's or Bon Jovi's — that's stretching things.

Still, looking at my Hall of Fame career from outside, someone might imagine a lifetime of success. But there have been failures, disappointments, moments of heartbreak and grief; family members who battled drugs and alcoholism, shaky financial deals, and lean times. A showbiz career is not the arena where one trumpets family difficulties. No one digs entertainers who suck air out of the building. Folks want recreation.

I juggled the best I knew how and made plenty of mistakes. Too often, I shortchanged my family, then did my best to make it up to them. Certainly, when everyone was younger, throwing money at problems seemed an easy fix. There were nannies and housekeepers. And from when my kids were little, I was an ordinary dad, just like others — except

I had a lot of guitars in the basement. My kids were sitting around the kitchen dinner table with me, most Sunday through Wednesday nights, getting put to bed, having a bedtime story read to them by their more remote authority figure, who counted the strokes of their toothbrushes. In my family, there was never any empty B.S. of a rock star lifestyle, but the downside was Dad's roadwork from most Thursdays through Sundays. Then there were Dad's preoccupations, his intensity, and his temper from his inability to cope with his own stress and anxiety. The kids suffered from having to live with an artist who toiled unpredictably under his own dark storm clouds.

Fame was never the goal of my career. So, when my kids were little, they were oblivious to it. Other kids at school would finally ask them about their *rock star* dad, and it dawned on them that there might be some mileage to be made of dad's notoriety. But Dad did not seem notorious to them. Dad was a guy who played "guitar, guitar, guitar," as my daughter Casey once sighed. (Which became a family running joke: if you wanted to describe Dad, you just said, in a bored sigh, "Guitar, guitar, guitar.") Dad drove them around, shopped for groceries, cracked corny groaners, and teased; made them eat broccoli and go to bed. When they got older, he imposed curfews. Their dad was matter-of-fact, routine, taking out the garbage, burping, scratching, looking terrible. My kids grew up hearing me practise all the time and make mistakes as I wrote songs. Dad was a constantly annoying, noisy, repetitive nuisance. They witnessed the boring drudgery it takes to become a good performer — and they were too young (and usually too busy with their own extra-curriculars, anyway) to travel to my gigs. No magic mystery in any of that.

I explained to them that fame is a by-product of hard work, if you get lucky. People obsessed with fame who didn't put in the work were not substantial. My kids grew up with those values instilled and were encouraged to hang out with friends who were interested in *them* — not their dad's business. They were happy to follow that advice.

My family life remained intact because I picked the right partner for the journey. Our family was always our number one priority, even if I was imperfect about how that played out. Perfection is overrated, anyhow, because it's nonexistent: mine was a *very* human race.

Now showbiz is mostly an act: you act like you have it together. It's a performance. It might have looked like I always had my act together, but you can ask my family, the guys who played in my bands, the roadies who worked with me, the doctors and therapists who have helped me along the way. I always battled my insecurities and hid my weaknesses, masked my deficiencies, and made the most of my humble assortment of gifts. Part of a creative gift is the ability to figure out how to work around one's faults, shortcomings, and weaknesses. On stage was a showbiz construct, a persona forged from years of playacting — never truly me.

The fabrications of my career had consequences for my family life; it was never a walk in a park of perpetual sunshine. Life happens. Shit goes down. Parents get cancer, sicken, and die. People get short-tempered, argue, and fight, or sulk and brood. Jeannette and I knew poor: in '78, we were using charge card debt to buy groceries as we waited for Triumph's U.S. record deal to land. She'd broken her neck in that car accident in 1980; later in the mid-'90s, she had to undergo emergency surgery for a perforated bowel, and we nearly lost her — but we survived that too. In a wider sense, my family is no different than any other: disappointments and tragedies happen. Hearts get broken, and then you try to find ways to heal and mend them.

On a late April day in 1982, Jeannette and our first baby, Shannon, came home from the hospital, and we were all upstairs in the main bedroom, where mom and daughter were settling in on a lovely new glide-rocker chair to nurse. It was a nice enough spring day that the windows were open for fresh air. Suddenly, a boisterous disturbance of the peace arose from the street. A group of rock-head fans emerged from an old car parked at our curb, shouting my nickname, with Triumph's music roaring from the car's speakers, a cloud of Cheech and Chong smoke surrounding these less-than-magnificent men emerging from their rock and roll machine. Their lead scouts had mounted the porch and were ringing the bell, pounding on the front door. Staring in horror from the second floor window, I was angry to have our special private family moment so rudely interrupted. Getting no answer at the main door, the troupe decided to wander the grounds and came round the back, climbed up on the porch, started peering through windows and blinds, calling out to each other as they saw evidence that confirmed their suspicions: gold records hanging on a wall, a guitar leaning in a corner of a room. We weren't being robbed, but it was a violation of privacy normally taken for granted.

Eventually they left, but my world view had been forever altered. With a baby, the game of celebrity had greater consequences. Within the hour, we were on the phone, arranging for security companies to come and give estimates for installing cameras, motion sensors, land mines, et cetera. In the end, the most sensible game plan came from a security company guy who told us, "A first-class security system costs a small fortune for a house like this and would be impractical anyway. Your property layout makes it crazy expensive to establish a perimeter. So, build high privacy side-fencing with gates to close off the backyard. Install an intercom at the front door. Here's the card of a friend of mine who raises and trains German shepherds for police forces. Get yourself a big scary-looking dog, then go to the hardware store and buy some Beware of Dog signs, and post 'em on those side fences."

Which is what we did, and it worked. We still had some incidents with fans at the front door — although most encounters ended with them accepting via the intercom that they had the wrong house. Other times, when strangers at the door would insist, "Doesn't Rik Emmett live here?" Jeannette would say, "Nope. You've got the wrong place. He moved away a long time ago." My wife is a convincing liar. I never want to give her cause to cross me, because if she did, I'd be dead so fast, I'd never even know I'd been had.

Meanwhile, the dog's beautiful, deep-chested authoritative bark — no yap, all diaphragm — made the curious beat a retreat. Rocky was deeply loved for over a decade, our family's best friend. A well-trained German shepherd is the best security system ever.

When my younger brother, Russell, was diagnosed with liver cancer in 2006, he rushed himself through the system in order to get a sectioning of the tumour revealed on his MRI. They opened him up, got a good look, and stapled him back up again. His cancer had metastasized to an inoperable condition. He got to go home a few days later, and his treatment included chemo and radiation therapy. He also explored an alternative method of treatment, bombarding his body with vitamins (which was expensive, accomplishing nothing but draining his finances). Through back pain, weight loss, and jaundice, he fought courageously for over a year — as long as humanly possible.

I will always vividly remember the last time I visited with him in his home, a few days before he was moved to the hospital for the final time. He ran through a long list of how his body was failing him. Then we sat on the edge of his bed together, and I hugged him. I told him he didn't owe any of us anything; he'd fought so hard, bravely. In the end, it was a fight that couldn't be won, only negotiated — through acceptance, with dignity and grace. I told him, for my part, he didn't have to choose to fight anymore. He'd wasted away to practically nothing. He said that when he died, we could just slip him into an envelope — making a joke, a brave face he wanted to show me. Through our tears, we just sat there and said how much we loved each other. Then there was nothing left to say. I realized later that in that moment, we had been saying our good-byes. I was letting him go. He was gathering himself to make his final earthly journey. That moment crushed me in ten thousand ways — but I know now it was also a great gift. It was ours, alone.

It took me years to find the perspective on this. I needed to write songs, poems, and stories to try to come fully to terms with it. I had to find words, get them down for the record. The words can live, somehow, beyond pain, suffering, confusion, guilt.

Creatively I can at least attempt to find a perspective of a universal picture I'll never understand but that consistently screws around with my emotions.

After Russ was gone, I took it hard. Other than Jeannette, my connection to him had been the closest in my life. It was brutal to witness his completely unfair cancer fight. But no one ever promised life was going to be fair, did they? (Such a cliché.) There was also something ironic in all of it (which I'd also felt as my mom declined, then passed on) because I was the guy who wrote songs about inspiration and positivity. So many people have told me how my music helped them through rough times. Unsurprisingly, trying to find consolation and strength was so much harder to practise than to preach (another cliché).

I couldn't come unglued. I had to stay strong, for my family's sake, and to honour my brother's wishes. ("You go to *work*, man — you go about living your life! You don't let cancer take away normal, everyday routine!") I didn't know anyone who loved life as much as my brother Russell — such an open, empathetic, sweet, and generous-hearted person (to a fault). He had so many friends within his circles and orbits, spreading himself so far and wide that his passing hammered hard, rippling a long way out. Yet he'd done his best to take the fight in stride: to handle it with grace and dignity.

In the course of a life / a lifetime running after dreams
that we chase
Where love awaits in every beat of your heart
there is a spirit of tenderness that can fill every empty
space / that can fill every empty space
You give it all: within every moment passing by
You give it all: and never lose the courage to wonder why
and you may find your place / in a state of grace

At the season-ending Central Michigan University baseball banquet in 2011, nine seniors were graduating, my son amongst them. Brendan Robert's life had centred on being a student athlete — elite since he was eight years old. At eighteen, he was an NCAA Division 1 ballplayer, playing on scholarship with a high grade-point average. Now his college life was ending, with a degree in broadcasting but no draft pick, no minor or major leagues. He'd been through Tommy John surgery and had played hurt; he worked out almost every day of his life. The team sometimes had to shovel snow from the stadium grass to get in some of their home games. No one could question his ambition, his work ethic, or that of his teammates. The dreams of nine seniors ended that night in speeches: they thanked their parents, their coaches, and their teammates, and they told their stories. Every single one of them shed tears, and our broken hearts grieved along with them, because this is what life is like.

Not everybody gets to be Derek Jeter. In many ways, it's a meritocracy, as well as a kind of lottery of both DNA and being at the right place at the right time.

In my son's speech, he quoted me, from the time he'd hit rock bottom and was facing elbow surgery. He recounted how I talked about experiencing some of my own incredible highs and lousy lows. I'd told him it's not about highs or lows. It's always about *what you decide they're going to do to you* — how you react, how you act in the wake of it, going forward.

Life is not always easy, and it's often unfair. Nothing good comes free. You pay dues and move forward. In truth, we're always trying to master our destiny, even when the moment has moved beyond our control. It takes courage. That's the good fight.

My older brother, Rob, passed in April 2016 after a two-year battle with cancer, during which he showed courage, dignity, and acceptance with a sense of humour and his faith in God. He was a gentle soul, a simple-hearted person who wished no man ill. But his was a tough life, full of challenges — the gawky kid with glasses, then braces; the teen who got bullied for his lunch money, mocked for failing grades. As he grew older, he was often lonely, mostly as a result of his own choices. After decades of hard living and abuse, he managed to work his way to a sober path through AA, but he was a lifelong heavy smoker to the end, paying a terrible price for all of that. The finality of death weighed heavy; that hollow feeling of grief sat in my chest. I knew that feeling, because we'd lost our younger brother, Russell, to cancer eight years before, and Rob's passing stirred up the black hole of negativity I carried around inside after losing Russ and my mom. I went to ground and tried to heal by spending time with my loved ones, with music, poetry, ballgames on TV, and movies. I was reminded of Willie Nelson's insightful lyric about grieving: "It's not somethin' you get over, but it's somethin' you get through."

Our family has endured some long, drawn-out end-of-life battles. I support the right to choose our final stretch run, when there's absolutely no doubt about the outcome. When it's my time, I want the choice to pass away on my own terms, with dignity and self-control.

I'm sentimental about Toronto. I loved to play Hugh's Room, because it was literally six blocks from the house I grew up in, around the block from Alhambra Avenue, where my grandfather grew up. The final concert gigs of my career were there in January 2019. When I played, Brendan walked the neighbourhood and took a selfie standing in front of his great-grandfather's house. That felt full circle.

I'm emotional about my Canadianness. I've seen a lot of the world, and while I do have affection for places like San Francisco and San Antonio (where I've played the mental game of "So, could I move here and set up shop?"), in the end, nothing compares to home sweet home. On airplanes flying in to Toronto, its skyline always gave me the warm and fuzzies. The north shore of the last Great Lake is where I belong; it's a part of who I am. Geography is character, family shapes character, geography is family: these are facts of Canadian life.

In the later stages of my performing career, mentioning the length of my marriage on stage drew applause. My wife deserved all that goodwill: she'd put up with my selfish shortcomings, inconsistencies, and artistic temperament. My loyalty to Jeannette, the only reality I know, feels right. It may be incurable romantic wiring, but I've also been lucky. I do think there's something to the adage that the harder one works, the luckier one gets — chance benefits the prepared. And I think love requires work: certain levels of discipline, humility, and forgiveness, along with a constant striving toward old-fashioned virtues.

Virtue seemed the path to choose in my life. Vice just seemed like too much work, too much stress for too little reward, and too much threat of damage to myself and the people I cared about. The "high road" wasn't the shortcut, but it seemed simpler, cleaner, better lit — always the more normal, natural choice for me. That disposition might just be lucky. Certainly I was lucky that Jeannette fell in love with me. That I can't explain. I'm simply grateful — happily, humbly. I also think luck starts with myself, and it always starts now. (And now. And now again.) I make a few simple decisions about the things I can control myself, about the things I hold in my own hands. I'm not saying it's always easy. I'm not saying my life has been wonderful all the time. But in most circumstances, love is the default that makes the most sense. Right here, right now — what can I control? My ability to love life. That's a choice.

Growing Old as a "People Person"

I'm either very close to tears, sniffling with happiness and corny over-whelming Hallmark love, or I'm tickled to be grinning like an idiot and goofing around with my grandkids. I love babies; I love kids. I enjoyed being a teacher in a room full of younger people. Despite my protective shell of cynicism, my griping unhappiness about how some people behave, and how ignorant, stupid, criminal, and evil some people can be, some part of me remains a people person, optimistically hoping for the best from folks, and disappointed when it's not on offer.

While talking about meet-and-greets with a musician friend, he remarked, "Yeahhh, *people* . . . Not a fan." While I grew to hate the obligation of meet-and-greets, surprisingly I still am a fan of people. I'm especially a fan of the young, who have giant amounts of innocence and wonderment and open-mindedness — so much potential. I always look forward to the moments when I can hold that in my arms and cradle it gently against my worn heart.

Broken Bones: Like Father, Like Daughter

Our daughter Cassandra's complexity was innate: her competitive intensity gave us a great deal of pleasure and pride when she managed to make it up to the travelling rep level of soccer. Nobody gave a more determined effort than our Casey. As a kid, her drawings were never doodles: they were detailed illustrations, baroque scenes with bordered rugs and family pets, furniture, and a backstory. Like her dad, she has the soul of an artist, creating with concepts and vision. An average student until a high school tutor got her to believe in herself, her self-determination carried her beyond her bachelor of applied science in kinesiology to a master's degree of science in human health and nutritional science — the first Emmett or Groulx to reach that degree of academic achievement.

One of the strongest memories I have of being her dad was when she broke her arm playing soccer in July 1999, on a Sunday night, and I had to take her to a Mississauga hospital where, in my presence, the emergency doctor (not an orthopedic specialist) reset the broken bone *without* anesthetic. There were tears, from both of us, but her strength of character astonished me, for I'd undergone the same thing when I was also fourteen, with a football injury. I knew what she was going through, and I know for a fact she handled it far better than I did.

On the clear spring night of May 4, 2002, I drove our sixteen-year-old daughter Ashley over to a local multiplex theatre so she could meet up with some football-player guy named Mike, from a rival high school, for a date. After I dropped her off, I watched her climb the grand stairs at the entrance up to where a tall, athletic, good-looking blond dude was waiting for her. When he turned and smiled at her as she approached, I thought my heart was going to burst. They looked so young and beautiful. The earth shifted on its axis. There goes our little girl, I thought. Driving away, my eyes were burning with tears. I had no way of knowing, but that night he asked her to become his steady girlfriend. Thirteen years and three months later, she married that guy (and I sang "God Only Knows" at their wedding ceremony). They have given us two beautiful grandchildren. I don't believe in fate, but I know what I felt — it was as if the universe was smiling on that moment, and it filled me up till I started leaking.

THE AUTOBIOGRAPHY CHAPTER

Celebrity is a mask that eats into the face.

— JOHN UPDIKE, *Self-Consciousness* (1989)

Self-discipline begins with self-awareness, delayed gratification, and learning how to say no. There are downsides: unreasonable self-righteousness can distort values. Self-loathing might arise when self-discipline is not as extensive and rigorous as some part of you says it should be.

When I was a little boy, I was shy. Painfully so — hiding in my mother's skirt when I had to transition out of kindergarten into my grade one class. I didn't want to go into the corner store to buy milk or bread, too shy to interact with a stranger. My parents and teachers — gently but firmly — said no, Richard, you are smart and talented enough that you should be doing these things; you need to find the self-discipline to make yourself do things that you fear. But I did *not* want to perform in public.

My father's and grandfather's generations went to war. We used to think that kind of self-discipline made men out of boys. Now we know it also creates many damaged people, struggling with PTSD. My older brother struggled throughout his life with drug and alcohol addiction. I did not have to look far to see the downside of self-medicating to try (and fail) to make other psychological problems go away.

Playing guitar and singing better than most folks is not so ordinary, I'm repeatedly told. I possess an artistic eye and temperament, the talent to create clever songs, to write poems and prose. Yet I deal with anxiety issues, even now in my senior years, reminding me of the ordinary man I am. Why was little Ricky so shy? Why did Richard become the class clown in grade nine, where he was the youngest and smallest? Why did a young Rick start playing in a glam rock band, wearing makeup and outlandish stage costumes? Why did a slightly older Rik join Triumph, a rock band that was all about The Big Show, tossing his hair in spandex jumpsuits? Why was he so eager and agreeable to play the major-record-label promo game, to provide the MTV money shot? Aspects of my nature can't be denied, but they also led to conflicts between overcompensating grandiosity and feelings of inadequacy.

As a child, it started when parents and teachers taught me to say yes, when part of my true nature buried deep inside was screaming no. I'm not assigning blame. It was considered proper, right. Through the balance of my life, I managed to keep myself away from drugs and the complications that could arise from rock and roll's extracurriculars. I kept myself relatively in shape physically, despite the growing list of chronic injuries sustained in the athletic (mis)adventures of my youth. I loved, honoured, and obeyed my wife; tried to be a good father and a good provider. This is how I saw myself through those years. But I was also an introverted creative and artistic spirit conflicted by grandstanding for self-fulfillment. There was a public power that arose from performance. I was always at war with the mask on my face (even when I'd been happily seduced by it).

Behind it all, creativity was my version of self-medication.

By 1988, I couldn't keep saying yes to the business of Triumph anymore. I finally began saying no, but it was hard to do. Some fans thought I was betraying the better part of my nature. In the song "Ordinary Man," I'd written "I will not be a puppet, I cannot play it safe," yet I had allowed myself to get strung up into a business partnership where I was a marionette. Decades after I'd gone out on my own, the irony of my own hypocrisy was still with me, every single night, on stage when I would sing those lyrics — "Look in the mirror / Tell me what do you see / Or can you lie to yourself like you're lying to me?"

When I wrote it, I meant it, and it felt true to me. But it was also the brave face of the mask talking, because, I mean, *come on*. Rock star! I'd long been an instrument for something else: I was the Rocket — the fuel for the engine in the *Rock and Roll Machine*.

By the second decade of the twenty-first century, I was long overdue to reconcile the true nature of the frightened, shy little boy, hiding behind the mask shaped from commercial success. But then, as an artist, I could always retreat into a shell where creativity reigned supreme. I'd always done so and was still up to those tricks.

After '95 or so, I'd figured out how to create and perform music with nary a care for mainstream commercialism. What kind of (different) selfishness was that? Someone ignoring the needs of his wife and family to retreat to the studio to create — for what? For posterity? To hide? Searching for peace of mind? Many folks who have shared in the lives of artists come out of it saying, "He was an asshole. A selfish, egotistical person who always put his 'art' first — a nightmare to have to live with."

So, there's a balance to be struck, a need for proceeding carefully, thoughtfully — and not necessarily instinctively or naturally, with "true nature" as my guide. Because as an artist, I don't have just one true nature. Humans are complex, with saints and sinners inside us all: selfish and altruistic, angry and loving, confused and resolutely determined, courageous and scared shitless. We are all human, running in the race. Sometimes, maybe, we summon the courage to say no to that race, in order to sit by the side of the road and try to figure out some of the crazier shit.

And hey, there's a lot of crazy shit going down right now.

The digital age ushered in the extinction of a lot of what I thought I knew — what felt comfortable to me. Change happening at the speed of light feels inhuman. So, I often have to say, Wait. Stop. I need to get off this superhighway for a while and get some perspective. I'm still learning how to say no more often. The mask had a price, as all masks do. I'm no different, but maybe I had to wear my showbiz mask more often than other folks wear theirs. Maybe mine etched deeper scars into me.

At the risk of sounding like a cliché paraphrasing my own lyrical construct, I just did the best I could. But sometimes things came at me from beyond my control. After I'd had a modicum of success — even when I was trying to leave the rock star mask off — sometimes the expectations of others stuck it back on my face. It ran the gamut from what business partners wanted down to getting recognized at the mall, or suffering through overreactions to my presence — that sort of thing. Radio interviews required the bluster of a rock star salesman; the mandates of promo extended the responsibilities of my mask beyond the stage. The spotlight sometimes found me when I didn't want to be found. A public life is a choice with consequences, ramifications. This isn't boo-hoo whining — I'm just pointing out how the territory cannibalizes its own boundaries.

Updike got it right, but when I was young and naive, full of the piss and vinegar of ambition, I *wanted* to wear that mask. Then I blinked a few times, found myself in my late sixties, and asked, Can I live without it? How addicted to it am I? Can I come to different terms with it?

Even the modest proportions of my showbiz life generated negative consequences for physical fitness, mental health, and self-esteem. When I lost the benefit of rubber-bodied youth, the slings and arrows of outrageous fortune left cuts and bruises, knocking me off my game. I became less inclined to place myself in positions of vulnerability. I was trying to establish better boundaries and, as time went on, to reconfigure them.

My showbiz mask created a mini-monster of selfishness, an unpredictable one that my wife and kids were afraid to cross. I was a guy with a bad temper who walked around under a dark cloud often enough that my grown-up kids and wife finally demanded that I go to family therapy for an intervention, a confrontation with my own shortcomings. I had all kinds of submerged and unaccounted-for fear and anxiety — a problem that had to be dealt with.

Fans saw my mask as heroic. My wife and kids saw something quite different. So, there I was taking stock, still getting pulled by perceptions, conflicts, challenges — shit that had created the mask way back before my kids were even born. And now I was dealing with repercussions that the mask itself generated.

There's a shorter window now to be the more consistent person I'd like to be. *Rock star* is a label I'm not denying. I own and wear it, good and bad. Many of my problems were self-induced, yet at the same time

I also earned the right to wear the mask and my road warrior scars. I paid dues, learned lessons, worked hard over a lifetime, and nurtured and protected my modest little bundle of gifts. When the spotlight turned on, I could bring it — a hambone in his mask. Why not simply revel in it? The answer is that, every now and then, a new deal needs to get cut between the inside and outside, on stage and off, church and state.

In the past, I didn't do it often enough or make it stick at critical times. Now, as testosterone abates, the body's ability to handle adrenalin and cortisol diminishes, and it's time for this retired senior citizen to rebalance, cut a new deal. So, no more mask. I'm writing this memoir, looking in the mirror, trying to find my real face. Still workin' things out.

Outgrowing the Mask

Consider the contradictions we carry around in us: animal instinct versus socialized, cultured, civilized behaviour. We evolve from childhood through adolescence into adulthood, taking our inner child through middle age, then senior citizenship. Who remains 100 percent consistent in nature through this process? As much as my own life celebrated my youth, and my keep-busy showbiz talents, some home truths belie the glorification of entertainment.

> When I was a child, I spoke as a child, I understood as a child,
> I thought as a child. But when I became a man, I put away
> childish things.
>
> — 1 Corinthians 13:11

When a man contemplates his own end and begins to question the things he's done with his life, trying to figure out what he'll do with the precious, dwindling time left — what's in one's nature at this point? This big question gets compounded in an age of "big lies, getting bigger all the time."

Sometimes I was a slave to circumstances, struggling with balance and what made sense; sometimes bonded into business partnerships, contractual obligations, the money to be made as a popular commercial musician;

captive to applause, social acceptance, peer admiration — so many fascinating bars in the gilded cage of an ordinary dude.

I remain driven by creative process and still love that work. I was always less interested in games of marketing and promotion; never interested in sex without love and affection; never interested in altered states; never liked how it felt to lose control of my own senses. In truth, I wasn't very good at wearing my mask when there wasn't a musical performance to give the mask its magic power.

Reconciling my inner life to the mask was getting beyond my abilities: the timeline of my life didn't correspond with the mask's youthful grin. It's a strange, beautiful thing that we have self-awareness and foreknowledge of our own mortality. The glory of our physical abilities begins to fade and deteriorate. As a performer throughout my lifetime, there had been a virtuoso element and a jock's attitude to my rock and rollin' heart. Then some notes became harder for my voice to find, until an octave of them wasn't even there anymore. The complaints of my bones and connective tissue refused to be ignored. The inevitable consequences of this erosion were things contemplated lying in a bed in the dark of yet another hotel room on yet another road trip. But the turning of magic tricks is what showbiz is all about, and the mask whispered, "C'mon, buddy, figure out ways to sell it. Be the wily veteran and use guile instead of chops — scale back, modify, redesign — but keep on keepin' on. Keep me up!"

Lots of showbiz folks are full of neurotic self-doubt. We start out that way, then our talent delivers our masks, along with the instant gratification of applause. Then we double down with a damn-the-torpedoes gutsiness. Along comes more recognition, acceptance, kudos. The addiction begins. After a while, quitting seems a cowardly way out, because you have a symbiotic relationship with the enabling mask: you can develop the work behind it.

Countless times I have written in a diary entry some variation of "I'm my own worst enemy." My strengths came with weaknesses; my gifts were my burdens. My doubt and fear sparked the eternal flame — and the business of the show was like gasoline, fed by the money that others could make as percentages of the take. Record companies, promoters, agents: just a game, and all I could do was play.

Rock Bands: Tribal Enablers

A group of folks get together in a garage or a basement, and it's almost a mutual support kind of aiding and abetting thing. We're all a bit whacko, a bit damaged (screws loose, ego issues, control issues, all *kinds* of issues), but as a unit, we can generate something greater than the sum of its parts. I had my own mask, and then I willingly joined a band that had a much bigger, collective one — designed to be epic, gigantic, larger than life. Commercial artists cannot ignore the marketplace, the culture of the business, so eventually, inevitably, there's also a fan base, bringing its expectations to bear. Then we willingly signed deals with record and merchandising companies which had their own wider agendas for exploiting the potential of our mask (our brand). Initially I had little idea what I was getting into, but I'd been more than willing to don the mask in the first place.

So, I had myself to blame, and I got very good at self-loathing.

Making Choices

There's a very human desire to look for shortcuts, to learn trade secrets, so that the magic ingredient for success might be revealed. But in the music biz, it's not secret; it's common knowledge. Success comes at a price: you must be willing to pay it. That willingness to pay it separates wheat from chaff. Do you accept the dues? When I was young, I was willing and eager to take on payments. Such is the bliss of ignorance, the arrogance of a naive rubber constitution.

My life story is not nearly as dramatic as many others. I chose music; it chose me. Career opportunities opened up before me, and I said okay. I didn't know any better. Becoming a rock star and putting on the mask, over the years, created my own inner Peter Pan. I never fully became the adult I was in real time. I'd go out on the road, play gigs, and at least some of the audience insisted on maintaining the illusion of my Peter Pan — sing the old songs, be clever, be talented, show us how you can fly!

Letting go of that wasn't all that easy, because I had become conditioned to make my inner Peter Pan happy. I mean, look at my life. Hadn't

I done all right by Peter? I provided for those around me, bought houses and cars, put kids through college, built up an investment portfolio. Who wants to quit flying, grow old, and lose out on having grand adventures in Neverland? I wanted to make associates and audiences happy too. I had a lifetime of that patterned behaviour. Changing from the inside out was hard.

I asked myself, Who am I, if I'm not what I've been doing all my life? Thus the need for a family intervention, then professional help to gain some perspective.

I had a breakthrough one afternoon with my therapist, who asked whether I loved my inner child, the Peter Pan rock star. I said I couldn't trust his selfish, immature bullshit and bluster. He was more false bravado than genuine depth, often running scared and anxious as a jackrabbit, because he lacked intellectual depth. He feared he was a clown, hiding behind a mask, a puppet on strings, a showbiz phony. His cynicism, sarcasm, and toughness was a junkyard-dog front. (The metaphors kept piling up.) She asked, Isn't that pretty much the definition of *every* teenager, trying to figure out how to be an adult? That set off a chain reaction: When might I forgive myself for my past fallibilities? Accept my mortality? When might I stop living in a loop of hating parts of myself?

Aha — a grandfather finally accepted it — time to grow up.

My boomer generation had a thing about *not* growing old. We wanted to maintain our "forever seventeen" outlook. But I'd abdicated responsibility for too long. It's good to embrace and love my two inner children: to still find the reverence for the mystery of life from when I was my mom's golden child, and to acknowledge the Peter Pan punk, taking on the world with his burning ambition and hyperactive imagination. Forgiving him his overreaching role-playing (his grandiosity) is not a one-and-done thing; it's an ongoing exercise. As is owning the rock star mask while seeing it for what it is: it's not my face. It was a tool of the trade. But it became as much a part of me as my golden child and my Peter Pan.

Like I said, quite the psychological gumbo, parboiling away.

Irresponsible denial wasn't working. I needed to let go of the baggage that weighed me down for such a long time. I was no longer interested in trying to sustain fantasies and exaltation of youth.

As the saying goes, growing old ain't for sissies. But losing wonder and reverence for life ain't good either. I want to hold on to that, all the way along. Folks talk about being "authentic," but change is inevitable, and once you're evolving your authenticity, reinventing, and letting go, how do you know where you're headed, as the process is ongoing? How do you know what it looks like from outside the process, when you're deep inside it? Perspective on creativity often comes long after you've finished something, walked away, and can see it from the distance of time. I can't say for sure what I'm after, where I'm headed, or when I know that I've arrived at a destination (or even a milestone). Surely, being comfortable with a childlike curiosity for the surprises of the journey isn't a bad thing and preferrable to the tyranny of destinations — wins! results!

Maybe the inner child — the part of us we're supposed to love and cherish — is the naïf who had a natural instinct for hope, a glimmer of awareness that the sun would rise tomorrow, bringing something new in the wonder and mystery of it all. Maybe getting real — being authentic and genuine — is about never pretending, never having the conceit to believe we've arrived, because we're all only en route.

Maybe *music* offers that: when I'm inside it, being it, there's only the music to think about, so I'm only a part of this larger thing that's happening. I'm committed, engaged, going with the flow, surrendering to the wonder and the mystery, and allowing myself to become fully integrated into the moment. No fear, no anxiety — just a beautiful, peaceful surrender, more unconscious and instinctive than premeditated and deliberate.

I dunno. Maybe.

I hope to live fully, reasonably, with wisdom, passion, common sense, love, kindness, compassion, and as much intellectual clarity as I can muster, as I grow old. I hope to become more virtuous, less selfish, less concerned about the judgment of others, and more concerned about improving my own good judgment. Now that I'm a senior citizen, I'm not sure where my path lies or where it leads — but I know I need brighter illumination just to read bolder, larger fonts. Back in my music career — in promotion, marketing, and sales — it was impossible to avoid some pathways that grew dim and a bit scary. Slowly, steadily, I've been trying to walk higher roads with better natural light.

My nature has both good and bad, and in my fallibility, my Whitmanesque multitudes embody some measures of hypocrisy and contradiction. My inner temperament conjured stress as an almost constant companion. It takes work every day to remind myself of my patterned behaviour and keep it at bay.

I went through some serious anxiety issues in 2016–17, with recurring panic attacks. My immune system was in revolt, giving me a case of shingles on the back of my neck and shoulder. In 2018–19, I started getting alopecia areata; loonie-sized patches of my scalp went bald. Retiring from the road started curing some of the things that ailed me, but those were only symptoms of something else going on inside. I'm in a much better place now than I was then. I had help from many sources, and the words of therapists, philosophers, artists, and psychologists all played a role in helping me find my sense of balance again. This adage became a recurring mantra: "If you are depressed, you are living in the past. If you are anxious, you are living in the future. If you are at peace, you are living in the present."

My simpler mantra: "Just let it go." Therapists helped give me back the gift of the present, which my past and future were stealing.

Naturally a very shy person, I'm only comfortable with a crowd when I'm in control of the program. (For example, panic attacks come on when I'm stuck in bumper-to-bumper traffic jams, and I let it get away from me.) Back in school, I discovered that the ability to make people laugh gave me a bit of power in the moment. So, I became a class clown, seeking attention and approval, needing praise and validation. Some people are ho-hum about the spotlight; others are scared to death of it. My competitive nature was surely a part of me making a living in it. When I was a kid, I wanted to run in the race, not for the experience, but to win. I always gave it everything I had. That natural wiring ain't always healthy.

If I had not become a touring musician, I likely would have been a (full-time) teacher of some kind. Maybe a writer, too, with a much more private, patterned life. When I coached baseball, I envied the other coaches — businessmen, teachers, salesmen, plumbers — their lifestyles.

These guys could organize their lives to be at almost every practice, every weekend tournament. I was regrettably much more hit and miss.

Disillusionment

Righteousness creates warriors of faith who head off on crusades: libraries burn, planes crash into towers, innocence is murdered. Seeing it in others makes me aim for less self-righteousness. I perceive a link to self-harm and collateral damage to the innocent in the vicinity.

In a world that increasingly favours competitive gamesmanship and partisanship, I prefer to choose fellowship, sportsmanship, friendship. If there's a loss of edge, so be it. We all make choices every day about the way we live. I've struggled with leaving myself open and trusting, but I'm learning to live with my choices: all of 'em, good and bad.

Another reason I decided to retire from touring was my disillusion with the tone and temper of the general public: the noise of the politics of the marketplace was costing me my liberal, subjective imagination of the magic power of music. I wasn't feeling strong enough to fight the general direction of culture, to beat my head against the walls being built. I was struggling to resolve myself to a society tearing itself apart, on its way toward Capitol rioters and Freedom Convoy protesters. For me personally, the good fight became one where I reassessed, conserved resources, rethought everything. I was overdue for retirement from the public ring. I got off the road and resolved to recommit to creative passions.

Prioritizing

In my head, my number one priority was family; number two was writing music and recording. Number three was playing live gigs (and teaching at the college); number four was career (PR, marketing, and promotion), and number five was website management, email, social media, et cetera. But the truth is I couldn't and didn't always keep these priorities straight. Especially in the ambitious early era of my career, family often drew the circumstantial short straw, which in hindsight will always be regrettable.

After a lot of soul-searching about forgiveness, I found that the hardest person to forgive is myself.

Fate

"Is it fate, or random chance? How can I decide?" Back in '86, I wasn't sure. Nowadays, I'm fairly certain: it's mostly random. I don't believe in destiny, or life being predetermined, any more than I can embrace the science fiction of multiple realities or universes, or the supernatural spiritualism of cosmic universal infinite eternities. While I don't believe in fate, I'm also not egotistical enough to believe that I can know anything for certain, which I might seek to impose on others, other than laissez-faire golden rules. I can't find the kind of faith necessary to commit to a higher power, other than to acknowledge that anything's possible, because my tiny brain is incapable of wrapping itself around an infinity of things.

Still I keep my head up and watch my step in the here and now, because the random chaos of the universe could come along any second and change everything. History shows that too many horrible, evil things get done in the name of higher powers. Far too many human beings cloak themselves in the guise of fate, destiny, or God — or wrap themselves in a patriot's flag — and then go out and turn standard, stupid, human tricks of deadly sins. Greed, ambition, envy, and lust always top the list. That track record leads me to believe that I can't accept someone else's notions of fate. I should maintain a good fight on behalf of my own game plan.

Teenaged questioning led me away from the business of religious faith. Reading some Bertrand Russell confirmed the agnostic, secular humanist in me. My natural curiosity through the years led to the writing of Dr. Robert Buckman. Humanism continues to make the most natural, organic sense to me. Its inherent humility appeals most of all. I have no problem at all with the idea that the universe and knowledge are infinite, and that we humans know practically nothing. If we decide to call the infinite universe, and all the stuff we'll never know, God — or Gaia or Yahweh — I can live with that. (As long as it stops there.)

The romantic in me likes to imagine that somehow it all connects — that the universe is an infinite house of cards naturally, chemically, organically, materially. However, the wild joker in all of that, for me, is the human element — the imagination that gives birth to all those wacky humanities (psychology, sociology, religion, spirituality, parapsychology, philosophy, politics, et cetera). I can't invest too much in an anthropomorphic interpretation of the way the universe works (even if we're only imagining). Voltaire said, "If God did not exist, it would be necessary to invent him," and I think we did. Jung equates the infinite unconscious to a god, which works for me in the abstract. Religious denominations claim to know the will or the word of God, but anything that anyone can ever know about God (including that which declares man as the master of his domain) has come to us through the filter of man. And we've got a bad habit of messing things up: polluting and misinterpreting things, demonstrating our selfishness, evil cruelty, and wicked greediness.

Destinies don't collide. Now I believe it's the chaotic accidents of unpredictable free will.

"You're the master of your own destiny." Argh. Just because I wrote and sang that lyric in the bridge of "Fight the Good Fight," do I really believe it?

No, it's not true all the time. But I do believe I have to live my life as if I can *make* it true, taking responsibility for myself and my actions. I must commit to something. But in the millisecond before any particularity happens, something random could come along to change things. In my humble opinion, no omnipotence makes that happen, and no amount of willpower prevents it.

I can't control my fate, not all the time. As I look around me at systems of government, finance, health, education, policing, and justice, the belief that our systems are still beholden to the worship of a supreme deity, who rules over the choices we humans make, seems delusional to me.

If we are going to do a better job for humanity, we need to start accepting our secular responsibilities to create a more humane and global culture. Faith and trust in the supernatural belongs in churches, not political states.

Mixing Art and Politics

As a humanist, my tendencies on social issues are usually liberal. On economics, I tend to be more conservative, probably because I paid a fair bit of taxes in my lifetime, was both a business partner and owner, and a teacher. I've been self-employed my entire adult life, a family man who lived in the suburbs, an artist, and an entertainer. So, I tend to work both sides of the aisle.

I've mixed art and politics in song lyrics over the years, taking potshots at politicians and advancing certain political and social theories of my own. In "Ordinary Man," when I wrote "con man, song in hand," I was saying — Look at me writing songs, performing them in (hopefully) a persuasive and entertaining fashion, promoting my values, marketing my wares, trying to manifest my point of view and profit from it — just another self-aggrandizing showboat. Art is propaganda, no doubt about it.

Throughout my career, I kept coming back to humility, admitting one might be wrong, willing to be gracious, humble, considerate. My wise friend Domenic DiGiacomo once said to me that in almost all circumstances, humility is great because it has no downside. It's all upside. The problem with arrogance is it has too much downside.

There's a whole lot of voter disenchantment in our culture: people are fed up with systemic failures. Public education and health care systems suck. Governments keep proving themselves to be corrupt and inefficient. Partisan power politics plays out in stalemate after stalemate. I get that frustration; I sympathize with the prevailing disillusionment.

I ask myself, Could art awaken more positivity, oneness, pluralism? That could be a good thing.

As an artist, I'm as entitled to a passionate point of view as the next person. But that's also why it's good for me as an artist to be a little skeptical, maintain a sense of humour, and not lose my sense of balance. Our best defence against bully pulpits is to keep moving, to remain agile and engaged.

Life's too short, with too many cruel twists and random acts of disaster. There's too much war, poverty, violence, cruelty, prejudice, injustice, ignorance, stupidity. I've always felt that honesty was the best policy, even if it meant some unhappiness in the short term. The great Nelson Mandela said that an issue was "not a question of principle; it was a question of tactics" — spoken like a true lifetime politician. Mixing art with politics is never simple, maybe always tactical. Still it always felt necessary to me, because politics is in everything.

Creative Juice

I've always tried to challenge myself to try new things — work with different people, teach, and also be a student for life. I had a varied palette to draw upon: writing, singing, playing, arranging, producing, teaching; different styles, gear, guitars. Mixing it up kept things percolating along. It was also important to get away from my palette — read books, watch movies, walk on beaches, catch sunsets, go to ball games. My philosophical penchant to try to maintain balance meant that if a well seemed to be running dry, the solution was to do some research, consult a map, and head off looking for fresh water. When I started feeling creatively blocked, it was often because counterproductive things were getting in the way. Focusing on the wrong priorities, I needed to lift my gaze to the horizon and contemplate other options. I could either stay miserable, believing life was dealing me a bum hand, or I could explore options about how to play the hand I was dealt.

I was also not above folding my hand to go looking for a new card game with a different dealer.

Blind Faith in Winning

When I was young, I was conditioned by competition. From my twenties into middle age, I maintained much of this cultural programming: the competitiveness of business, the may-the-best-man-win, dog-eat-dog nature of capitalism. There were gnawing doubts. After all, how does one reconcile the instincts and ideas of being civilized and humane, caring for the innocent, the weak, respecting the elderly?

I blinked and found myself a senior citizen, feeling somewhat ancient and vulnerable and certainly seeing things differently. The competitive exercise of the hit parade had lost its youthful innocent charm for me.

I look at my grandchildren and wonder, What kind of world will they inherit? Reduced ambition and optimism haven't made me more conservative, however. I'm reminded how liberal-minded I've always been, deep down.

In the dangerous politics of capitalism, there's a vainglorious modern obsession with winning. Who cares about losers? In a constant, combative, self-congratulatory state, winners have set the tone for democratic capitalism everywhere, with an awful lot of folks buying into those ideas of winning and losing and the gerrymandering of power and wealth. They *like* that style of leadership.

When I was a younger man, with higher testosterone levels, I was more into the competitive law of the jungle. Now pro sports seem shallower and more inconsequential to me, like mercenaries in the gladiatorial spectacle of the Colosseum. Bat flips, strutting, trash-talking, and touchdown celebrations strike me as hollow, showbiz theater. Not much sportsmanship in evidence.

As a jock in my youth and as a baseball coach in middle age, I understood only too well the adage that winning is chemistry. Winning masks blemishes and creates an atmosphere of tolerance for practically all peccadilloes. Plus, how does one come to terms with being a loser? No one likes to accept that status, so it's an enigmatic paradox. One competes because it's supposed to be character-building — but what has happened to character? Gamesmanship bullies its alpha dog status over sportsmanship, because it's about winning at all costs.

Isn't that what terrorists believe when they do what they do? I always played to win. Was I an unholy terror? Older now, I wonder, What do you *lose* when you win like that? Everything comes at a cost: nothing good is free. Each one of us makes choices every day, and each choice carries consequences — things we gain and lose. Learning how to handle defeat with class, dignity, and integrity intact is a deep life lesson that sport offers to everyone. It's a shame that so many have failed to learn its value in our modern world.

Some think their gloating and bullying behaviour brands them as invincible warriors, revelling in the hot-dog-sizzle moments of their achievements. I prefer athletes who control their intensity, channel it, and respect opponents. When that shows up, I'm delighted that at least a portion of the world is not going to hell in a handcart (with vanity plates).

The world has become more and more divided, between left and right, rich and poor. This culture of division and fear surely worked its evil spell on me, because in the last decade, I grew afraid.

In 1964, Marshall McLuhan wrote that "the medium is the message": content gets overshadowed (and rendered much more inconsequential) by the much more powerful influence of the medium that carries the information. He was primarily thinking about how TV was becoming such a force in society; his perspective certainly foreshadowed the arrival of a digital, social media age in which tweets function as PR and the dissemination of policy, in which Orwellian false flagging and brays of "fake news" have created an unholy mess of misinformation and propaganda.

> Americans no longer talk to each other, they entertain each other. They do not exchange ideas; they exchange images. They do not argue with propositions; they argue with good looks, celebrities and commercials. . . .
>
> The television commercial is not at all about the character of products to be consumed. It is about the character of the consumers of products. . . .
>
> If politics is like show business, then the idea is not to pursue excellence, clarity or honesty but to appear as if you are, which is another thing altogether.
>
> — Neil Postman, *Amusing Ourselves to Death* (1985)

America elected a B-movie star as its president and later put a reality TV star in the White House. As social media and TV play to the entrenched, grifters bellow about "fake news" and are all about winning dangerously shallow games. For us agnostic, humanist liberals, it feels like the whole world is losing.

Freedom of religion has come to mean that there's never freedom *from* religion. Power on the right seeks to impose its beliefs on others — church wants the power to control state — and power corrupts, scheming to hold on to what it's got and get more. It gerrymanders all it can, so it can win and keep winning, so that its power will accrue, to protect itself and crush enlightenment.

Since I became a teenager, I've never felt that "In God We Trust" was a good sociological or cultural strategy. The Wehrmacht had "Gott mit uns" on their belt buckles, but God is never on anyone's side when they go to war. God never cared who won the Super Bowl or an election. God is a concept used for leverage. To an agnostic, any notion of godliness is, at least, ecumenical: at its best, pluralist. But that's not the world we've got, with gaps widening between winners and losers, haves and have-nots. In our digital universe, it scares me that the moral, ethical, virtuous leadership that democracy historically offered to the world — the good faith side of democratic capitalism — has become such a polluted export. The brave new world isn't *brave*. Much of it seems to be driven by desperate bullies scrambling for turf, full of false hype.

I became fearful to express myself — in my own backyard, on my own website. Having voiced this angst, I want to state this: I'm not misanthropic. I still believe in the inherent goodness of most human beings.

Leaps of faith, I get. Blind faith, I don't.

Idealism versus Pragmatism

As an artist, I'm a lover, not a fighter — a pilgrim for peace, love, harmony, and beauty. But since I worked all my life in showbiz, I'm also a pragmatic realist. Loved ones would rightly say I have a tough, cynical side. I try to entertain people — reach 'em, teach 'em, connect with 'em. By the same token, some people can be frightening in their stupidity, ignorance, and hate.

The reality of this life is that there are all kinds of people who don't care what you think or feel. They have their own agenda, and they believe, with zeal, that their agenda is more important than yours. Those folks are dangerous.

A paradox of leadership is that no system, no plan, no theory, or amount of complexity or simplicity in doctrine, dogma, or political, economic, or military mechanics can ever solve all the world's problems. There will always be old problems that dog us and new ones that arise to challenge us. There will always be:

- ignorant and wilfully stupid people
- victims of any system one might care to invent
- criminals and lazy people looking to beat the system, the odds, the man, the game, the table
- good people with the best intentions who make human mistakes
- suckers born every minute, and those who are willing to fleece them
- hurricanes and tsunamis and force majeure "acts of God"
- innocent babies dying of leukemia
- neighbours fighting over the fence line.

Life isn't fair, and justice is a notion we keep trying to apply, but there are no ultimate solutions. Every system we invent requires maintenance and upgrading because nothing's perfect, and every system we invent will have victims who require justice. That's why the law can never be static: as society evolves, some laws become unjust.

There will always be a need for humility as one takes on responsibility. In my life as an artist, and in the music I made, I tended toward certain themes: justice in an imperfect world, evolution of the game, an attempt to spin something positive out of my cynicism, time, and the abiding graces.

Ego and Abiding Grace

Acknowledgement or acceptance from others doesn't make me believe I'm great at anything. It's gratifying, yes, that occasionally I found acceptance from folks. But generally my best intentions were to keep moving forward, to not spend valuable time and energy in the evaluation of past efforts. Good music is the thing that's great; I liked to pursue the idea of offering it. The rest, which is to say, the establishment of a reputation, ends up being largely marketing, and while I understood its value to a certain degree and knew that I must play along, there were always so many artists far greater. I tried to ignore conventional turf lines of genre as dictated by the market, and instead I simply pursued (and survived) my own capabilities, articulations of my own stylized pastiches. If other artists acknowledged me, it was perhaps for *that* quality — not for a quality of technical or artistic sophistication that I possessed, but for my combination of vocalist, songwriter, and guitarist, as a creative survivor. Some might perceive this attitude as false modesty, but it's not. Some think I'm too cynical and negative, but I think it's simply practical realism. Humility kept my work ethic honest.

It didn't feel wise to take too much praise to heart — nice when it happens, lovely to hear, and in some ways important to a career. Others had that perception of me, and sometimes winning awards helped with marketing and word-of-mouth. But if I started to believe my own best notices, I'd venture too far into the realm of showbiz and wouldn't be keeping the art and craft in its prioritized place of respect. If I believed the full extent of praise, shouldn't I also have taken the worst critical reviews to heart?

No: an athlete who recognizes that he's not bigger or better than the game has got it right. Ego and confidence are essential qualities to a performer, but greatness is in the eye of the beholder. The artist in me beheld the art and craft as the great thing I pursued. Buying too far into the praise of others might make me lose my own humility, and that felt unhealthy. I wanted to be myself, focused on my creative mojo, with my own perspective and sense of proportion.

When artists talk about someone having great taste, this may be what they're describing. Tasteful artists are really in touch with their own perspective, with the dimensions of their talents and abilities. They don't try to do too much: they might push the envelope, but they don't get out of their bag, their pocket, or their comfort zone because they know their limitations, and they don't start thinking of themselves as great. Consequently the music seems appropriate to its own ambitions — tasteful. That quality kept growing in importance to me.

Some celebrities, flush with success, start to think that this is their destiny, their birthright, and their charmed life is richly deserved — so they act that way. It's regrettable but hardly unusual in an age where certain graceless, discourteous behaviours are found to be entertaining and funny. TV characters are rude and selfish, intentionally written as unrepentantly self-centred. Reality TV is often cruel and heartless. It's been a graceless age — an age that holds nothing sacred, an age of irony (all phrases that found their way into my lyrics).

Still I hope for the best in others and try to give everyone the benefit of the doubt. I'm a very fallible human who can get short-tempered, cranky, and sarcastic. But at heart, I prefer to try to live under the influence of the abiding graces.

Reading Influences over My Life

As a child, I had every Win Hadley sports book in the series written by Mark Porter. I loved Ian Fleming, Ray Bradbury, J. R. R. Tolkien; devoured the Sir Arthur Conan Doyle Sherlock Holmes books and the *Complete Mark Twain Reader*. Kurt Vonnegut was a writer whom I stayed with from teenage years up into adulthood. I still have everything he ever wrote in my library. I read Dickens, and so, as I grew older, I also read and enjoyed John Irving, but his latest stuff got to be too much of a gordian-knot plot slog for me. There were periods during which I tried to catch up on English lit — the Brontës, Jane Austen, anthologies of the Romantic poets. I would also go through periods on the road, back in the day, when I would read everything by Anne Tyler, Alice Munro, Margaret Atwood, Jane Urquhart, et cetera. My subscription to the *Globe and Mail* newspaper was crucial to me as a writer. I used to read it every morning and do the Cryptic Crossword later in the day.

My wife and I joined the Book of the Month Club when I hit the chips in Triumph, and as a magazine columnist, it seemed wise to establish a proper reference library of my own. By my desk, I always had *Roget's Thesaurus*, *Bartlett's Familiar Quotations*, the three-volume giant-sized *Webster's Dictionary*, and many of the Oxford reference books (*Companion to English Literature*, *Book of Essays*, *History of the*

Classical World, Companion to the English Language, etc.). I kept handy the Strunk and White and the *Globe and Mail* style books, as well as Arthur Plotnik's *Elements of Editing*. I also had an extensive collection of music, songwriting education, and guitar history books; some were life-changing.

On long car drives, with the band, we'd play games to pass the time — the goofier, the better. In Triumph days, we'd kill time by naming obscure hockey players from the Original Six era, recalling names from the trading card and coin collections we'd had as children. (Collectible hockey coins came in packages of Jell-O and Shirriff products.)

In the Rik Emmett Band, on long car rides, we'd often come up with a category and play the Best of All Time.

Best Rock Bands of All Time: The Beatles, Deep Purple, Led Zeppelin, Steely Dan, Yes.

Best Produced Albums of All Time: *Aja* and *Gaucho* (Steely Dan); *Sgt. Pepper's Lonely Hearts Club Band* (The Beatles); *Pet Sounds* (The Beach Boys); *Bellybutton* (Jellyfish); *Songs from the Big Chair* (or a Tears for Fears greatest hits, because "Woman in Chains" is also insanely good); *The Dark Side of the Moon* (Pink Floyd).

Best Male Vocalists: Paul McCartney, Steve Perry, Freddie Mercury, Stevie Wonder, Sting, Peter Cetera, Don Henley, Lou Gramm, Steve Winwood.

Best Electric Guitarists Ever: Jimi Hendrix, Jeff Beck, tie — Page and Clapton, Steve Howe, tie — Ritchie Blackmore and Jan Akkerman, Wes Montgomery, Chet Atkins, Hank Garland.

Best Fingerstyle (electric): Chet, Joe Pass, Ted Greene, Lenny Breau, Tuck Andress, Tommy Emmanuel.

Best Drummers: John Bonham. I'd pick Steve Gadd as a close second (and he's perhaps more to my taste, even, than Bonham). Vinnie Colaiuta. Closer to home, Randy Cooke, Dave Langguth, Paul DeLong.

Desert Island LPs and Tracks:

- *Still Life (Talking)* and *We Live Here* (almost anything from Pat Metheny really)

- *Aja, Gaucho,* and most of *Countdown to Ecstasy* and *Royal Scam* (Steely Dan)
- *The Nightfly* (Donald Fagen)
- *Alone / But Never Alone* (Larry Carlton)
- *Breezin'* (George Benson)
- *JT* (James Taylor)
- "Lil' Darlin'" (Joe Pass — the sweetest guitar tone in the universe)
- "Girl Talk" (Kenny Burrell)

A scattering from recent playlists in our home:

- *Back in the High Life,* "Higher Love" (Steve Winwood)
- "Woman in Chains" (Tears for Fears)
- "God Only Knows" (The Beach Boys)
- "Still the One" (Orleans)
- "People Gotta Move" (Gino Vannelli)
- "I Wanna Stay Home" (Jellyfish)
- "Breaking Us in Two" (Joe Jackson)
- *The End of the Innocence,* "The Last Worthless Evening" (Don Henley)
- "Baker Street" (Gerry Rafferty)
- "Cause We've Ended as Lovers," "Where Were You" (Jeff Beck)

Two of the best live concerts I ever experienced were James Taylor shows — one at Massey Hall in Toronto (November '92), and one at Tanglewood, outside of Lenox and Stockbridge in the Berkshire Hills west of Boston (July 2011). James Taylor records are great, but live his music takes on another dimension, which comes from his confident comfort within his own wheelhouse, which is a beautiful, tasty thing.

The best live classical guitar solo concert I've ever attended was John Williams at Roy Thomson Hall in Toronto in the early '80s. I've seen Pat Metheny several times. His Pat Metheny Group tour for *First Circle* (1984) was amazing. I wish I'd been at a live concert on the *Still Life*

(Talking) (1987) and the *We Live Here* (1995) tours, because those are the two band albums that have emerged as my faves over the years. (I love his solo albums, especially *What's It All About*, as well as his *Beyond the Missouri Sky* album with Charlie Haden.) I recognize that this puts me squarely in the "most accessible Pat" category of Metheny fan, but even though I contend that Pat is probably the greatest guitar artist on the planet, often his artistry soars over my head. I happen to love the Pat repertoire that I can almost grasp.

On the road, I never partied with other bands. I was polite and respectful but always professional. I never fraternized or looked to make new friends. My attitude about touring was that I was working. I didn't bring my wife out on tours; she might join me for the last show somewhere, or we'd hire limos to bring our families to hometown gigs or down to Buffalo. But I wasn't looking to use gigs as excuses to hang out, party, or befriend guys from other bands. To me, making music was a gift — something to be honoured. It was important to me to approach touring with integrity. Like being a pro athlete, I was supposed to take care of myself: get enough sleep, eat well, stay hydrated, exercise, stretch, and — the biggest challenge of all — keep my throat healthy for night after night of singing super-high tenor parts. I willingly maintained the discipline to protect and prolong my humble gifts and talents, because it was my privilege to do so.

The past is a source of curiosity and good memories for fans. I get that. But there's a fair bit of cringe-worthy embarrassment for me in trips down memory lane — memories I'd prefer to package away in a vault, so I can move along in my present without constant reminders of youthful follies.

Maybe we tend to revisit the past because it's comfortable, reassuring. Our own history is a knowable, quantifiable, measurable place that validates us and makes us feel that our lives have mattered. Plus we can massage fuzzy facts into a better story, overlooking the bad and focusing on the good stuff (writes the man in his memoir).

Artists worth a lick should be hard on themselves. That's how the work evolves. The thing about the past is it's gone; it changes with the way we choose to put it into context. It's like Santayana's old expression about those who forget the past being doomed to repeat it. Life evolves, and we stumble blindly if we don't roll with it.

Given a choice, I'd opt for living in the moment in a creative and newly productive way. I really enjoy the process of creating recordings. Once they're done, I prefer to keep moving along to the next one.

Mental Health

Some people seem to enjoy stress: they seek it out and it gets them off. They like riding roller coasters, watching horror movies, and walking down strange alleys in strange countries until they get lost.

I *hate* those things.

Cognitive behaviour therapy was useful for me in trying to understand who I was, where I was at, and who I wanted to become. There's no shame that I feel in sharing this. It's become an ongoing, routine daily activity to keep coming to terms with my anxieties. Life had gotten too complicated, too hard. It had too much pain and sorrow in it for me to function properly. But our lives are always flowing in the river of time, and it's up to us to make our lives work for us; to try to make them simple, beautiful, and kind; to make them feel naturally good, both inside our heads and bodies and outside, where we interact with the natural world and the human beings we encounter. I always need to remind myself to circle back and do the work necessary to find my centre of gravity.

Despite a bit of discomfort as I warm up and work my way through it, I still love almost everything about playing guitar, and I enjoy the fact that I'm good at it, with some skills and abilities that reward the effort put into it. I feel a duty and an obligation to keep myself active as a guitarist, because it's my avocation — my calling — even though it's not my gig anymore. Making music helps keep me sane, giving me a very real sense of purpose — things that retired people need to have, by all reports. Since guitar has always been my hobby, as well as my gig, I don't see myself ever giving it up totally. Arthritis might eventually make playing too painful to be fun. But making music is also writing, and I enjoy writing of all kinds — emails and essays and letters and magazine articles and poetry and memoirs. I still love writing songs. So, creativity can still happen, even if I'm physically restricted. I don't think I'll ever stop making music. Nevertheless, one of my heroes, Ed Bickert, retired in 2000, put his guitar down — which had been in his hands as much as fifty hours a week! — and never picked it back up again to play or perform, for the remaining nineteen years of his life. During that time, he claimed he didn't miss it at all.

On My Tangents and Melting Pots

Triumph's live show was truly larger-than-life. But away from the stage, it was never in my personal nature to inhabit that style. I did get mighty sick of myself sometimes, wishing I could exercise more of what I lack: wisdom, patience, a scholarly and cosmopolitan diplomacy. I admire people of few words, who make them count. My articulation has always come from thinking and talking out loud, playing or writing my way toward something.

Over time, I became something of a Tangent Man. I'd been so type A, wanting to win the damn game; I didn't want to let the team down. But as I aged, I started chasing some butterflies.

From the mid-'90s, my career became ever more indie, low budget, and under the radar. My best option was to use my skill set to create boutique experiments in styles (tangents, in a way) that I imagined I could handle. No matter what bag I dipped into, it would still be inhabited by the DNA of a rocker and the spirit of a songwriter — a choirboy who loved British rock bands and the Great American Songbook.

A melting pot of tangents: every good musician is one, to some degree — just depends how much. I'm very happy to surprise listeners in positive ways. There was something to be said for challenging my own inventiveness, on limited budgets, and managing to come up with something worthwhile. I liked a business model where I got to be an original writer and performer, keeping my life straightforward and my business relatively simple.

Tangents are true to my nature. In moments when I'm racked with self-doubt or self-loathing — when I wish I was someone else, someone better, someone different — I'm comforted by the thought that at least this flawed human being is attempting to be honest with himself.

What's the sense of making recorded music if no one ends up hearing it? Problematically the digital world is one infinite shopping mall, a ridiculously oversubscribed and uber-competitive marketplace, filled with young folks who have more energy and ambition than I do, competing for their chance in the sun (so get outta the way, old fart white dude). Dignity and integrity colour the equation. I don't want to act or look desperate. Sometimes the marketplace bends and distorts you into shapes you never thought you'd find yourself in — something to avoid, since I'm not as flexible as I used to be.

Often striving for an optimistic voice in my work didn't make me mindlessly starry-eyed about anything. As I aged, there was no meaningful commercial music business climate for a lifelong writer and recording artist doing what I do. I'd checked a lot of the boxes on my career ambition lists, anyways. Collaborative business arrangements had lost their appeal. I'd played a few novelty cards and felt I'd gained whatever value they had. By my seventh decade of life, and my sixth decade in professional show business, the music business had changed so dramatically, I'd lost my ambition for commercial initiatives. I was looking for ways to distill it — get back to basics, make it simple and fun. Are there ways to make good music without business getting in the way? This required reinvention, thus new simpler recordings distilled to a basic format: a singer-songwriter, solo, with his guitar. I started thinking about bucket-list things: songs and music that would reflect roots, a book of poetry, a memoir.

Transitioning

As far back as 2010, I had begun quietly to consider less travel, less roadwork, less of the pressure of logistics and overhead. Administration behind the scenes was stressful, but I'd become addicted to the routines of constant psychological stress and pressure. My job defined a big chunk of my self-worth (as it was slowly but surely killing me).

Annual U.S. immigration work visa paperwork was an arduous, tiresome process for this Canadian musician, and that was only the leading edge of the grind. Airports were ever bigger and busier; lines were longer, the hauling of bags and instruments more wearying; there were more flight delays, with customs and airlines treating passengers like cattle and losing our luggage.

What if I could dispense with sidemen, agents, and roadwork? My attitude had shifted: I didn't fear retirement as much as I dreaded travel. Still there were the gigs: 90 to 120 minutes of play, of getting to be The Man. What would I become without that gravitational centre of my universe? If I gave up gigging, I'd be losing that lifelong part of my self-realization. What might happen to my self-esteem? Who would I become?

Granted, throughout my career, working around limitations had been part of the game. My music performances relied on physical skill sets — hearing, seeing, sensing. Time had begun catching up on me, bringing its arthritis, tinnitus, cataracts. Intellect was duller, memory not as trustworthy. But I'd always found ways to adjust. Maybe giving up the stage was just another adjustment to be made.

I try not to give regret much time and energy, because it's counterproductive. Yes, one uses experiences of sadness and regret to shape one's choices for today and tomorrow. But wishing that reality had been different never held much fascination for me.

As it played out, it took me eight years to finally transition away from touring, so my showbiz mask obviously had mighty deep hooks into me. When I finally took a leap of faith and retired, it turned out I could become more myself again, coming back to terms with my life, my family, our friends. I became more aware of life's changing nature: that the end of one chapter meant a new challenge, another new beginning. (I also had Lasik surgery — *awesome*.)

But there was a hard road to travel before I got there.

By the middle of 2017, the depth and range of the shit our family had gone through in the last year and a half went beyond the beyond, like nothing we'd ever known. My wife got breast cancer, had surgery, treatment, and got better — then got politically canned from her job. In the wake of that, we renovated our house of thirty-eight years (to sell, in an upmarket) and bought a new downsized place, living through the stress of also renovating that new home. Then the purchaser of our old house reneged on the closing day, and a lawyer spent a few months chasing the release of the deposit payment. In the meantime, we had to bridge finance to carry the two (renovation budget) mortgages on two properties. Then we sold the old house again — happily for even more money than we got the first time. (Still with me?) That allowed us to pay off the bridge financing on the mortgages and let out a deep sigh.

But my older brother got cancer and died. (As my younger brother had in 2007 — so it stirred up darkness.) My father aged to the point of (us) selling his house and moving him into a retirement home, where he started to show advancing signs of senility. So, there was also increasing elder care.

I kept playing concerts, and I wrote and recorded a rock album at the Metalworks with guest stars, including a Triumph reunion. During that period, in June 2016, my closest associate and brother-in-arms, Dave Dunlop, lost his wife, Deanne, to a sudden and tragic illness.

It made me question all of it, right down to my strength to remain in showbiz.

The Lifesaver of RES 9

I don't commit to stuff in superficial ways. To paraphrase Homer Simpson, I don't go half-assed at stuff, I commit whole-assed. I was all in on the RES 9 recording project. It tied up a lot of my life's loose ends.

The Mascot offer was a nice gift, with the resources and freedom to make the album properly, a lovely surprise at the age of sixty-two. I was grateful that the opportunity turned out so well — for the brother-hood, the hosting generosity of Gil at the Metalworks, and the karma, going back to work there. I appreciated the support and the kindness of positive reviews. In recent history, there'd been so much loss, pain, grief — so much divisive anger and fear in our culture. Why did this beautiful embrace of our music happen along? How did I get so lucky? I truly didn't understand and wasn't even going to try. It simply humbled me, in a profound way.

2016–17 had also been a grinder in other ways. As a college music teacher, I kept catching the whiff of political correctness and entitlement in the air. The familiar meritocracy was on its way out, and a new kind of meritocracy was awakening. I was losing ambition, optimism, mojo, and my sense of balance. Plus I was going to be up against it with my 2017 fall travel schedule for live gigs. I didn't like disappointing people, but the stress and anxiety of my college classes in the spring of 2016 had been draining me.

I always envisioned retiring from the road first, while keeping my hand in at the college. But in the end, the paycheques of live gigs won out over the long-running part-time college gig. Touring continued but unhappily. Value-added meet-and-greets were burning me out. Before I became too misanthropic, I needed more barriers to keep myself intact.

Another truth was becoming obvious as 2017–18 dragged along: the constant top-down coarsening of the public mood was killing the notion of graceful dignity for me. Some days, I could still dial it up, put on that mask of self-assured showbiz confidence up on stage, and pull off the music with a facade of cockiness. (As Chet Atkins once said, showbiz is making the hard stuff look easy, and the easy stuff look hard.) But as my friends and my long-suffering wife could attest, I'd always struggled with my own anxieties and introspective shortcomings too. So, even though I was ultimately disappointing many fans, I *needed* to hang it up.

In January 2019, I quit the road. (My timing was pretty good, because the COVID lockdown came along and the road got pulled out from under everybody else.)

Last Two Gigs: January 26 and 27, 2019, at Hugh's Room, Toronto

I didn't want to get boxed into a "last show" thing. At the time, I wrote on my website forum: "I can't predict the future: I don't know what will happen: it's uncharted territory." Here's what I wrote after the gigs to one of my daughters.

> [Last night] was an exercise in self-control, trying not to let the moment (emotionally) get away from me: I think I did pretty good. I enjoyed almost all of it, was "in the moment," and will have no regrets if I don't bother to gear back up for gigging in one way or another, in future. It all feels pretty natural to me — a relief, more than a sorrow. But — of course — I love music so much, it's hard to imagine a life where I don't get up and play it. I'll take my time and figure out how I get the fun of it without the stress and anxiety and aggravation of it. Meanwhile — in a way, I feel like when I was a little kid, and school's out for summer — my retirement beckons, like a big long summer holiday. (On a day of minus 17 with a snowstorm rippin' through. Hoo haw.)

Thoughts on Retirement

Health inevitably becomes a major focus. Getting from forty to sixty established a baseline of more-or-less healthy habits for exercise and diet; now I hope that my genetics remain kind. In my darker moments, I think Shakespeare might have nailed it in *Macbeth*: life is "a tale told by an idiot, full of sound and fury, signifying nothing." But on better days, when the golden years light shines to show the way, I sense some dignity, independence, and a measure of control in body and mind. I want to remain creative and positive about every new dawning day. I want it to feel like a gift — not a tale signifying nothing.

Aging is challenging, so living well is the best revenge. For me, a good retirement will mean staying on good terms with my finite existence. I'm not religious, so my spirituality is a humanist quest. There's a responsibility to continue the work toward becoming more conscientious, wiser, and that starts close to home, with family. As much as it was important to retire from ambitious hamster-wheeling, the great joy of my avocational life was the major element of play. The biz was a soul-eater in certain ways. But retirement can be about curiosity and creativity, expanding the palette of things that give me pleasure — good food, good friends, music, art, books, movies, and TV. Nice, comfortable clothes. I worked hard to build a solid financial base for my family; now I can offer them a sense of what constitutes the good life. That hard-earned wealth delivers a graceful, dignified final lap featuring lots of laughter and virtue — kindness, charity, patience, humility — and wisdom leading to serenity. Moving forward, evolving, learning, expanding, thriving. The final laps become a question of mind over matter.

School's out — will it be an endless summer vacation? I married the right woman. We have four amazing kids, who are wonderful people, and four grandkids (so far). We're rich with friends. So, I'm good.

I sold off the copyrights to my catalogue of master recordings and publishing because my children and children's children will never have the knowledge or desire to run a record label or a music publishing business. I barely had the motivation for my corporate assets anymore. So I began winding the company down. I don't give a shit about the vast marketplace. I have a little store at RikEmmett.com on the infinite digital internet mall. If somebody wants my new music, they can come and find it. If they don't want it, I don't really care about trying to make music retailers (or "influencers") recommend it to them. Retailing brings its own agenda and pressures to bear, which I don't want. Those complexities no longer suit my complexion.

Wanderlust (Inside Out, Outside In)

My wife likes to travel, and my kids have the same bug. I don't think of travel as something exciting, exotic, and fun. I spent my entire adult life travelling for business, so I can't really separate out the pleasure from the packing, unpacking, checking in and out, lining up, going through airports, hauling luggage — *hassle*. I went on a European river cruise with my wife and it wasn't too bad (except for the flights there and back — yikes). I liked how being on the boat meant not having to check in and out of hotels every day — going on site-seeing excursions but ending back on the boat. Same table for meals. That was okay by me. Another time we did the Rockies train ride — also okay by me, civilized.

We ticked off some bucket-list things for her: went to Arizona and visited Monument Valley up in Navajo Nation, did the helicopter ride over the Grand Canyon, saw the surreal Antelope Canyon gorges cut through the sandstone. (For me, we attended a spring training game in the baking hot sun of Phoenix.)

We've also flown to St. John's, Newfoundland, and stayed in the lighthouse keeper's cottage on the easternmost point of land in North America, getting to see the sunrise and hear the fog horn blow (thinking of Van Morrison and "Into the Mystic"). I don't do these things because I ache to try them. Occasionally I join my wife with a small amount of curiosity, but a larger desire to share in her happiness. So, in retirement, we'll likely go on a few trips here and there. But I'll be looking for luxury and no-surprise itineraries.

In truth, I'm a homebody, perfectly content in my comfortable abode with a cuppa tea, a guitar that stays in tune, a pencil, and a spiral notebook (a laptop now too). I've always been able to provide my own entertainment.

I've found that I don't desperately need an audience, of any size, and I don't need a paycheque. I've had plenty of both in my life. I never really had any wanderlust. More of an inside-out person than outside-in, I travel the infinity within.

THE TRIUMPH CHAPTER

Ars longa, vita brevis, occasio praeceps,
experimentum periculosum, iudicium difficile.
Art is long, life is short, opportunity fleeting,
experiment dangerous, judgment difficult.

— HIPPOCRATES

"This Is the Guy"

Gil Moore and Mike Levine hatched plans for a power trio mega-production project, and then went looking for a guitar hero who could sing, write, and front the show with a winning image. On a fateful August night in '75, they came talent-scouting at the Hollywood Tavern in Etobicoke, saw me performing, leaned over to each other, and agreed: "This is the guy."

After our first meeting, a jam session that served as my audition, it was clear that they were two of the savviest and most ambitious musicians I'd ever met. But yes, they could use a strong creative partner. With the job offer on the table, I had a few conditions. They needed to commit to conscientious rehearsing, to develop our gig stamina chops. I'd get an equal third say in band affairs. And importantly, they agreed to pay me

$175 a week whether we played bookings or not, which meant I could move out of my parents' home into a tiny little house at 530 Dufferin Street in Toronto with my girlfriend, Jeannette, as well as my pal Andy Brakas (who was, at the time, a French horn player graduating from the performance program at the University of Toronto).

The original mutual respect and balance of our skill sets established an effective, successful partnership. It was flattering that they valued my creative talent so highly, but it was even more critical that they guaranteed a steady income. In the end, the deterioration of these fundamentals led to my departure from the band. But in our developing years, Gil and Mike proved to be a dynamic duo of ambition and perseverance: Mike with a focus on marketing and promotional wheeling and dealing; Gil with extraordinary smarts for business planning, finances, and bookkeeping. Their appetite for the enterprise was impressive. (I loved Michael Cohl's description of them in the *Rock & Roll Machine* documentary: "They were pushy." Yes, *they were*.)

Our first rehearsals in an abandoned bowling alley at the corner of Mississauga Road and Lakeshore Boulevard West in September '75 began a high-risk enterprise that took a few years to get established. The first album dropped in October of '76, but things didn't start looking up until '77, when our cover of "Rocky Mountain Way" became enough of a success on Canadian AM radio that we could play concert venues as opposed to bars and high school gyms.

Things began to solidify when we signed the RCA U.S. record deal in '78, then locked in career-wise when "Hold On" and especially "Lay It On The Line" became solid FM radio hits in the U.S., off the *Just a Game* LP in '79. A bumpy, uncertain series of speculative bets got us to that point: my partners masterminded a growth plan that projected — *declared* — success, whether it was objectively true or not. Much of it was the helium of chutzpah, bank loans, a propane torch, dry ice, disco balls, cop car lights, and flash bombs: smoke and mirrors. Somewhere in the heart of all that, I was playing guitar, singing at the top of my lungs, smiling for the cameras, and learning how to write more effective commercial songs.

Triumph's business plan was an act of faith, committing ourselves to the carnival ride. Once I'd decided to live by my own entrepreneurial wits as a self-employed musician, I accepted that roller-coaster existence.

There's always a whole universe of other options one might try, but only one choice to make in the here and now. There's the old "right thing, right place, right time" cliché, and there's also knowing when and how to prioritize, to convince Lady Luck to come knocking, get up off your butt and answer the timing of her call — then work hard to satisfy the things, places, and times that she seems to prefer. (Yes, she's wearing overalls, so it's going to be arduous. Were you expecting a lottery win?) Plan A always requires more of a strategic work ethic than the average person possesses or routinely demonstrates, along with a tolerance for delayed gratification. Triumph had what it took to start the high-risk, low-percentage mountain climb of rock and roll showbiz.

It was not all luck. Gil Moore and Mike Levine worked some wonders, but they also believed in me. They encouraged me to put classical guitar pieces or jazz songs on hard rock albums, letting me write and record mini-symphonies for FM radio. They allowed me long lengths of rope, which I used to defy hangings. For that belief, I'll always be grateful.

From day one, the other guys worked double overtime on their priorities. Gil's abiding passion was for a razzle-dazzle stage production, and once we could afford to compete in the big leagues, Triumph's presentation kept evolving toward world-class — as was the marketing, promotion, and negotiating that my partners doggedly pursued. Gil also took justifiable pride in business administration, accounting, and bookkeeping, embodying his dad's business background. Mike worked the record company, radio, promo, and the industry. He was a salesman, comfortable in the disarming T-shirt and jeans uniform of a hippie rock star, looking to make a deal.

Yet by the time the characters in a partnership like ours got past the itchy seventh birthday, there were as many plan Bs developing as there were band members. Our trio of musketeers had our own personal lives, with growing responsibilities. In our particular rock and roll machine, the all-for-one-and-one-for-all ethic began to erode with individualized choices and priorities. They could never sustain their commitment to keep their chops up to where they might meet my expectations. Differing imperatives bumped other ambitions down our increasingly individualized lists.

In 1980 I accepted the invitation to become the "Back to Basics" columnist for *Guitar Player* magazine. That changed my public profile, differentiating me in the marketplace via the association with *GP*'s legitimacy and credibility. Rik Emmett wasn't just another rock-star wannabe: he could really articulate his love of the guitar beyond the trappings of a commercial image. Every month, I overdelivered conscientiously, with editorial research ranking the column as a reader favourite. That high-profile side hustle led to endorsement offers. (I'll always be grateful to Curt Smith, the Yamaha Canada artist rep, who ushered me into that wonderful company.) Delivering a monthly column broadened my writer's discipline. It led to a career highlight and an achievement of a teenaged fantasy: a cover feature in January '85. Another dream came true when I pitched a concept, had it enthusiastically approved, then co-produced the July '87 *Guitar Player* soundpage and cover story relating to Beyond Borders, an all-Canadian guitar quartet of Ed Bickert, Liona Boyd, Alex Lifeson, and me. Those opportunities would never have come along without Triumph, but it also became clear that endorsement deals and profile weren't based exclusively on the band's image. After I left the partnership, fortunately, execs at Yamaha and other companies continued to do business with me.

I was relieved to find this, after leaving the band, because Triumph was not universally admired. That's likely true of most showbiz acts, but within the industry, the fact that the band managed its own business and had its own production company was seen in some quarters as too cocky — suspect, an ambition of evil corporate rock. In some quarters, resentment and envy rose and curdled into scorn. A prevailing perception within the critical community was all sizzle, no steak. Our business attitude of brash confidence meant that bridges got burned, as my partners skirmished with booking agencies, managers, promoters, and record companies. I was spared the confrontational bloodshed but not all of the consequences. Still, most of it turned out to be simply par for the music biz course.

Plus — Triumph's chutzpah wasn't all bad. For example, Mike Levine negotiated us into the closing slot of Canada Jam in the summer of 1978, which was a nightmare to actually play, as the clock crawled toward four a.m. But, like Hendrix closing Woodstock, it became an undeniable, eyebrow-raising symbol of the band's speedy rise into public recognition. That was all Mike Levine, talking his A game with promoter Lenny Stogel.

Another example of good business management: early on, a bank loan arranged by Gil secured us a tractor trailer, and we would roll into gigs making a larger-than-life declaration. But it wasn't hollow — that trailer accommodated production values that other bands never even contemplated. For instance, years later, Gil ordered a custom-made, state-of-the-art crowd control barricade for front-of-stage. When we weren't out on the road with it, our production company rented it out to every concert promoter and event producer in our neck of the woods. As one of our steadiest wage-earning assets, that barricade stood in eloquent testament to Gil's business acumen.

Those are only two anecdotal stories from the hundreds of ways my partners assembled and drove Triumph to its successes. There's just not enough space for them in this book. Maybe someday they'll write their own.

Constant larger-than-life declarations of the act's career were both the trademark and the Achilles' heel of Triumph's business. Creative dimensions of the band were supposedly my principal turf, but I could simply get outvoted on any initiative and often was. My partners kept me distanced from the business, for understandable reasons: in the first six or seven years of our partnership, I was underqualified and inexperienced, happy to be spared the B.S. and the battles. Over time, however, the power dynamic grew problematic for me. The growth of their control over business affairs streamlined their day-to-day process, but gradually kept diminishing the value of my input.

Still — that's not how it felt to me back in the '70s. I kept looking for artistic, creative ways to build our reputation. Off the first album, the track "Blinding Light Show" gave the act some artistic credibility, via radio airplay in San Antonio, Texas. And credit should go where it's due: that song was actually composed by Chris Brockway, Denton Young, and me, in Act III, the band I'd been in before joining Triumph. Chris had coined that title and hook within a concept that had intentional, ironic layers. Triumph's adaptation of the song meant the band's dynamic light show now had a production number with lyrics talking about how the spectacle could be a hollow, soul-destroying exercise. Its classical guitar instrumental section also challenged riff-rock clichés (and became a recurring staple of Triumph albums).

But I hit upon something with legs when I wrote the song "Hold On" for the third album. Triumph was now a band with a self-empowering message for people, a hit song on the radio that optimistically spoke to motivation and inspiration. The follow-up tune, "Lay It on the Line," was even stronger: musically hip but heavy, with signature hooks and a message that said *give me the truth*. The name of the band was now imprinted on a unique freak flag, flying for its fans. Our content outgrew the petty resentments of our declarative ambitions: the proof was on the charts. The band calling itself Triumph was about its *music*.

Those commercial successes of '79 changed the band's dynamics out in the world. Yet inside the rock and roll machine, it gave rise to things that eventually forced me out the door. But first . . .

Understanding timelines and the development of priorities is critical. Our first daughter, Shannon, was born in '82; our twins, Cassandra and Ashley, in '85; our son, Brendan, in '88. One of the many reasons I left Triumph in September of that year — but perhaps the most important — was because I wanted to have more of my own life back, to try to be a better husband and father. I'd missed the first steps of some of my kids; the first time they spoke a real word or rode a bike; birthday parties and parent-teacher meetings. The truth is I'd been trying to figure out how I might extricate myself from Triumph since '84, but circumstances never offered a viable strategy. (Also, leaving the band partnership didn't automatically make me a better husband and father, regrettably. Trying to arrive at a Triumph settlement made parts of my subsequent life miserable, and over the years I realized that my career experiences had pulled my whole world out of whack, so that the balancing of life and career remained a huge challenge.)

Core Issues: Lead Vocal Profile on Focus Tracks

As the lead singer of both radio focus tracks ("Lay It on the Line" and "Hold On") in '79, growing public impressions of Triumph pegged me as the lead singer and front man of the band. But make no mistake: Triumph was *always* Gil Moore's band.

RCA's promotional commitment to those two songs fuelled and solidified the band's growth. Touring got stronger in both the U.S. and Canada, and the business of the band expanded. Gil was spending more time in the office, building the tour production, booking agent and promoter connections, and merchandising. Mike was always working the phones, doing radio promotion, and travelling to radio conventions and industry events. There was significant advancement on a lot of business fronts: the band had more cash flow; our office staff and payroll were increasing. We were making a major investment with our studio, Metalworks, which was being built and staffed right next door to the offices and warehouse. There was more overhead and more risk, but it all made good sense to me and was well within my comfort zone.

Songwriting Credits

On the first three albums, whoever brought an original song idea into pre-production got a sole writing credit. So, when my radio airplay royalty checks showed up following *Just a Game*, they reflected solid earnings for me personally, especially due to American radio success. This gave me pause for cautious thought about the future: would my partners, who were devoting long hours to business management, grow to resent inequitable songwriter earnings if the trend toward the popularity of "Rik songs" continued? After all, songwriting credits and earnings had played a role in the discord of the Beatles, and lesser bands, where singer-songwriters earned far more money through airplay royalties and publishing income than other band members (customarily, rhythm section drummers and bass players). So, I proposed to Gil and Mike that, going forward, our songwriter's credits and royalties should get split equally three ways. They agreed, and I began signing over my royalty cheques for deposit into the band's general accounts.

The writing credits of the pre-1980 *Just a Game* songs remain solely mine, however, to this day — and when I left Triumph, I took those royalties with me.

In any case, this attempt to preserve the team spirit of the partnership didn't solve the fundamental divisive issue. Gil wanted to sing Triumph hits. The issue grew when "Magic Power" and "Fight the Good Fight" off '81's *Allied Forces* LP became two more tent-pole, evergreen FM radio anthems. While both of those songs carried the new official three-way songwriting credit split, I was the vocalist, so once again, from the outside in, public perception of Triumph's brand became more Rik-centric.

That wasn't the way it worked from the inside out. Ironically, these particular band successes were eroding the musketeer ethos.

Suing RCA and Moving to MCA

After the *Never Surrender* LP release in '82, and the subsequent touring that carried us well into '83, my partners grew unhappy with our RCA record contract because the label wouldn't renegotiate the deal. It locked us in for a lot of albums over what promised to be an eternity, thanks to automatic suspension clauses for late deliveries. These suspensions began piling on top of each other, as we'd toured incessantly to establish a foundation for the act, thus delaying our ability to deliver albums at the contracted calendar deadlines. More to the point, production advances for the budgets of major label rock recording acts had boomed, so there was chafe at what had become our relatively modest production advances, locked in at the label's annual discretionary option. Compounding this unhappiness: chatter leaked back that RCA perceived Triumph commercially as only a "cult" band, selling gold, never making it into the multiplatinum big leagues, only ever being an AOR FM radio act — preferably with Rik as its singer. Consequently, RCA likely only projected cult-level marketing and promotion budgets toward Triumph. Meanwhile, already comfortable in a big-leage pop world, in the Elvis Presley universe that the record label was predicated upon, RCA had begun signing and investing heavily in priority acts from other stylistic pop genres in the music biz — decidedly not hard rock. I was pretty content with the creative career success I was enjoying, but my partners had larger career ambitions than being in an RCA-contracted cult band, so they went looking for a lawyer to make the case for a lawsuit that could break us out of the contract.

I was never keen on this lawsuit gambit. After eight years of a passive business management role, I was growing restless. But I remained a loyal musketeer, accustomed to being the odd man out, committed to paying my one-third share of the legal bills and my partners' New York travel, hotel, and meal expenses.

Ultimately we lost in court, which really shook my faith in the business plan and the scale of risks we were undertaking.

After that, the prevailing assessment was that our future working relationship with RCA had been fatally poisoned, so — plan B — a timeline for a contract buyout began. RCA set the price tag at three million bucks, which led to an industry-wide shopping expedition for our next album release. Mike and Gil made the rounds with some tracks from the pre-production of our new *Thunder Seven* album. Two high-level execs flew up to Metalworks in a corporate jet for a private listening session and wine-and-dine evening. As they left for the airport, they said, "In our opinion, this is the very best album that you guys could possibly have ever made. Congratulations." They went out the door, and there was jubilation in the lobby of the studio — but not from me. Frowning, I said, "He chose his words *very* carefully. He said it was our best effort, not that he even liked it or that he personally thought it was any good. He didn't say he wanted to make a deal." My interpretation of the way it had played out was dismissed, but the next morning, they officially passed. Misreading the room in a high-stakes situation, right before my eyes, didn't exactly bolster my confidence in our shared venture.

Irving Azoff, the president of MCA Records, eventually did step up, willing to write a three-million-dollar cheque to RCA and build a new Triumph contract. In my eyes, at the time, this wasn't necessarily a win. It was our biggest gamble yet, placing Triumph under a daunting three-million-dollar debt — an advance against our own royalty account. Based on the record company's own bean-counting, we would need to sell enough records to pay back all that money from our own royalty earnings. We'd never gone platinum (sold a million units), and now we likely needed to go at least double platinum, if not more, just to break even.

In my dark moments, I would run scenarios of how I might extricate myself from the situation, but I kept coming up empty. Giving notice and leaving the partnership had grown so complicated that I couldn't envision any other sensible option but to musketeer along, even though the dynamics were growing more uncomfortable.

In the title song from the '83 *Never Surrender* album, I'd written, "I've only got one life to live, it's gonna be mine." That proved to be prophetic. While disenchanted with the direction of the partnership, I lacked the courage to generate a constructive confrontation. I also lacked the creative ability to develop any strategic vision that my partners would have found acceptable for disentangling myself from Triumph. I didn't want to poison the atmosphere inside the rock and roll machine with too much unhappy noise. We had a partnership agreement contract, drawn up in our early days, with punishing "leaving partner" provisions: heavy financial disincentives for calculations of partnership assets and book values. That held me inside and kept me quiet.

I actually went to Triumph's in-house lawyer, Ross Munro, to talk about the ramifications of leaving the band. Ross was then, and still is, a very good friend of mine — an ethical, decent, and emotionally transparent guy. Whenever I raised my unhappiness confidentially with him, voicing my desire to bail out of the partnership, as a part of the management team, he always maintained his loyalty to his office and to the partnership of Triumph. (He always advised that those "leaving partner" clauses of the contract agreement were more than enough to quietly keep anyone in place.) As I climbed out on the ledge, over different issues during the years up to '88, Ross would talk me back down, recommending I cope with my unhappiness. I will always feel bad, because I kept putting him in a compromised, conflicted position. Ross and I were close friends who got along well, and he ended up managing my solo career for about eight years after I left Triumph. But his loyalty and duty had been to the partnership that employed him, and his advice for almost four years was to find ways to make it work, to stick it out.

I don't want to create the impression that Triumph didn't have some glorious and truly beautiful moments of brotherhood during the surreal journey we experienced together. There was a heart of Triumph that I really loved. It always makes me smile when I think back to the crazy days of our surreal growth. Like the time in 1978 when we signed the RCA contract for our U.S. deal; it was a complicated legal undertaking, with a central agreement as thick as a phone book, spawning several side letters and schedules. The venerable downtown Toronto law firm Lang Michener handled the signing of the paperwork. On the big day, we were ushered into their giant boardroom, featuring a table that had to be thirty feet long. At one point in the proceedings, every lawyer had gone off to make copies of addendums, make confirmation calls, or send faxes; secretaries were tracking down fresh coffee. The three of us were left alone in the solemn, hushed room. I could not resist the opportunity to entertain my partners: in my jeans and running shoes, I took a running start, leaped up on the table with a good head of steam, sprinted a few strides, then dropped and pulled off a long hook slide the rest of the way — safe into second base, right in front of the gigantic portrait of founding partner Roland Michener, a former Governor General of Canada. The guys belly-laughed. I'm not proud of my behaviour, but it's still a sweet memory of being in Triumph — when it was just a game, before the musketeers started taking themselves too seriously. Truly the glue that held the band together as long as it did was that we could laugh at the surrealism of it all, and at ourselves.

What I Can See from Here that I Couldn't See from There

It's often impossible to get the objective perspective of a career when you're inside it and living it, day to day. But careful consideration, distance, and history provide both overview and insight. Looking back, it's obvious that Triumph never dominated the commercial record sales market. Our strong AOR FM radio airplay from '79 to about '86 never converted into the top ten songs or mega-record sales of Boston, Journey, Styx, Rush, Foreigner, Bon Jovi, Def Leppard, or Mötley Crüe. Without those giant multiplatinum sales, our revenue stream was a bit more complicated. Our touring and merchandising earned us more than our record royalties, with more commercial success in the U.S. than Canada. And with the U.S. market ten times the size of Canada's, we also benefitted from the exchange of U.S. dollars into Canadian. Being self-managed saved a huge slice off the top of our gross earnings: we held on to our own publishing, with sublicense deals in foreign territories. The Metalworks Studio had grown into a viable integrated business operation. Gil provided accounting and bookkeeping oversight that saved us huge expenses for financial management. The production, lighting, and staging business that he ran from our warehouse provided a solid base. Through his entrepreneurial instinct for business development and management, those aspects of our enterprise thrived on being practical and Canadian, modestly operating within its means.

By '85, pursuit of tour endorsement and sponsorship had become the partnership's main business focus, with Gil solidifying his official position as the GM, CEO, CFO, and executive producer of every move of the Triumph brand. He came by this power-positioning honestly. The only son of a financially astute dad, Gil had grown up in an affluent suburban community, fully understanding a fundamental power dynamic that so many musicians fail to grasp: controlling the cash flow means controlling the enterprise.

The *Thunder Seven* Production Project

Circumstances had allowed me great personal creative freedom in the Metalworks of 1984. As my partners were away in a New York court fighting the lawsuit, then shopping around the U.S. for buyout candidates for the contract, I was left alone for weeks on end to pursue my own agenda, getting to create the B-track studio pieces "Time Canon," "Midsummer's Daydream," "Little Boy Blues," and "Stranger in a Strange Land." These weren't songs built for the hit parade of radio airplay; they were recordings made to feature artistic imagination and studio chops.

As a recording artist who came into his own during the album era, I loved the depth that B-tracks provided to the arts and crafts of making recordings. To me, that depth defined an album artist, as opposed to a pop star. I always identified more as a musician and a creative writer than as a rock star, and *Thunder Seven* allowed me a generous education as a recording artist. But in hindsight, it was not the kind of chart-conquering, bulletproof commercial-song-oriented production that was coming into vogue. Nineteen eighty-five featured commercial hits from Tears for Fears, Sting, Dire Straits ("Money for Nothing"), Foreigner ("I Want to Know What Love Is"), Starship ("We Built This City"), and Richard Page singing "Broken Wings" in Mr. Mister. Producer Ron Nevison had delivered the *Heart* album to Capitol Records, which sold over five million units. Smash hit singles and crossover power ballads with money-shot MTV videos had become a heavily established, industry-wide formula.

Our band failed to grow along with these trends, and I was probably more guilty than anyone else, since in '84 I'd been left alone, deep within a Metalworks bubble, playing to my own eclectic indulgences. Plus the partnership's prevailing vibe at that time was that since I already had evergreen vocal tunes, the focus tracks were destined for Gil. The strongest hooky commercial song I wrote during the *Thunder Seven* sessions was "Follow Your Heart," and from day one of its pre-production, Gil was slated to be its lead vocalist.

After the MCA deal got signed, Eddie Kramer was brought in as a producer, lending his expertise and industry credibility to finishing some overdubs and the final mixes. Eddie's solidly legit track record included Hendrix and Zeppelin, and I was delighted to get to work with him. Still, out in the industry, there was a more modern school of commercial production development that Bob Clearmountain delivered for Bryan Adams, Mutt Lange built for Def Leppard, and Bruce Fairbairn contributed for Bon Jovi.

We were behind that curve, and despite optimism going into the MCA deal, the song "Spellbound" and its video hadn't really popped, and even though the live "Follow Your Heart" concert video did well for us at MTV, it wasn't a particularly big radio hit.

The *Thunder Seven* tour, however, was an unqualified success, with Pepsi sponsorship and the band travelling in a private jet.

Nevertheless, *Thunder Seven* record sales failed to shrink our debt; worse, the new MCA contract made us liable for annual payments on any interest generated by the unrecouped advance, which was in the neighbourhood of a few hundred thousand U.S. bucks, at least. Consequently, the live album, *Stages*, got rushed out in '85, the result of a side deal hurriedly concocted to replace that payment due to MCA. We'd dodged a financial bullet but were still living under the shadow of three million dollars in debt. Already unsure and nervous, I began to suffer from the stress and anxiety of catastrophizing, looking to the future and twisting in the futility of my powerless position.

In June of '86, our family was blessed with the arrival of twins. With more dependents, I found my misgivings deepening, locked in the partnership at ever higher stakes. My faith in our success was diminishing while my doubts about the band's business grew in proportion to the ballooning consequences of the debt. Radio had transitioned into tighter formatted playlists, and the competition had outpaced us. With Triumph heavily unrecouped, the label's influence and pressure mounted, and the two subsequent album projects had radically changed processes, each in very different ways.

Between the label and band management, it was decided that Ron Nevison's undeniable track record, delivering big hits for Starship and Heart, demonstrated a winning strategy. He had a reputation for bringing surefire commercial hit material from outside writers and publishers into pre-production, so we wouldn't even have to write our own radio-friendly focus tracks. My own songwriting ability was being slighted, and I wasn't totally happy to surrender opportunities to add to the commercial potential of our own publishing catalogue. But I kept my mouth shut and soldiered on.

Nevertheless, a critical dynamic had been compromised: the partnership was on a commercial path where the very things I loved to do — write, sing, and play good music — were shrinking and depreciating within the confines of our business plan.

We cut the drum bed tracks in L.A., where Ron and his assistant engineer, Mike Clink, were comfortable. On the day before we flew home to begin overdubs in our own studio, the issue of lead vocals on focus tracks arose once again. Ron pulled me aside and privately directed me to ensure that overdubs on the focus tracks he'd brought to the project got cut in *my* best vocal keys. But Gil had already claimed the strongest commercial tune of the bunch, the Neal Schon, Eric Martin, and Tony Fanucchi power ballad, "Just One Night." I told Ron he didn't understand the political dynamics of the band, and his plan to put my vocals on his focus tracks was never going to fly. He assured me I could leave that up to him.

I didn't know Ron well, but I sensed that an issue of this magnitude required diplomatic tact and should be raised between musketeers. So, on the plane ride home, I decided to broach the subject with Gil.

That was a huge mistake.

It's an industry standard cliché: artistic differences. But it's a common problem of creativity by committee.

During that flight, the issue hanging in the air was: what's the best way forward for the career success of the band? Somewhere over the vast Midwestern USA, carefully buried fault lines of the partnership's internal tectonics finally cracked. Discussion and debate became argument, then blatant anger. Irreconcilable artistic differences erupted into the open, causing damage that would take decades to heal.

Triumph had given me great opportunities and privileges — joyful and fulfilling. I got to write, sing, and perform my own original music that reached a wide audience, becoming successful on radio and in concert. Understandably, Gil wanted that same privilege: to be the lead singer on Triumph's focus tracks. Given the band's direction, the value of my role and the future potential of my privileges would be narrowing.

I stepped off that plane feeling more than ever that my growth as a creative artist depended on getting out of Triumph.

Despite the serious internal damage to the partnership, a superficial working solution for the business brand was quickly arranged. Ron came up to Metalworks, had a short meeting with Mike and Gil, and immediately left the project. Mike Clink moved into the producer chair (later proving himself multiplatinum-legit by delivering Guns N' Roses to the world). Gil performed the lead vocal on "Just One Night." But as the album was headed toward its delivery date, at the eleventh hour, the label said they still didn't hear a lead commercial focus track, so I was dispatched home by Levine and Clink to compose a peppy pop song. I went home, wrote "Somebody's Out There," and the band hurriedly recorded it exactly as written and arranged. Climbing to number twenty-seven on the *Billboard* singles chart made it the highest charting commercial tune the band ever had, but the follow-up promotion campaign failed to catch on, and the *Sport of Kings* album had no market legs.

My commitment to the partnership had been damaged beyond repair. The pressure of record company debt and the shift of the market forces had stolen the band's sense of humour and our ability to enjoy each other's company. For three years I'd been quietly, personally struggling to figure out what a graceful exit might look like. Now, everything was awkward and uncomfortable — and headed for worse.

Retrospection allows me to look back at how the music industry changed from '78 to '88 (and beyond), and realize that the competitive nature of the biz kept narrowing its commercial focus. Despite my own affection for eclectic album rock, it was rapidly losing market share. Plus, I was simply getting older, in a business predicated on large-scale demographic marketing that sells the music of new young stars to teens and pre-teens. It wasn't all Triumph's fault that Rik Emmett's prospects were shrinking. The business itself had begun shapeshifting on its way to the launch of Napster in 1999. In a way, Triumph had been struggling with these realities without the benefit of a bird's-eye perspective of the grind of history.

More Red Ink

Before the *Kings* tour started, a million-dollar nonreturnable advance from the upstart Virgin merchandising company was offered to Triumph. It was rejected in favour of a deal from the band's previous tour merchandiser of T-shirts, hats, gifts, and novelties. The advance from our known associate was smaller and — critically — also returnable. But doing business with them brought a level of comfort, and if tour sales went well, the royalties offered more profit potential.

I had a bad feeling about the potential popularity of our ticket sales on the upcoming tour, which brought along serious doubts about those future potential merchandising royalties. Given radio and MTV trends, I believed that our competitive market value had weakened. Therefore, that million bucks of non-returnable "upstart" money left sitting on the table had looked extremely good to me, simply because we wouldn't have had to pay it back if tour sales failed to recoup the advance.

My cautious instincts didn't determine partnership decisions: Triumph's risk tolerance was solidly established. In this case, the edgy strategy went bust. Ticket sales were weak in a lot of markets, so merch sales were too. Additionally, for our normally lucrative hometown stop on the Canadian tour at Toronto's Maple Leaf Gardens, originally intended as a two-night event, advance ticket sales only justified one show, with the entire gate going to charity.

Once the tour dust cleared, there was a huge debt owed for repayment of the lion's share of that merchandising advance — yet another huge hit to my confidence.

***

A further crushing blow came unexpectedly. Gil's dad, Herb, passed away — a difficult loss for the whole band, as he had provided bookkeeping services for us during our early years and had been a calm, trustworthy counsellor and figurehead who was a grounding influence for us all. But it was devastating for Gil, an only child, whose grief was profound. Clearly, it was the wrong time to broach the extremely difficult and complicated scenario of my exit strategy.

***

Before we get to my story of finally leaving the band, let me say — I truly enjoyed the Banger Films *Triumph: The Rock and Roll Machine* documentary. I think Sam Dunn and Mark Ricciardelli did a fantastic job, saddled with the impossible — taking more than 40 years of history and fitting it into a feature-length movie. Obviously, it was a mammoth editing job. I willingly, happily participated in that project, fully aware that the band's history was going to get reduced into a singular showbiz narrative arc. That story suggests the guitar player suddenly quit the band at the height of its success, but there were many challenges behind the scenes — and my departure wasn't sudden. Our positioning didn't feel all that lofty to me either.

This is my perspective of where things were at, up to the fall of '88, and why I decided to finally bail out when I did.

The Beginning of the End

The production of the contractual obligation *Surveillance* album was the last gasp of the MCA deal, as they reluctantly honoured the contract for one more LP from Triumph. Thom Trumbo was MCA's U.S. west-coast-based

A and R man, and as a sign-off assignment to his planned job departure from the company, he parachuted in as our executive producer, and diplomatic babysitter, to get the album delivered on time.

By then, being in Triumph was disheartening — there was little engagement, and we were hardly ever in the recording studio as a unit.

The final straw that broke me dropped over a tune I'd written entitled "Rock You Down," its lead vocal assigned to Gil by Thom and Mike. When I got to hear the mixed track with its vocal for the first time on the afternoon of the day the completed album was due for delivery to California for mastering, I discovered that wthout consultation or collaboration, my lyrics had been rewritten — changed from my topic, about each generation's instinct for rebellion, into a song about physical lust.

Thom advised me to let it go — that an album B-cut doesn't really matter much in the grand scheme of things. From certain perspectives, he was right. But for me, it was symbolic. Yes, I took too much pride in the old-school artistry that could be found in deeper album cuts. Yes, I was insulted that my creativity, taste, and work ethic had been compromised. I felt that a sacred trust had been broken. A combination of anger and heartbreak extinguished any remaining loyalty to Triumph, but in order to extricate myself from the complicated workings of the Rock and Roll Machine, there remained troubling legal and business details.

The End of the End

As 1988 began, I gave my notice and was looking to negotiate my way out. But Triumph needed to generate cash flow, somehow, to repay the debt to the merchandising company. There was no large-scale *Surveillance* tour, as there was no market traction from the new album. An elaborate video for "Never Say Never" failed to get decent rotation anywhere.

Some opportunities presented themselves for big paydays on special concert events and outdoor promotions in the spring and summer. The band proposed that I stick around to play gigs, helping to pay back Triumph's debt. After some back and forth on a myriad of prickly issues, I proposed a simple compromise: I'd stick around and play as many gigs as Triumph wanted to book, in order to settle financial matters.

As it turned out, four gigs were booked in 1988. March 19, spring-break week, we played a windswept beach at Isla Blanca Park on South Padre Island off Corpus Christi, then March 25 at Roberto Clemente Coliseum in Puerto Rico, then another big outdoor event July 30 at the Redwood Amphitheatre in Great America Park outside San Francisco, and finally, a gig on the Labour Day weekend, September 3 at Wonderland, north of Toronto.

Throughout those nine months of 1988, everything felt surreal. Essentially, I was hanging around, waiting for a settlement that never materialized. I figured Triumph's entire merch debt had been offset by those four gigs, so I said — no more. I'm out. All of the issues went to lawyers, who took years to eventually sort it out. Even after accepting a settlement, it took me another dozen years to figure out how to come to terms with what had gone down, forgive it, and move past it.

1983 to 1988 were crazy times in my life and my music career. In the Banger documentary, I talk about how I ended up angry at myself. What I failed to articulate was my frustration — a few decades of resentment toward Triumph had eventually boomeranged on me because I couldn't summon whatever it took to find forgiveness. If there was going to be any kind of reconciliation (and maybe an eventual reunion), I had to figure out how to be a man who could get over his history, which seemed like a non-starter.

After many years, it took one major catalyst.

The First Steps Back — Russell

I thought I could never reconcile, but when my brother Russ was dying of cancer, I discovered that some sacred beliefs and strains of righteousness don't guarantee much at all. Life was getting rewritten around me, whether I agreed or not. Declining from cancer in 2006 and putting his own affairs in order, Russell said he'd love to see me mend the Triumph bridge and take care of my own baggage. He had the same sense of nostalgia that fans had and was advocating the virtue of forgiveness: honouring the better parts of friendship and having the courage to always try to do the right thing, even if it seems fearfully difficult. I had to let go of my self-righteous anger at perceived betrayals and grievances. My brother Russ was like the fictional voice that whispers to Ray Kinsella in *Shoeless Joe*: "Ease your pain."

He asked me to promise, so I took on reconciliation primarily as a tribute to him. I would try to come to terms with the grand parade of time, which had made me realize that stubborn pride was insignificant in the struggle for liberation from the swirling darkness of sorrow that comes from loss, grief, and guilt.

I had to learn how to face my own mistakes and narrow-mindedness, and attempt to expand my horizons. I needed to open myself back up — push towards a forgiveness that I naturally lacked. It was a promise I made to my dying brother, but that didn't automatically make it easy. My fears and anxiety had kept me from making any attempt for years, but the vow to Russ proved to be the necessary tipping point. After all the times that I swore it would never happen, here are the reasons I said yes to reconciliation with Gil and Mike.

Nostalgia

I have many positive, powerful Triumph memories of my own. It hadn't been easy, living in denial of that career history. It had been even harder to build a new life for myself. But Russ had become the point man for all the people who kept asking, "Can't you do it, for old time's sake?" On my own website's member forum (patrons in the best sense of that word), folks kept encouraging me. Couldn't I put myself at the service of a larger community spirit than the one I inhabited? For decades, I couldn't. But an allegiance to nostalgia also spoke to a virtue of forgiveness that I'd suppressed — maybe entirely lacked.

End Selfishness

I decided to change my perspective and think about the happiness of others. Maybe Gil and Mike might also experience some relief. Ironically, by going out on the road and playing the evergreen songs in concert, I'd kept the memory of the band alive for fans who'd never let the legacy of

Triumph fade. The video evidence was all over YouTube. So, if I could get through reconciliation, maybe I'd become happier and more peaceful as I let go of stressful negativity and my stubborn, proprietary obsession with my aggrievement. Of all things, the Zen of it was Russell's strongest argument: let the negative go. *Let it go.* There was something metaphysical and spiritual to learn. As I learned from Russ, we all must try to come to terms with letting our lives go and be at peace with that. I'm not quite there yet, but I know I'm closer to terms with my unfinished spiritual business.

Harmonizing Past, Present, and Future

My past career was my constant companion, even when I was promoting new work. No matter how positive and proud I might be about new work, it couldn't eclipse the past or put any of it to rest. (I had a book of poetry published in 2021, fourteen years after our reconciliation and reunion. Most interviewers still asked, So why did you quit Triumph? When's the reunion tour?)

Triumph will be in my obituary. It's a past that always inhabits my present and whatever my future might hold. So, the only reasonable, practical version of my present had to be reconciled and harmonized with what remains an inescapable past in order to give the future more comfortable prospects.

I had a lot of support in my efforts to reconcile. The band's friend Neill Dixon (who had been my manager briefly both before Triumph and during a short stint as he represented the band during the RCA signing period, remaining close with Gil) deserves recognition for always working behind the scenes to facilitate a reconciliation, finally establishing a groundwork in October 2006. By the middle of November, paperwork was signed and exchanged, including official apologies. A press release went out November 20, 2006:

> Arrangements have been finalized to have Rik participate along with his former partners in Triumph as the band is inducted into the Canadian Music Industry Hall of Fame at a luncheon on March 10, 2007, during CMW, Canadian Music Week. This is

about honouring good memories of the past, and respecting the spirit of fans and industry friends . . .

There's another name that needs to go in this record. My friend Rick "Spud" Wharton started out in promotion for MCA in Ontario but had always been a believer with heart. He was and still is a brother, a friend and a mensch when I need someone to lean on. He kept the spirit of Triumph alive, and between us, we worked toward what is honoured in the Triumph documentary and Hall and Walk of Fame awards. Spud has helped me since the early days of my independent solo career, up to the present. Fans of Triumph know that Richard Joseph Wharton was always a good fighter acting in good faith, deserving of gratitude. The reconciliation, reunion, and this memoir should all reflect on Spudman and show him the love.

After some healing, it was satisfying and gratifying to have my contributions to some of the prime architecture acknowledged. Maybe that doesn't sound too humble, but I'm just talking about how my fear and darkness gradually turned into a quiet kind of confidence about who I was and what I did, which is a part of who I am and what I do.

With my two former partners, there's something in existence now that had disappeared for over two decades. Our estrangement was unhealthy, unhappy, and unbecoming to all concerned. I can find a way to smile about it now, because Triumph has morphed into something different than a rock and roll band. It's now a casual, mature friendship — most unlikely, considering its history. It's surreal: street dedication ceremonies, legacy conversations, the Walk and Hall of Fame, documentary, lifetime achievement . . . These things are not linked to the existence of contracts or a tour itinerary with nightly grinds through a set on stage under the lights. It's not about business for me. But Triumph once again became a part of my current and future reality, which I thought had been lost to me forever.

I had a few decades of my own music-making and record releases to worry about. I'd found fulfillment and contentment with my own creative output, as well as security about my humble little place in the universe as a solo artist. I'd been prolific and built new partnerships with a successful, award-winning reputation. All that stuff got checked off the bucket list.

There's much to be said for having a simple life, flying under the radar, with many kinds of alternative compensations. Yet history will always keep returning, washing over me, trying to drown me in nostalgia, haunting me — or simply offering an amusing blast from my own past.

In order to make my late brother proud of me, I wanted to try to be a better person. It boiled down to something that simple — simple to say, so hard to do. But what seemed impossible became something else — awkward at first, in a stage where I was embarrassed and ashamed, but it got easier. Now it seems a more logical and natural place. Onward and upward sometimes means getting off a high horse and getting down, humbling one's self, opening up, in order to be in a better position for the give and take of forgiveness.

Embracing the Mess

An older, wiser part of me says, Own your mistakes — every scar and wrinkle, every cringe-inducing memory and regret. Life is messy: it's a real house of cards kind of place in which we're subject to choices that others make around us and to random flukes in the chaos of life. Shit happens: force majeure, acts of Mama Nature, random acts of violence and stupidity that sweep us up into the messiness. What else is there to do but embrace the mess within and without?

The flow of the river of time only ever goes in one direction. This is as fundamental a truth as there is, about the nature of the universe. Light can bend, but it can't travel backward in time. I'm no quantum physicist, but I know this: there aren't any do-overs.

The Reunion Gigs

One thing led to another, and another, then another.

Our old agent Troy Blakely put an offer on Triumph's table from Martin Forssman to play the Sweden Rock Festival on June 7, 2008. Large enough to be enticing, it had a bonus side package of a budget for a CD and DVD recording as well. We started talking about it in earnest and decided to bring the reconciliation full circle by trying to play a reunion gig. Troy then brought a second offer to play Rocklahoma, outside Tulsa, on July 11, and we decided to accept that offer too. The gigs felt conditional, experimental, like logical things to explore, to round out the adventure.

It was a grand experiment, an adventure taken in baby steps, to see if we could pull it off and be any good at it. At the very least, it would put some questions to rest. I was chasing something symbolic and far-reaching to do my brother Russ proud. He had wanted to live to see it happen, but he didn't make it. (He passed in September 2007; Gil came to his funeral.) Still, when the reunion gigs and the halls and walks of fame events happened, it kept Russell's spirit alive for me — a living legacy in his honour. I'd spun some of my own nostalgia into it.

I had no interest in business partnership again. But I happily agreed to participate in anything that conveyed a spirit of friendship. In my mind, I was simply an independent contractor, fulfilling the role of Rik Emmett of Triumph (live, in person).

I recommended that we add Dave Dunlop as an extra guitarist and background vocalist, and his contribution was critical. It brought a musical brotherhood element into it from my present circumstances, and I was glad that Gil and Mike embraced the idea. We rehearsed at the big room in Metalworks for six weeks to bang the old machine back into shape.

There was an enjoyable rehearsal in a hall close to our Swedish hotel on the afternoon of June 6. We regretted not having cameras and recording gear running for that, because we got jacked up by how good it felt and sounded. To be honest, the next evening's northern summer twilight mainstage performance didn't capture the same magic of that rehearsal. The show itself was a one-off after all, fraught with technical issues with monitors and PAs typical of gigs with outdoor stages and no soundcheck.

The stress of that show day brought on one of my migraines, and a doctor shot me up with a Swedish cocktail of ibuprofen and Gravol. I was groggy but good to go by five p.m. local time. (If I seem a bit lacklustre to those watching the DVD, now you know why.) Before we went on stage, I walked over from the backstage compound of trailers and clambered down under the big mainstage scaffolding to place some of my brother Russell's ashes on the site. If not for him, we would never have made it to Sölvesborg.

Rocklahoma also had several oddities. We'd had an interesting rehearsal in Tulsa on July 10 (my fifty-fifth birthday) the day before the show, in the famous old historic country dancehall venue Cain's Ballroom. I love being in venues where the walls and floorboards creak and whisper with eighty-three years of ghostly musicians playing and singing their hearts out. During the night before the gig, a tornado ripped through the state, knocking down a few tents and structures over on the concert site. On our afternoon limo ride over to the grounds, Oklahoma state troopers pulled our driver over for speeding and arrested him for driving with an expired licence. We weren't allowed to get out of the car, so it was surreal and nerve-racking, like something out of a B movie. We were late for a press conference, but it gave us yet another bizarre but true story to tell.

The gig was anticlimactic: a typical one-off on a multiact event, with monitor and stage issues and cues for special effects that were way out of synch. Still we pulled it off, completing something that started all the way back in September 1975. The rock and roll machine left the Rocklahoma stage on July 11, 2008, and a thirty-three-year roller-coaster ride (with a twenty-year pit stop) had come full circle.

My Most Memorable Triumph Gigs

The gigs on this list are significant not just because they had a seismic impact on my career, but also because I recall them being great gigs from the point of view of the band kicking ass and taking no prisoners.

- January 28, 1978: The first time we ever played a headline concert venue in the U.S. was in San Antonio at the Municipal Auditorium. We were a last-minute replacement for Sammy Hagar. Yesterday and Today were on the bill, but more significantly the Runaways, with a teenaged Joan Jett. (Later in our career, we got the key to the city out in front of the Alamo.)
- March 21, 1978: Our first time in Maple Leaf Gardens in Toronto was magical, on a Tuesday night.

- July 4, 1980: The Day on the Green at the Oakland County Coliseum.
- June 7, 1980: The first time we played the Memorial Auditorium in Buffalo. (We also got the key to the city here, from the mayor.)
- December 4, 1981: The Reunion Arena in Dallas.
- August 1, 1981: The Heavy Metal Holocaust in England, on the bill with Ozzie and Motörhead.
- June 27, 1982: The Toledo Speedway Jam, with Foreigner and REO headlining.
- July 2, 1982: The Rose Bowl in Pasadena, with Journey headlining.
- March 24, 1983: The first time we played Joe Louis Arena in Detroit, though we'd earlier and memorably played Cobo Hall on October 3, 1981. Detroit was Rock City, the home of Bob Seger, Ted Nugent, Alice Cooper, Motown, Iggy and the Stooges, MC5. To sell out a building in that town was like climbing a music biz Mount Everest.
- May 18, 1983: We played Nassau Coliseum in Long Island, the night after the Islanders won the Stanley Cup in that building. There was definitely something in the air.
- May 29, 1983: The US Festival in Southern California.
- June 18 and 19, 1983: The Texxas World Music Festivals at the Cotton Bowl in Dallas and at the Astrodome in Houston.

Low Sparks of Rock Star Boys

On the *Thunder Seven* tour stop at Maple Leaf Gardens, I tripped going up a short metal staircase on our stage and barked my shin, which bled a little through my pant leg. That wasn't as bad as the time we were going on stage in the early '76 Triumph days, in the De La Salle College gym in Toronto: a roadie caught his foot on a cable and pulled a strobe light down from a PA cabinet directly onto my head from about twelve feet up. I had to go back to the dressing room and ice it, waiting for the bleeding to staunch. Long before concussion protocols, it probably should have had a stitch or two, but the show had to go on — and it did.

Fried by Flashpots — Twice

I got blown up at the "Follow Your Heart" video shoot in Providence, Rhode Island, on the night of February 8, 1985. The shock of it made me really angry. I lost a fair bit of hair, and what was left smelled awful. (There's outtake video footage of me retreating with a smoking hairdo.) I was overtired, because the shoot took place after a full show, and we'd kept the crowd around for excitement and energy. Take after take — then somebody accidentally threw the master switch and blew off all the flashpots across the front line of the stage simultaneously. It wasn't even supposed to be a pyro shot, so I'd been up close to the front lip of the stage. After some hair and makeup salvage, I had to go back out and finish the shoot. The show must go on.

Never mind getting scared witless, I was instantly reliving the traumatic event of being very seriously blown up and burned in Port Hawkesbury, Nova Scotia, back on May 16, 1978, on one of our first arena tours. In that accident, I lost my vision for a bit — very blurry, very scary. Fortunately there was a registered nurse in that crowd who came to the dressing room and helped me wash out my eyes properly and cleaned my face. In that accident, I lost hair and skin, but since it was before my days of gel and hairspray, the hair burning wasn't as much of an issue. Nevertheless I lost eyebrows, eyelashes, and all the hair in my nostrils, as well as a few layers of skin on my left upper lip and the tip of my nose. For the rest of that tour, I had to pencil in a left eyebrow and a bit of sideburn, then use concealer makeup to cover the burn marks. Ah, memories light the corner of my mind.

On the Popularity of *Allied Forces*

The turntable brings me back around again changed, different: still ordinary, chasing the magic power, fighting my good fights, older, maybe a bit wiser. Always working things out, coming to terms with the past. For me, looking back on its fortieth anniversary, the *Allied Forces* album was one of the brightest shining moments in our history. Life teaches you that sometimes one's fate is not within one's own grasp. But during the stretch of time that we were building Metalworks and completing *Allied Forces*, we believed in ourselves and hit our stride, which is evident in that recording. That's a pretty cool, fairly rare thing to be able to celebrate.

The sword within the flying V guitar was a symbol inspired by the shoulder badge logo of the Expeditionary forces, tied right into the cover concept I sketched up. From album to album, tour to tour, Triumph always had a running kind of subtext, a theme that tied into the name of the band and played into the notion of the constant battle, the game, the war, the struggle.

When I listen back to the tracks, I'm struck by the great guitar sounds and tones that Mike Jones engineered. They really stand up over time, sitting in great places in the mixes that Mike Levine, Mike Jones, Ed Stone, and Hugh Cooper built.

Allied Forces was a very unifying chapter in the band's history. A lot was going right around '80, '81. It was my favourite time to be in Triumph and holds my happiest memories.

On a live midnight interview with Eddie Trunk, we talked about the nature of Triumph's FM radio career: how, as a touring act grew into a large-scale arena production, the evergreen songs held up because they weren't just about hormones and anger but offered hope and faith, the search for something better. The catalogue that stood up over time gave the band a kind of common man, easily embraced coolness. Gil had blended the military tone of *Allied Forces* into a denim army vibe; the spirit of rock and roll married the spirit of radio and iconic V guitars, as metal went pop. We figured out how to live up to our name. Our fans heard songs about figuring out who they were, as people. The band figured out what core values and purpose we had (in the nascent Metalworks recording studio). We never made it into the multiplatinum ballpark of a home-run career. But we weren't a one-hit wonder kind of act either. In a sense, we got enough exposure and recognition that folks knew who we were but never so high a profile that we wore out our welcome. We were under the radar just enough that we remained an acquired taste.

The "Rock & Roll Machine" Guitar Solo

The inspiration for that guitar solo is obviously Jimmy Page's "Heartbreaker," which led most rock bands to feature an extended electric guitar cadenza in concert. "Rock & Roll Machine" was Gil's concept: a heavy rock tune updating "Johnny B. Goode," about a guitarist (me) playing blazing solos. When we arranged the song, I pushed it toward Deep Purple territory. (I'd worshipped the Blackmore era of *Deep Purple in Rock* and *Machine Head*—two of the greatest rock albums ever.) The solo itself was live off the floor onto two-track tape. Several takes were edited down (because it needed to make a kind of story sense, where one idea led to another). For that main cadenza solo, I used Doug Hill's Les Paul Custom (which I was borrowing, even for touring, by the time of the sessions for our second album). I played it through a souped-up Marshall fifty-watt head (no preamp knob, but a voltage control knob on the back for the power supply) and a four-by-twelve-inch slant cabinet with Celestions. The solo was recorded in a hurry. Playing it out on the road for years added dimensions, and it evolved into something more than what a novice kid captured on a tight studio budget.

Jonathan Gross, a concert reviewer for a hometown paper, the *Toronto Sun*, once wrote that I "didn't have an original lick in [my] body." The guys in the band often used that phrase to tease me whenever the subject of my talent came up, in any circumstance. Looking back on my life I realize that for the most part, I had my ambitious energy and a reliance on my own momentum going for me. That's because it was a time when music critics and reviewers generally didn't like hard rock bands much; arena bands, not at all. Canadian music writers took their cues from U.S. and U.K. publications where punk attitude was what mattered. In Canada, the uppity ambition of Triumph's success required humbling.

Hot air balloons required pricking. We had to fight and scrap our own way to our success, digging out from under to try to keep making our own even break.

U.S. FM radio, MTV, and a world-class stage show had contributed to the band's success. It became obvious that Canadian print media music writers were spitefully bashing their own when the band could go to Chicago, Detroit, Dallas, Long Island, or L.A. and get a fairer shake. So, their tone changed to a muted, lukewarm message: "Apparently they're doing very well as an export success story. Can't fathom why, but the public gets what it deserves, I guess, so congrats are in order." They still wouldn't say we were any good, only acknowledge realities. Eventually we emerged from under that negativity. Maybe because the constant roil and reorientation of the music biz changed the perceived power of critics and reviewers. In '82 and '83, we played on a number of U.S. stadium and outdoor events with no special effects, only our songs, and those gigs went very well. Maybe that turned the critical tide. What gets you into the Hall of Fame? Work ethic that survives.

———————

At Gil's Metalworks studio, the lobby walls are covered in gold and platinum records, awards, and signed tributes from Drake, Prince, Christina Aguilera, Rush, David Bowie, and dozens more.

Gil took the Metalworks ball and ran with it, turning it into a worldwide brand. He built relationships with artists of all stripes, bringing them to his own Mississauga turf, expanding the studio into a school and a major production company — a bricks-and-mortar metaphor for his competitive ambition and persistence.

When he played the drum track on "Grand Parade," he sent me a hilarious email about having a defibrillator standing by and the Red Cross on alert, saying how much fun it was going to be, how glad he was to have me working back in the Metalworks as his guest, as his brother. It was just a wonderful, beautiful thing to have that easy sense of humour of a brotherhood back, which I'd thought was lost forever.

The backdrop of the Metalworks studio where Gil laid down his part on "Grand Parade" features a black-and-white photograph, blown up across the full wall, showing an architectural frieze above a doorway that reads "Art Is Long, Time Is Fleeting."

Life is short, but it's also been long enough for me to reclaim some good things from my checkered history, long enough to reinvent the boundaries of my creativity and forge new paths. Life is also a beautiful mystery, a glorious mix of opportunity and dangerous experiments where difficult judgments prove worthwhile.

Which sums up the chapter of Triumph in the story of my life.

THE MUSIC BIZ

The music business is a cruel and shallow money trench,
a long plastic hallway where thieves and pimps run free,
and good men die like dogs. There's also a negative side.

— HUNTER S. THOMPSON

I don't recommend a career in the music biz, unless a young musician is a motivated self-starter with an undeniable persistence, a gift for networking, and an entrepreneurial spirit. On the other hand, music is also a spiritual pursuit. As a hobby or as a part-time calling, I believe it can bring a tremendous amount of satisfaction and aesthetic depth. The musician Steve Swallow might have put it best: if you want to be a musician, don't do it, because it's a hard life. But if you *have* to be a musician, go ahead, because it's the best life you could ever imagine.

A vocation is just a job, but a true avocation means you hear the call. And if you hear it, you should answer it. You must feel the combination of ego, ambition, and devil-may-care insouciance to imagine that you will survive the music biz. Which, in a way, is how Hunter S. Thompson put it. But in my experience, all of it wasn't always like that, even if

Thompson's matter-of-fact embrace of its dark side is always a necessary, ongoing part of it. It requires that kind of cynical sense of humour.

Music is supposed to be about recreation, so it's easier for the media to mislead the public with the glitter of celebrity and the misdirection of mythology than to try to unravel the Gordian knotted layers of the biz. There are such huge gaps between the perceptions that people have about the biz and the realities of it, that most efforts to explain it sound like the convoluted rantings of some lunatic on a soapbox. Nevertheless, Thompson's definition is closer to the truth than a Disney fairy tale; the biz requires persistence and an uncommon willpower.

Strength can also come from other things. A sense of humour was something we shared in Triumph, and it kept us sane when everything around us was surreal. Beyond that, I always kept a few small parts of myself sacred, parts that showbiz was never going to get to touch. I always nurtured the kid inside who loved music and singing in the choir, and who loved going to band practices (when there was no money in it, no guarantee of any future) simply because music was fun. I think that inner persona requires consistent care and feeding. Another part of me was a cocky teenager who got swept up into the lower rungs of the music business and felt, "Well, isn't this a hoot? Like a roller-coaster ride through the freak show at the carny midway! This play-acting is certainly more entertaining than working for a living. As long as someone finds a way to pay me, I'm gonna work it."

Roller-coaster rides come to an end; sometimes the ride breaks down. There are always other rides in other carnivals. You keep your head up and your wits about you; that's how I personally modified the Thompson perspective. Yes, there were thieves and pimps, and sometimes I went along to get along. Sometimes I was just being wary about my back, sitting facing the room, head on a swivel. But inside I always felt like I was protecting my integrity, and I had confidence in that. I felt responsible for creative work that had some substance and depth, some quality (some of the stuff that money can't buy). So that "good" man was never going to die like a dog. The business might kill off the showbiz facade. But the good man could slip out of the character and move on to the next adventure, living to fight a good fight on another day.

The moment the lights go down and the curtains open in a theatre, there's a magical potential in the air. This positive communion is a mystical, powerful force that can be awesome and beautiful. I've felt that strange power — stood in front of it — felt awed by it. It's like the flow of life force going through you, and when it's working its magic, it fills you with a peaceful, joyous kind of light. When Ray Charles passed away, Quincy Jones memorialized him on 60 *Minutes*, saying, "He had this incredible gift of taking his own private darkness and turning it into a joyful shining light for everyone to share."

The music biz and its media love to find a promise of outrageousness, the danger of weirdness. A Lady Gaga meat dress, Boy George, a Flock of Seagulls haircut. And if the outrageousness comes with core talent that can keep delivering — voila, a media darling. Giving great quote and being "interesting" because you're so consistently media-conscious can make you cool. But it doesn't prevent about 90 percent of music acts from becoming "cartoons in a cartoon graveyard" (to quote Paul Simon).

By my mid-thirties, I'd lost any ambition for cartoon cool, even though showbiz leans toward it. I was never all that interested in fashion or makeup or even making videos — a pain in the ass from the drop, really. Triumph was cartoonish from the beginning ("Their mission is to BLOW UP THE COUNTRY!"), but I chased music without showbiz getting too much in the way of the work. It wasn't mainstream nor media friendly. After '94 or so, I lost interest in stylistic, cultural trends and the hit parade. I didn't completely ignore it, but I survived by carving out independence, reinventing myself to adapt to a digital universe. I evolved the way I made recordings and marketed myself through indie channels. I simplified by concentrating on writing and making music, not chasing celebrity. My knowledge base was mostly from the old music business paradigm, in which the artist was the last to get paid (net) from the (gross) pie that provided all the management and business partners with slices. That needed to be a big pie. On my own, controlling the cash flow from my own modest little pie, I made a decent net living, because the gross never got slices off the top, and the net never got divided up by partners.

I started out as a union musician playing in wedding bands. In the '80s, part of my paycheques came from wearing Converse running shoes, drinking Pepsi, and playing a Budweiser guitar. I'm a guy who played classical guitar for a television commercial while Elvis Stojko came skating out of a Canon photocopier, and who provided screaming rock guitar for a GM truck commercial and a pizza company's radio spots. So, while I can respect and understand narrow-focus, high-minded artistic principle, I've also had a career strongly associated with commercialism, with no discomfort about that. Nevertheless, when I made music, I hoped to sell it as my profession, and not necessarily have to hawk T-shirts or go on the shopping channel like Esteban. My basic focus had always been to play a gig I could be proud of, that my audience would consider to be my best effort. I wanted to make the best music I could. There's other stuff — the necessary noise that helps pay for groceries. It's not high-minded; reducing to simple denominators made the complicated dance between commerce and art a bit easier to navigate. "Render unto Caesar," and all that.

Ten Tips

I taught a variety of college music courses for a few decades; I wrote guitar instruction columns for *Guitar Player* magazine for thirteen years; I was a Yamaha-endorsing artist in its international program for over two decades, hosting master classes, seminars, and workshops over the years. Here's a column I wrote one year for Long & McQuade's annual retail catalogue pamphlet with a digestible top ten.

1. **Be Yourself.**
    American Idol judges advise contestants to "make the song your own." Ricky Nelson wrote, "You can't please everyone, so you got to please yourself." You may never become the greatest star on this earth or even make music full-time. But if you really know yourself and make music with honesty and truth, you'll always enjoy the

process. Music offers us the opportunity to be happy doing what we're doing. For me, it's often a life of chasing an infinite dream, for music itself is so ephemeral. My favourite song is always the next one that I'd like to try to write, the next concert, the next album. Most artists I've known are usually restless for new challenges, hungry for the horizon, enjoying journeys, not destinations.

Yet rules have exceptions, and any rule about music is bound to contain a paradox or three. In this game, you have to please people in positions of power and influence, then capture the imagination and support of an audience, and try to hold on to it to build a career. So even though every success story is its own unique self-help story, with no hard and fast rule books or magic secrets, most successful individuals are people who remain humble researchers and students, who are excellent team-builders, forming great business alliances and strategic partnerships.

2. **Gain and Keep Perspective. Be a Student for Life.**
Where are you now? Where are you headed? What are you really good at, and where do you want or need to improve? What values and qualities do your role models and heroes possess that you would like to emulate in order to capture the imaginations of their constituencies? What values and qualities can you project that make you unique? A student for life always does market research, and also searches their own heart and soul for the changes happening in there. Education offers perspective and information; it helps you to become a better you, realizing your potential — not to copy or imitate, but to learn how to articulate your own spirit and ego. Modern comprehensive artistry develops as much awareness as possible, so it informs the work.

3. **Be Prepared. Give It Everything You've Got.**
Can practise make perfect? Perfection might be an unfair expectation for us to place upon ourselves. But great preparation — technically, physically, mentally — increases the odds for great performance. Get yourself into the zone; give 110 percent. Music should always be

a labour of love, including practice and even the business of "Takin' Care of Business," every day, in every way. . .

4. **Be Comprehensive. Diversify.**

Learn how to read music, arrange, and produce. Learn how to build a website and construct a marketing plan. Be a valuable asset to others; deliver essential services. I found work because I was a guitarist who could sing. I got some gigs because I could write; others because I could play rock or pop, and dress (and play) appropriately for the wedding band circuit or a glam band. I got work because I could be articulate (writing magazine columns, teaching). I also have repertoire for solo acoustic, duo, electric rock band, and smooth jazz gigs, and I recently had an acoustic instrumental world album nominated for a Juno three decades after being up there as a rocker. A jack of many trades reinvents his wheels and only knows one way to play: always willing to give it his best shot.

5. **Ty Cobb's .367 — One of the Secrets of Life.**

Ty Cobb has the best career batting average of all time, .367. The most successful hitter in the history of major league baseball failed more than six times out of ten, so learn to live with failure and hearing no. Don't be afraid to make mistakes. Learn from them. Evolve. Adapt. You don't need to be perfect. Getting a hit three times out of ten will probably get you into the Hall of Fame.

6. **Balance Ego with Humility, Ambition with Respect. Manage Your Expectations.**

Dignity and integrity are woven into choices. Musical product expresses discriminating taste. Others will have opinions, exerting influences on your journey. But the choices remain yours, and your choices should give you a feeling of staying in balance. If chasing music is like facing the infinite, shouldn't that be enough to keep you humble?

Showbiz image should be consistent with one's true nature, balanced with self-image. Your spirit should be evident in your product. Get knowledgeable and comfortable with the marriage and balance of all elements of hype — packaging, publicity, marketing, and promotion. This is branding.

Manage your own expectations. Be practical; be realistic. Advance in stages. Dreams are important: gotta have 'em. Just remember, "Step by step makes dreams come true / Only bite off what your teeth can chew."

7. **You Can't Make Time, So Manage It.**
Time is the most precious of all commodities. The single greatest challenge that a modern musician constantly faces is time management. Prioritizing is a crucial skill; building practical and realistic game plans, strategies, and timelines with achievable goals is fundamental to the evolution, adaptation, and progression of successes.

8. **"Music Is Spiritual. The Music Business Is Not."**
— Van Morrison
In other points, I've mentioned heart and soul, spirit, ego, love, and truth. But there's also practical, realistic, calculated plans, so Van's quote deserves its own number. Always remember that business is just business; that a business needs to make a profit if it wants to survive. You can't eat or pay the rent if your integrity gets no gigs. Even the most determined spirit needs to find a paying audience. That ain't selling out; it's just business, so "render unto Caesar." Music is not just technique, math, or intellect, because (when it's very good) it's also spiritual and connects with folks emotionally. Learn to make that kind of music and you'll always find work. Feed your heart and soul and share that with audiences, capturing their imaginations by offering them the kind of stuff that money can't buy. That particular "value added" is the most compelling quality of all.

This inevitably leads back to the balancing act of number six and forward to number nine . . .

9. **Form Strategic Partnerships. Be a Good Team Player.**
Music is a collaborative endeavour. You need other musicians, engineers, and producers who can do cool stuff that you can't; managers

and agents who can find and make deals that you can't; you need champions who are business executives and corporate patrons. So, you must be able to get along with these folks. You need them to believe in you, and it helps if they like you. Also there's James Taylor's bus factor: does a sideman have a sense of humour? Is he pleasant to be around? Does he make life more enjoyable?

10. **You Go Back, Jack, and Do It Again.**
Our little blue planet spins on its axis, orbiting the sun as the clock hands chase round their circle in the cycle of the seasons. Sometimes the smartest thing we can do is get back to basics, our roots, put things into the context of our own history, and hit refresh. Remind yourself why you got into it in the first place. How far away from your original ideals have you strayed? Take a good look at what you've learned: if you could go back, and do it all again, what would you change? Go back through this list and recreate, for your product is always you. Fill your work with your character and personality, so you will always differentiate organically.

Winning the Lottery, or the Work Ethic of a 360-Degree Approach

Career decisions in the music business are not clean, easy, or simple in real time. You never truly know what you're stepping into or where the decision will lead. There's an instinct at work in taking a calculated risk and sometimes a half-dozen practicalities competing for precedence. You must be willing to accept this messy hodgepodge of instinct, unknowns, and entrepreneurial risk.

The record business that I knew was tough, and making a career exclusively from the sales of recordings grew impossible. I became a touring, gigging jobber toward the end. A lucrative career from simply creating music and making recordings maybe still happens for a few lucky lottery winners. I'm guessing the odds are just about the same. Recording is mostly a PR, marketing, and promo activity that justifies other things — touring, selling merch, making guest appearances on TV shows, licensing songs into soundtracks, making social media videos, being web savvy, and forging strategic corporate partnerships. Just to remain competitive.

In Triumph, we borrowed money from the bank and the credit union to buy a PA, lighting rig, and a truck trailer, so we could get paid for providing sound and lights at our concerts, which supplemented our band gig paycheques enough for us to survive as a business with a band inside it. We started a recording studio so that we could convert our record company album production budgets into rent, leasehold improvements, and equipment purchases, so that other clients would be paying us rent while we went out to play gigs (where we'd get tour sponsors, sell merch, license songs, and turn a profit with our sound and lights). Banks lent us money because they approved a valid business plan based on a legit projected cash flow.

Promo

Radio promo was dog-eat-dog, where the most competitive, no-holds-barred radio promo man could win. It wasn't just about payola, or the cocaine and party favours at conventions. But it was still a personal industry, and music and program directors at radio stations liked to be in positions of influence and strategic importance. Sometimes, music would win on its own merit. But sometimes it would win on the merit of hard, competitive business work done behind the scenes.

When a Triumph album came out, Mike and I would spend long waking hours for two weeks working the phones, well into the evening (because, of course, the West Coast runs three hours behind). Mike was a tireless champion of promo, attending all the radio conventions, becoming a personal friend to the industry's top indie promo guys. Every time a new song was going out to radio, more weeks of phone work. I don't know if other bands did this or not; we did. We played radio-station-presents gigs on all tours; we had backstage meet-and-greets after almost every show. On later tours, we'd get corporate sponsorship and then extend the backstage meet-and-greets to include the sales staff of beer, soft drink, or shoe companies, because that was the way the hard work presented itself. Maybe our songs got to a certain point because of their merit, but we could never relax and think that was enough. Because it wasn't. Hard work arose in a lot of different places.

In Search of a Career

Lots of acts are one-hit wonders, as much of the biz generates sugar rushes, or carbonated fizz from soda pop or beer — fast money, quick bucks. Back in the day, in my own mind, I pictured record executives standing in a pitch-dark room, blindly chucking darts up against the wall in search of the dartboard. Whatever stuck got a marketing push. But nine out of ten could fail, and the boardroom boys didn't care, because a 10 percent success rate paid for the whole game — the bottom line, the salaries, the expense accounts, the nine dead darts on the floor, plus all the blow and payola.

Getting a hit is hard but only short-term thinking. Building a career means making hit after hit (after hit after hit), and it's harder to do. It takes a comprehensive approach — management, PR, and booking agency power — and some showbiz acts are simply incapable of that vision and effort.

After MTV's '81 launch, its video rotation offered quick impact in terms of breaking and establishing markets. Radio airplay had to start sharing its predominance, but it was still a major component of breaking a band or album and of growing a career. Acts with a vision toward brand-building never lost sight of the importance of grassroots live concert touring. The ability to sell hard tickets as a headliner was always (still is) a bottom line of brand establishment. Still, by '82–83, all labels were in focused pursuit of MTV rotation. Image had always been important (movies and TV created stars of Elvis, Ricky Nelson, the Beatles, the Monkees . . .), but MTV widened those dynamics, creating more demographic categories than ever before, moving image back into the foreground of career development. The growth of video broke the stranglehold that FM radio held on the rock and roll industry, just as FM radio (album sales) had morphed a lion's share of the biz away from the AM radio of the '50s (singles). All acts understood the value of how radio (both FM and AM) still managed to build the solid infrastructure of fandom that bought tickets for shows. But as David Lee Roth once said, rock and roll is (also) really all about haircuts and shoes. Yes, some question are of style. And by the mid-'80s, MTV style was filling concert venues and stadiums.

When it came to video image, Triumph was forced to keep playing a game of competitive catchup. By '85, Triumph and MCA's offices couldn't swing as much weight at MTV as other labels' priorities could. Our video presence was never as highly prioritized as chasing heavy radio rotation in concert-touring markets and having the biggest eye-candy live stage show that could be mustered. The music business was now also shifting its priorities: Bon Jovi, Def Leppard, and U2 were the biggest rock acts. Michael Jackson was the King of Pop. In an era of MTV superstar acts, with bulletproof songs geared for record production, Triumph lost brand positioning.

A Perspective on the Music Business

Large conglomerates owned and ran cassette machine manufacturing facilities — conveniently also blank cassette manufacturing plants. Those conglomerates also owned the contracts of recording artists and the publishing companies that signed them. They weren't conflicted: they knew, better than anyone else, what padded the bottom line best: continue to reinvent the paradigm of music delivery. Get folks to put their turntable into storage and get a cassette player. Then make everybody ditch their Walkmans for CD players.

Similar multinationals now own the plants that manufacture your cellphone, your plasma screen TV, your laptop ... Plus all the plants that manufacture the chips and the doohickeys that go inside all that hardware. The music business has been assimilated into the business of a new iGadget every couple of years. They partner strategically with service providers for monthly automatic billings. These industrial-commercial conglomerate concerns have far more powerful lobbying groups than artists and musicians. We are but tiny "content" cogs in their very large multinational machines. It took decades for artists and creators to get legislative bodies and regulatory agencies to consider the dynamics and consequences of the digitization of the universe. (Too little, too late.)

I'm not pessimistic about music; I remain a firm believer in its power on many levels. But I'm very ambivalent about the business of music, and the business of the arts in general (and how it plays out for the musician and artists of what used to be a decent middle class). I see musicians reduced to an old-world eighteenth-century model, in which we are servants of nobility, humbly grateful for crumbs from their tables. The nobility are now global mega-corporations, as politicians have been reduced to insignificance, fashioned into fiscal bean counters of arts culture. An artist is required to find a way to build a marketing brand and to affiliate with corporate sponsorship — to chase grant money, seek endowments. I realize that I'm one to talk, a guy who thrived on tour sponsorship and endorsements. Perhaps a stronger perspective is this: we did those things and were never an A-level band with multi-platinum releases. The 10 percent success rate of the old music business paradigm used to trickle down, enough to embrace a middle-class artist guy like me. Now it's a business for digital social media lottery winners, with no significant middle class at all.

The tech sector has a burgeoning bourgeoisie though.

Despite the drawbacks of the modern digital universe, music can still be a valid historical stylistic vehicle for artistry, because it's a highly liquid, elastic, mutable form. Styles of commercial music are highly bastardized from their inception, and since music is a mongrel that shape-shifts, it's made for the twenty-first century — our digitally morphing universe in a wired world, truly the global village that McLuhan envisioned.

Style categories aside, the music industry is ruled by class issues, driven by economics and technology. I shrug with overwhelming ambivalence. I have no idea where it's headed.

My Days of Advocacy

When I was sitting on the board for the Songwriters Association of Canada, I was an advocate against filesharing, for reasons both obvious and complex. I quickly became disheartened by an obvious losing battle against the growing Borg-like corporate noise that couldn't be defeated.

In the early stages of digital technology, it was clear that artists would lose even more control of their work than ever before. In the old days, executive directors on boards of corporations made profits from planned obsolescence and the reinvention of commercial music's delivery platforms — far more than they ever made from selling artists' recordings. For many long years, those corporations never shared a cent of software and hardware platform profits with their corporations' own record company and publishing divisions, where artists were contracted. If artists complained about the fact that they were getting screwed while someone else was making huge bucks, replacing technology and reinvigorating industry profit based on the value of music (because that's the ingredient that drives consumption — access to the music in whatever form suits consumer needs), corporate strength used the media and PR to make artists look greedy and ungrateful, contemptuous of music fans. Meanwhile, of course, companies gouged consumers' pocketbooks for their new delivery platforms — hardware that played the new software. The marketing of planned-obsolescent machinery was always just around the corner: compact disc, mini-disc, MP3 files, filesharing online, that phone buzzing and dinging in your pocket.

That bonanza means there's no more music stores at the mall, but there's an Apple Store. All of the telecoms have storefronts. That paradigm has certainly made for more music in the marketplace, although it discounted old catalogues that saturated the marketplace. Everybody and their uncle could make a CD on their laptop. Lots of silver plastic CD coasters got handed or mailed to me every week from amateurs, hoping I might be able to help them with their careers. (No one burns CDs anymore.) More competition for listeners' attention meant more mainstream commercialism than ever before, as corporate television competition talent shows dominated their own demographic segmentation. The commercial juggernaut of rap and hip-hop overpowers the marketplace, a product of digital production and proliferation.

The digitization of the universe continues to slice the demographic shares of old-fashioned, older-paradigm musicians ever smaller and thinner.

In the mainstream, big sharks feed (gaming! betting apps!), while small fry struggle in the indie mini-streams of a digital universe. It's a very small margin game for wee schools of fish. Projects can't cost much to make, because you're only ever going to sell a few thousand, and it's going to take a long time to do it — a classic example of Chris Anderson's Long Tail theory.

The value of historical recorded moments captured for posterity was eroded by filesharing. Recordings amassed in digital computer files lost their intrinsic magic and value and became banal and ordinary (libraries for sampling!), as common as photos and easily shared. People give music away for free, hoping to enhance the viral heat of a 360 deal, where the brass ring hangs on merchandising and endorsement.

The entire digital Big Tech universe makes certain kinds of noises to justify its own agendas. But the simple fact remains that all established and developed digital technology business plans assimilate the values inherent in copyrights generated by creators and recording artists.

To now point at massive amounts paid for Dylan and Springsteen publishing catalogues only serves to reinforce the argument. New writers attempting to enter the marketplace face a now-entrenched consequence of the digitization of the universe, since only historical lottery-winners matter, and the middle and lower classes of the creative copyright community have been decimated. There's no trickle-down effect. Digital streaming companies, like ISPs providing filesharing opportunities, never respected traditional copyright levies or royalties. Large-scale digital-minded companies have paid Springsteen and Dylan hundreds of millions for their catalogues; that doesn't provide reparations to the tens of thousands of artists who got hosed for three decades. The rich getting richer only proves the point.

This is how horizontal and vertical conglomerate integration works: scratch each other's corporate-partnership backs as the money shifts from one pocket into another, with the intention of driving up everyone's monthly service charges along the way. Musicians and artists lubricate the goodwill and good faith of the humanity flowing around on the internet, as their work is one of the first things that people gravitate to for a good time. But music copyright creators are the last ones to get paid fractions of pennies, after somebody else has made millions — crumbs off the table of the new robber barons of the digital age.

The Work

I wouldn't have put recordings out into the world if I didn't think that they had value and quality. But as time goes by, some age more poorly than others; some become fan favourites. An old recording might not diminish in value and quality for a listener nearly as much, or as quickly, as it might for me, as I kept prioritizing my time and energetic capacity for new artistic work. The fact that older work can take on whatever interpretation others might have (good, bad, or indifferent) made me passionate, philosophically, about the next idea I was cooking up. I cared about the present moment and what I could make work. I cared about creative performance.

My past could eat into my present too much. On a timeline with plenty of learning curves, I prioritized the work in order to preserve my creative evolution.

Games within the Game

As a young man in the biz, I wrote, "It's just a game, and all I can do is play." The *game* part of it was the biz, but the work — the music, the creative process — had a dual kind of nature. Music was play, like a game (and I was nothing if not an eagerly competitive player). Yet it was also more than a game to me, because it was spiritual with a sacred quality. That was the territory where I felt I was obligated to pursue, articulate, and demonstrate the best parts of myself. The business parts of the game sometimes led to feeling compromised, which I was reluctant to accept or would flat-out rebel against. This became an awkward paradox: sometimes playing the game meant I had to fight for something that felt more important than someone else's interpretation of the rules. And sometimes it meant I had no alternatives left. The game was rigged.

I came to the realization that I needed to walk away from tables where I couldn't win and go looking for different challenges.

An artist should feel that growth is possible — out ahead of them, something to look forward to. There are different kinds of growth and different perspectives, especially as one ages. I developed a more Zen approach to my artistry: I want to live in the moment, inhabit it, not thinking too much about the past, which is gone, and not worrying too much about the future, which causes anxiety. Growth is possible by having and keeping an open mind, an open heart, a positive curiosity about what can be learned right here, right now.

All well and good, but in a memoir, I'm quite sure the average reader craves retrospective and perspective on that nostalgia. Fair enough. To indulge those dynamics, this book contains mostly thoughts on experiences from the past. But it's important for me to reassert the context of my current philosophy on the artistic, creative timeline.

Advice for Musicians: Being Self-Critical

There's an adage in the music biz self-help manual: always be the worst player in the room. Early on, in my shallow, pale, inexperienced youth, it was almost always a given. But opportunities came to me because of my natural talents and not necessarily because I possessed a wise musicality beyond my years, or an uncanny head for business. When I joined Triumph, I was the junior partner. Even though I possessed the musical talent that attracted interest in the first place, the other guys had the business acumen and frankly much more ambition for commercial success — better organizational skills, more financial savvy, far more tolerance for risk, guts. I was a neophyte at strategizing. I was not all that cunning or critical. Like a lot of young people, I was probably more self-obsessed, feeling insecure and inadequate. My awareness ranked somewhere between organic and naive.

Awareness develops through making choices in your process. Most high-end musicians are extremely self-critical. Music is ephemeral. Recordings are of the moment. At a certain point, it's time to acknowledge that you have a good grip of the repertoire, but it's never going to get so perfect that it will pass microscopic analysis. *Forward momentum is a crucial part of process, not analysis paralysis.* Experience teaches this. What's very common is a kind of humility, in the face of the enormity of the artistic, musical challenge. Talent floats a lot of the boats in the marina, but a practical kind of humility keeps yours on an even keel. It then becomes a question of choices. What talents do you admire, and which ones would you choose to avoid, if you could?

I've seen many musicians who rankled under authority, who didn't mind confrontation, who had a talent for courting trouble, who had a real talent for alcohol consumption or drugs, who had a superhuman greed for power. In moderate doses, these traits might prove helpful. Too much of anything sabotages career plans. It's a question of knowing and identifying which talents you seek to emulate.

College music majors (especially in a performance-oriented degree program) considering professional careers as artists are taught the mechanics of performance — technical skills, theory, and harmony of practices. But they are rarely taught about the internal dynamics, ambiguities, and paradoxes of an artistic life.

You can't cope with an artistic, creative life if your ego doesn't cooperate. You must believe that the work you create deserves an audience, that your opinions are worthy. The work needs to be informed with your character and personality, to be unique and stand out. Ego isn't just negative — nor can it dominate humility or sensitivity. An artist needs to be able to handle the ambiguous paradoxes of a complex, messy, heartbreaking, and yet awesome, wonderful, beautiful life. Artists need a measure of pride but not arrogance. Everyone needs a modest amount of self-respect to get out of bed, bathe, shave, smile, and say good morning to the mailman. If you're trying to sell the mailman your latest download and a ticket to your gig, you need to feel that your work is worthy of his attention. You need to believe in the work.

It doesn't mean you go to war against strangers; it just means that you aim your work straight at them. It means you respect your audience: aiming honestly, truthfully. You don't work down to an audience (as if you are better than them, as if your ego elevates you above them), and you don't work up at them (as if you aren't worthy, as if you're embarrassed by the weak-ass crap on offer). If you feel you have to make excuses for your work, before people can judge for themselves, then you're working up — and you're simply not ready for prime time.

To become a pro, ready for prime time, you must give yourself permission — and not just permission to be okay. You must give yourself permission to fail, so you can learn from mistakes. But you also must entertain greatness. To be great, you must believe that you can. If you don't have faith in yourself — if you are full of doubt and fear — how can you expect someone else to have faith in the quality and value of your work? This belief in one's self must manifest itself as work — as character and personality — embodying humility, soul, spirituality. An artist does a rare and beautiful thing in taking the complexity of life and reducing it down into a song, a painting, a dance. So that people can go, Yeah, I get that, I feel that. ("Don't you know that part of you is part of me?") Sharing takes a certain kind of confidence — enough to handle an audience that doesn't like your work, or a critic who tells the world your point of view sucks. They're entitled to their opinion and have the right to express it. You must hold on to the balance of your pride and humility within your own soul when that's going down.

When I struggled, I conjured the thought of Bob Dylan at the Newport Jazz Festival in 1965 (and on his subsequent '65 and '66 tours) getting booed and critically trashed as a Judas for going electric. Neither traitor nor hero, Dylan was simply honouring his own artistic instinct, which takes some courage and a healthy measure of self-worth.

Theory and harmony deal with the relationships between notes; learning about them means learning how to communicate quickly and accurately to another musician in the common language that all musicians share. Theory can even teach you how to access emotional interpretations. Young musicians should be exposed to a certain amount of reading music in order to understand music better intellectually. This isn't about academic non-feel versus soulfulness — a debate that tends to be blown out of proportion.

For example, I've spent many hours in the studio cutting lead vocal tracks. Nothing requires more drama — more acting, emotion, more interpretation, and commitment of heart and soul. (Lead guitar parts sometimes get into that ballpark, but they're not at the same level of a total holistic, physical commitment right from your respiratory system.) Trying to capture certain vocal lines, I'll often pencil out the melody notes, writing the shape of the phrasing, so that I can lock it into my head. It improves my pitch and gives me more confidence in committing to the notes, making the physical interpretation come alive. Visualizing the shape and context of music speeds up the process and leads to a more complete integration.

On Leadership

I've had a wide range of interesting life-work experience, always self-employed as an independent contractor and in partnerships. I've gained a variety of knowledge from participating in board, committee, and faculty work, as well as associating in various aspects of businesses from studios to touring sound and light production companies, to arm's-length endorsement relationships with multinational companies that did record sales and instrument retail. I also coached youth sports for many years. I've witnessed some management and micromanagement of both large and tiny organizations — some successful, healthy, well-run businesses and organizations, and some in trouble, going through tough times. My life experiences led me to a mellowed-out perspective. My son Brendan turned me on to the leadership wisdom of Nelson Mandela, and I became a believer in transparency, accountability, inclusivity, and communication in leadership via consensus and team dynamics, with clearly defined role awareness, expectations, goals, and boundaries. That reads like a bunch of pop psychology jargon, but I've experienced it, and when it's in play, it's fluid and it works.

Leadership is decision-making: what one does with the power of positioning. It's not easy, because of the whole "great power, great responsibility" dynamic. Power also brings great headaches, sleep deprivation, self-doubt — great pressure. And since we know that power tends to corrupt, and absolute power corrupts absolutely, grace, strength, perseverance, courage, and calm deliberation are virtues that define great leadership and are increasingly rare. Successful businesses reflect the incorporation of healthy leadership values, because quality leadership sets a positive tone that filters down throughout the company.

Simplifying toward Positivity

In my line of work, role models are important. In my lifetime, no one ever had as much success (and therefore power of choice) as the Beatles. I would often think of the pressures that impacted their private lives, their triumphs, and their struggles. I'd think of Paul McCartney, the Beatle who seemed to emerge content and well adjusted to the industry's greatest good fortune. His personal gifts were approached and addressed with light-hearted ease, consciously trying to stay in a positive, artistically instinctive frame of mind. Intentional positivity ("You say goodbye, I say hello"; "We can work it out") requires the effort to lift oneself out of black holes.

One's psyche gets banged around pretty good in showbiz, and music is indeed its lowest shallow plastic hallway. But I made a very good living (not quite as good as Sir Paul's), so I'm not going to backbite and indulge in too much cynicism. In the games of smoke and mirrors, I did all right.

Despite my philosophical defaults toward simplicity, I can enjoy complexity (sometimes). That's why I try to embrace life's ambiguous paradoxes. The pendulum swings both left and right. The secret is in finding the balance, the grey matter between black and white. That's the stuff that makes us human.

I believe truth is a point of view. So, "the whole truth and nothing but the truth" means I try to consider all points of view. Then I make my choice, and art allows me to share my truth, my point of view, without imposing my choices on others. Others make their own choices. I'm big on choice.

Life is complex, but the gift of life remains simple enough. Sometimes I need to watch the sun rise or set, or listen to the wind in the trees, watch the clouds blowing across the sky, and imagine that my deepest heartache, my sadness, can be relieved by bearing witness to the evidence of the universe. I can step outside and take a deep breath, smell, hear, lift a glass of water to my lips and taste. This helps me with mourning, anxiety, and the pressures that life brings. Sometimes I need simple ritual: a hot cup of tea, a change of strings on my guitar, a walk in the park.

It's in my nature to choose, to try to simplify.

Branding

Understanding showbiz requires an understanding of branding. You and your music are product. Product gets packaged and marketed, and branding is about the images you project in the marketplace. The perception of you and your music in the hearts and minds of potential customers is your brand. You don't just sell you or your music: you sell the *idea* of you that will reside in the hearts and minds of folks in the marketplace. That idea is branding.

Many of my college students had never thought of music as product, never considered marketing at all. Yet the separate stages of creativity, marketing, and consumption all generate very complex dynamics. Once the creative work has gone public, the marketplace takes over. Branding is how the general public perceives and interprets you and your work in the marketplace.

Being a College Teacher

I liked teaching; it was another interesting type of performing for what potentially could be the best kind of audience — one that wanted to learn, not just be entertained. Over the years, I taught Music Business, Songwriting, Directed Studies, Creative Development, some private lessons, as well as a small ensemble for songwriters. As part of my work with the Songwriters Association of Canada, I did some resource leadership. Guitar education was something I always kept my hand in from my *Guitar Player* magazine columns to the national summer workshop programs to various Yamaha clinics and seminars. For many years, I also had a role as the director of the SongStudio songwriting summer workshop. Teaching was giving back. (Jokingly, I would add "community service" for my crimes against humanity, having been a rock star earlier in life.)

By 2013–14, I was sensing changes from within and without. Some students arrived with heightened airs of entitlement; administration was starting to accommodate the cultural force of political correctness, while I was increasingly an aging, loose cannon. I could feel myself burning out on the expectations placed upon me, as it was becoming clear that my qualifications for the gig in the first place — my school of hard knocks, rock and roll experiences — were becoming liabilities. Old-school meritocracies were fading, as colleagues and contemporaries were retiring. I managed to hang in for another few years, but in the spring of 2017, I decided not to renew my contract for the fall semester.

I taught college to help young musicians gain a clearer view of themselves in the real world, making music that could fulfill them and make the world a better place, because it might put more of a ring of personal truth in the music they offered. I wanted to help them have wide-open eyes when they started bands, made recordings, cut deals, and signed their first contracts. Maybe I could save them a few bumps and bruises in the school of hard knocks where I'd studied all my life. They might benefit from a few road warrior horror stories.

I also hoped to dismantle some of the wilful use of ignorance to control people. Managers did it with artists; the music biz did it with everybody. It was patronizing, reductive condescension: "Don't worry your pretty little heads about it. We'll take care of all the difficult stuff. It's too complicated for you to understand, so let's not even get into it. Just leave the business administration to us." The status quo of exploitation might get dismantled a bit if people learned some of the truth about how it works. They might be able to protect themselves from it and from their own eventual disillusion.

In my wiring, I am something of a didact (some might say pedant). I believed that information got passed along so that others could use it to build a better world out of this one. ("It's too late for me, but maybe you can avoid the mistakes I made.") In the long run, in the big picture, despite my skepticism and cynicism, I believed in the search for truth.

Still I retired from teaching music biz, because the industry had become a vast blur of digital technology, impossible to solidly grasp. My lifetime of personal experiences and circumstances — different deals, contracts, songs on *Billboard* charts, huge tours, damnable lawsuits, partnership disputes, band perspective, solo career, mainstream, indie, the scuffle of paying dues over and over, and surviving to tell tales — in the end had become irrelevant, untimely, and inconsequential.

Now reinvented daily, the music biz requires people to demand transparency and accountability from digital telecommunications conglomerates and their multinational corporations. It requires politicians to upgrade their own domestic copyright legislation quickly and constantly. Canada still doesn't address fundamental inequities for copyright creators in this digital universe. Despite my dogged sliver of optimism as a human being, I'm also a realist, leaving me pessimistic about politics.

But I do have this thing about good fights.

Once I went indie, I just did my own thing and hoped it would be self-sustaining. A magazine writer once said, "His own worst enemy. Too talented for his own good." I used that in my bio. After the mid-'90s, I never made any recordings to enter sales competitions, charts, or commercial horse races. My career was nobody's business but my own.

The game of measuring is shallow, but in a digital universe somebody's doing it somewhere, all the time. I chose the paths I walked because I wanted to push myself. I needed to be creative, not one-dimensional. It was a question of simplicity and self-control. I'm not keen on being measured, because someone's always taller, smarter, stronger, better-looking, more successful, more amazing. Someone somewhere will always be accounting. Whatever. I account for myself and my work.

Eras change in pop music because of technology. The entire history of recording technology has favoured the owners and manufacturers of tech: every delivery system of music has been designed with disregard (and, in many cases, disdain) for the creative artist's moral and intellectual rights. The makers of song rolls for player pianos in the very early 1900s were no different than the owners of radio stations, record companies, the makers of record players, cassette machines, CD players, or Shawn Fanning with the hardware and software of industrial digital delivery. And now streaming. The artist is always the last to get paid fractions of penny rates. Meanwhile these corporate tech delivery-system owners lobby government at every single copyright hearing in history, complaining that the cost of paying artists for their work is too high.

There will always be lousy songs made into great records, and even lousy songs that are also perfectly awful recordings that become huge commercial successes anyways. A good song is not the same thing as a good record. And a hit record doesn't have to be good by any qualitative measure to become a huge commercial success. If an idea really captures novelty, that's something that works in showbiz. It doesn't necessarily speak to deep artistic values but certainly can speak to commercial ones. A cultural and business zeitgeist fans the sparks of novelties into catching fire, just as it blows out ones that die ignominious deaths.

"Nobody ever went broke underestimating the intelligence of the American people," said P. T. Barnum. Not just American people, of course. Plus Barnum's not 100 percent right on this. Nobody should ever underestimate human nature when they embark upon a marketing scheme for a piece of product. High-minded, low-brow, whatever — one is trying to create that viral quality that captures the public's imagination. Sometimes the public is imagining itself as cultured, hip, and cool; sometimes the public is at a tailgate party and just wants a good laugh. Often what songwriting, record-making, and the commercial music business boils down to is the tickling of fancy. TV played a big role in this for a long time, and then along came the internet and social media — the biggest human-nature fancy-tickler yet.

History of the Rock Music Biz

Rock and roll was the bastard child of an integrating pop culture world — certainly from the union between art and commerce and hormones. It stands as the first real cultural trend that came out of mixing media (television with music that got on the radio) as well as styles (blues with country with swing and jump jazz). It opened the door on racial integration: Elvis was "singing Black" as he'd heard on "race" records he loved, while Chuck Berry was making records aimed at white teenagers. Rock opened the door on gender bending (Little Richard, Bowie).

We now have a world where cultures have been fusing for a while — a global marketplace where digital and analogue make amateur and pro compete and interact on highly integrated and levelled playing fields with lowered bars of admission.

Rock combined technology with arts and crafts, fashion, and political, cultural awareness. But technology has always been the progenitor of commercial music genres. This kind of integration continues to evolve at lightspeed now, as cellphones access infotainment and recreation instantly. Broadband wireless assimilates and streams rock and roll attitudes into the cultural lifestyles that have given rise to the current dominant market power of rap and hip-hop, for example.

Rock music became the valid historical stylistic vehicle for bringing artistry to youth because it was such a highly liquid, elastic, mutable form at a time of a boom in the teenaged demographic. Digital beats are now the form that shape-shifts the polymorph in a virtually fluid universe. The era that rocked and rolled from the late '50s and '60s, tailing off toward the end of the century, was a perfect storm of affluent baby-boom teenagers listening to FM radio, buying albums, drugs, birth control pills — a cultural revolution that aligned with an explosion in audio engineering and technology, the rise of stereo and multitrack recording.

Shawn Fanning's filesharing opened Pandora's digital box. The competition is fierce in the modern marketplace, and the wired world is multicultural and fragmented. It's hard to imagine how anything stands much of a chance against music product that aligns with the interests in internet service provision, because it's about streaming and digital distribution.

I adapted and reinvented myself in the digital universe at its most basic level, carving out an indie career, using digital technology for my own recordings. The advent of digital technology and the internet gave rise to competition for attention, lowering the bar for production and flooding the market. ('60s and '70s rock music was not competing against gaming platforms or streaming services.) Really good musicians, writers, and recording artists (there are far more of them too) now have a harder time getting heard, reaching and building an audience, earning a decent living. Being an artist has been discounted; being a recording artist is even cheaper than that. A viable middle class shifted from the music business to the tech sector.

I knew I needed to simplify my own life and spend more time doing better personal work, for whoever I might be able to attract under the radar, out of the mainstream, and away from "the walls of noise" out there that kept growing "higher day by day" (to paraphrase my lyrics from "Calling St. Cecilia.") Acting on good faith, curious to see how the experiment might work out, I used digital technology for more direct access to my patrons. In my own little humble corner of the world, I envisioned a paradigm without an industry of mainstream middlemen manipulating their magnificent marketing machines.

I don't know anything for sure, and never did. My career choices might prove useful to others as an object lesson of what *not* to do.

The digital age increased the rate of change to the speed of light (the rate of bits and bytes flowing through fibre optic cable and bouncing off satellites). Having high-speed adaptability, keeping centred and balanced are both tricky, and success is often measured by simple survival. As I got older and my skill set, um, *matured*, the challenge was to try to maintain the integrity and dignity of my purpose, as the business swirling around me created its own pressures and compromises. There's delicate, gentle diplomacy in compromising, collaborating, and cooperating without sacrificing arts and crafts. Easy to think, to say, to write — so much easier than the way it plays out.

I coped the best I could, made all kinds of mistakes. Knocked down easily, I was also predictable, (eventually) bouncing back up on my feet to try to regain my balance again. Long ago I realized I could never win the war; it was all about working guerilla style, winning some minor engagements here and there, picking my moments, remaining the master of my own destiny in smaller ways. I got myself in trouble when I lost sight of what I was made of, who I was. Not heroic, by any stretch. The survival of integrity is not epic and outsized; it's internal.

As it said in my bio, my career was based on a loyal friendship to my gifts, instead of slavery to fashion (with luggage to match). The less baggage I carried along, the easier it was to manoeuvre with my aging capabilities. A fancy way of saying keep it simple, stupid. A sense of humour was also critical. I had to be able to laugh at myself and in the general direction of the slings and arrows of outrageous fortune.

Post-Triumph, the work was satisfying. I was lucky that opportunities kept coming my way. I found that my audiences and fans were very gracious, forgiving, and willing to cut me plenty of slack, giving me latitude if I also honoured their expectations of me. (There's no point in denying a hall-of-fame lifetime career of luggage; I just didn't want to get buried under it and lose my sense of direction.)

I learned from mistakes and tried not to let myself get too far up or down. Even-keel balance was simply common sense. But I struggled with those things, always. I tried to keep my ego in check, behind the music, and let it lead me and hear what it told me it needed. It was about enjoying and loving the process, the chance to make music. I may not have been the world's greatest anything, but if I showed people that I remained dedicated to the work with good faith, it seemed to work out often enough. Optimism resonated within me because I wanted to believe it was true: whether it was or not, honest work felt healthy.

The fighting edge of integrity is a double-edged sword if ever there was one. You can do damage to yourself with it. Showbiz also requires compromise and collaboration; sometimes you get pushed to conform to someone else's ideals. Integrity then becomes a question of what feels reasonable on any given day and then requires the ability to forgive yourself for making a bad decision. Integrity is also resilient; it can get compromised, then salvaged. It can get damaged, yet some folks are lucky enough to be able to rediscover it in the most unlikely of circumstances. Life throws so many curveballs; integrity goes hand in hand with that essential sense of humour, bouncing from misadventure to adventure. Artists must take chances, have fun, and not take themselves so seriously that their integrity makes them look like a pompous arse. Beyond honesty and virtue, integrity requires a balanced mix of sensible things related to good faith: common sense, a sense of humour, and a sense of risk.

Success comes (to so few lottery winners) and brings along the doubt of imposter syndrome. Do I even really deserve this? Is this even going to last? What does anyone ever really know about coping with sudden fame and wealth? What training did I ever get about maintaining this lifestyle? How shallow might I end up being?

If you live long enough, you end up paying all sorts of dues. There's no escape. You can always try to renegotiate the terms and conditions, the going rate. But the oversubscribed competitiveness of the business, with its harrowing narrowing of demographic slicing, keeps demanding, "What have you done for me in the last soundbite nanosecond?"

Eventually I found a solution — yeah, okay, talk to the hand. Enough.

Showbiz is predicated on showing. What it shows is intended to entertain, and even the stuff that seems hyper-real is usually an artfully constructed docu-drama at best, and an out-and-out con job at worst. ("Reality" TV?) Showbiz is a reflecting pool of the world we've got going. The internet hasn't changed human nature with its haters-gonna-hate ignorance and stupidity, its Russian hackers and ransomware bit coiners, its social media bubbles of fake news and false flags. It doesn't change the downside of spurious business models or exploitive assimilation business practices of megacorporations. We're living in an age of social media and of the mining and harvesting of data for algorithms, both generating a wearisome routine of disappointment in humanity.

For me, the conflict was wearisome — unnecessary, counterproductive. I shrugged and walked away. I decided to do creative work purely, simply, in order to prove something for my own therapeutic sense of self, which became more important as my window of abilities narrowed. I went looking for precious moments inside the music. Circumstances were forcing my hand more out of self-preservation than anything philosophical or intellectual. What path would lead to an escape from the wearisome, counterproductive, negativity of the business giving me the business?

I'm a writer, so I wrote a bunch of bonfire songs. Some jazz guitar pieces. A couple of books of poetry.

And yes, I wrote a memoir.

THE ART OF MUSIC

Surely there was a time I might have trod
The sunlit heights, and from life's dissonance
Struck one clear chord to reach the ears of God.

— OSCAR WILDE, "HÉLAS" (1881)

W hat comes closest to truth, to capturing the infinite mystery
of the universe? In my humble estimation, music is the closest
thing we've got to a place where humanity meets our desire to connect to
the universe. I don't know anything for sure, except that while I'm here,
I have a responsibility to use my modest talents to celebrate and honour
the history and bloodlines of what so many other musicians and artists
have shared so well. I want to be in that club.

Music is the soundtrack that enhances all of the most significant
human events: weddings, anniversaries, dances, parades, births, and deaths.
Music is the great catalyst, the facilitator, enhancing and celebrating life
at its most profound times, connecting our emotions to our realities. It's
the living metaphor of emotion in motion, filling the spaces between us. It
celebrates; it comforts; it delivers joy and engages heartache — all in the
same piece. It's the stuff of life, with mortality and spirituality celebrated

on the fly, in the air, in the moment of truth. Surrender to music and you flow in the river of life, immersed in its language.

When I was a little kid, I used to love to run, to feel the rush, be the rush. I loved to play sports, because I could just cut it loose and give it everything in that moment — become the moment. Music offers that same poetry, the Zen of living in the moment. I hope to keep making and offering moments like that my whole life long. I want to keep living in these verbs: playing, singing, listening, writing, creating, feeling, laughing, crying, thinking.

As a child, there were feelings I would get from the music in church. More than anything else that ever happened there, the music could go from pin-drop, goosebumps magic to all-out raise-the-roof anthems. I loved the atmosphere of things like Christmas candlelight choir concerts. As I started to write songs and sing and perform myself, I thought if I can get this right, those qualities will be in there. That was the idea: pour everything I've got into a song and make it reflect the light within — go from a whisper to a roar, speak a whole truth, and nothing but. Sometimes I could get that resonation, that fulfillment.

As an artist — a performer, a writer, a musician — the writing, playing, and performing of music will never retire from me. I can't presently imagine that. I breathe, eat, sleep, dream with music in every part of my life. So even though I retired from the road and cut back on the amount that I make myself public, I can't see myself ever withdrawing from a creative life.

Why play, sing, write? Because it connects me to the flow of life. Because it's so natural it feels supernatural. Like fear and joy, happiness and sadness, it balances out and flows, like a river. Why? Because I can. Because I must.

I don't make music thinking I can change the course of any kind of history except my own. I make music to try to harmonize my life with the natural universe. I don't try to expand into control; I try to reduce into manageable; I try to come to terms.

Music is very powerful — persuasive and engaging. At the same time, it can be discreet. It's a way to make inner points of view palatable to anyone interested in listening and connecting. And they are free to take away from it whatever they choose. But that won't change your own creative reasons for your own groundings. Music is an open medium for communication.

The power of music therapy has only begun to be understood. Our brains are highly chemical things — and music provides a great deal of chemistry for catharsis. Lyrics can give music a more direct quality, of course. But even lyrics can have poetic licence: bobbing and weaving, using metaphor, they can leave themselves open to interpretation.

Alex Ross has written that music is "infinitely variable, acquiring a new identity in the mind of every new listener . . . subject to the ever-changing human landscape in which it moves." That's such a perfectly articulated insight. Music can be liquid, taking on the shape of its container. It can be what we need it to be, what we want it to be, what we will it to be. It defies gravity; it floats in the air, and when the wind changes, it's gone. But it can stick inside your head and take root in your heart.

Crossing over Party Lines

The music biz has a "circle the wagons" tendency — turf marking, party lines, tribes, camps, gangs. It's the nature of the beast, and I try to be cool about accepting certain realities of human nature. But party lines, and the dogmatic orthodoxies they imply, never appealed to me very much. On the other hand, one of the glorious things about good music itself (all good art, really) is it allows listeners to make their own interpretations, invest their own emotions. It invites participation on intellectual, emotional, even physical and sensual kinds of levels. Granted, sometimes it imposes its will. But most of the time it invites and welcomes interpretation. It's that openness that I dig. It's hard to articulate, but it's as if the exclusivity of a good piece of music also features its inclusive vibes.

Accessing the Amygdala

Nostalgia plays a large role in music: themes often play on nostalgic emotion: "It was the summer of '69." (One of my favourite pieces of music is "September Fifteenth," a composition by Pat Metheny and Lyle Mays, a beautiful tribute and elegy related to the day that Bill Evans passed away.) History gives lives meaning and importance. A soundtrack helps us recapture the emotional power. And the most emotionally tempestuous and intense period of most people's lives happens as puberty turns into adolescence and transitions into adulthood. After that, most of us settle in and settle down. But to revisit that past, through the music that accompanied it, that's "more than a feeling, when I hear that old song." And we begin dreaming.

As our culture accelerates ever faster in our modern digital age, we are bombarded with choice, information, marketing — a never-ending assault on our eyes and ears. The tiring complexity of our lives is stressful. So where can we go where everything is clearer, simpler? Where is that destressing, relaxing, fulfilling place? The past is fixed — reliable and trustworthy.

Our taste in music is a pleasure we get from personal reaffirmation. Without irony or negativity, we get to congratulate ourselves on our excellent ability to spot good value and great quality. Every generation has its soundtrack and cultural icons. The music goes right to the amygdala, and neurotransmitters fire those endorphins.

The Poetry of the Moment

When I was a child, and my instincts became actual conscientious knowledge, I learned that I could become the song I was singing — go into it, and be there for the duration of the piece. That's when I realized I might have a future in it. But it wasn't much different than the feeling I had when the ball was in the air and I was running, my body in motion, the ball falling out of the sky toward the moment it might settle into my hands. That was play, the poetry of the moment. I couldn't have cared less if someone witnessed it or not. I mean, it adds a lovely thing, after the fact, if a bunch of people applaud the catch, but I didn't make the catch so I could get the applause. I made the catch purely to enjoy the poetry of that moment — to be totally alive in that moment and not worried at all about being who I was, trapped in this finite existence, betrayed by time. The poetry of moments is that they are timeless; it's why dancers dance, actors act, painters paint, singers sing, and banjo pickers plunk away. We step out of time and into the poetry of life, waiting for us in that moment.

I like when instrumentalists phrase as if they were singing, breathing and articulating with vowel sounds and consonants, raising their voice with interrogatives, yelling and whispering dynamically. It should be like vocalizing when it's good, because the human voice is truly the most expressive instrument that exists. So, good playing should naturally inspire language — and good phrasing should resonate with the inherent rhythms of language. Although one of its great appeals, for me, is that it can be extra verbal, because it does not necessarily have to tie itself into words or find satisfactory rhymes. It can just be in a musical sense and allow each listener a wider range of emotional and personal interpretation. I do think that song is one of the highest forms of expression, and that song takes on a more ambitious multilayered essence when it has lyrics. But lyrics can sometimes be pedestrian and weak in capturing the beauty of the music or melody — just as a melody or harmony can often fail a great lyric. Sometimes the best thing for music is just to let it speak without words.

As we struggle with the maybes of life, the amazing thing about music is its abstract nature, always adaptable to each person's individual interpretation and circumstance. It has such beautiful potential to morph, mutate, cross-platform — an equal opportunity employer and exploiter.

I've never been a big fan of the arrogance it takes to interpret the universe in absolutes. I cannot bring myself to accept on faith an understanding of God's will or mind, or Mother Nature's grand scheme. Music appeals to me because it has a more natural political kind of resonance, existing on a more Gandhi-esque, inclusive kind of plane. In order to make life more bearable, some people turn to religion, but organizations establish themselves along lines of dogmatic exclusivity, seeking to powermonger. I choose art, and of the arts, music highest of all, because it helps me cope. It helps me understand my perspective on the world from moment to moment, day to day, year to year.

Moments in Time

A take on how life works: beauty is only ever in the moment, waiting for us to celebrate it. All of life — even beauty, our happiness and joy — is also suffused with our sadness and pain and grief, because (once we have reached adult awareness), we know that everything about life is temporary. Like a flower, our decay and death are present in our most beautiful moments, our most alive experiences. Which is what makes music so powerful in the moment: it is fleeting and ephemeral, floating in thin air, and will dissipate and be gone — as the moment will be, forever. Time only seems to stand still, captured, frozen, in art, but it is, at the very same time, proving to us the poignancy of how time is never static, never waiting, never slowing down. So, there is the music, so timeless — and yet it is all about time. It derives much of its power from the story unfolding along the timeline. The passing of time has always been hard for me to come to terms with, but I think I'm doing better than I was. This linkage of the spiritual with the musical is the stock in trade of the artist.

Music in the Abstract

As I got older, I began to imagine that maybe the universe itself (not just the people in it) makes music in the abstract. Gravity makes spinning planets end up as perfect spheres: orbits of planets around stars take (essentially) circular paths. Oscillations and wave forms appear in nature: the Golden Ratio, the ridges of sand on ocean bottoms (wave action), and how they are so like cloud formations, depending on wind action. In my lyric writing, I often alluded to tides, waves, the moon, gravity, orbits, shooting stars, planets spinning, et cetera, quite intentionally, because I sense the musicality of the universe in these natural manifestations. Unoriginal, I know, what with Pythagoras developing his music of the spheres and Kepler's *Mysterium* following up. For a non-physicist like me, it's almost impossible to try to articulate this. It's a purely poetic kind of instinct (or perhaps an early sign of mental illness), and I fear I can't do it any justice, trying to elaborate on it in prose. Nevertheless, what's writing for? (Let's give it a go . . .)

The greatest truth I can know about being alive and conscious resonates in my being when I am connected into music. Rhythms arise naturally, and the human brain has evolved to be attracted to, fascinated by, and compelled by pattern recognition. It is one of the things that surely gave rise to intellect, to conscientiousness.

Much of the cultural awakening of the average person to organized, communal music (as soundtrack in a way) arises from hormones awakening dominating messages. Maturing and socializing into adults, both primitive and sophisticated human cultures dance to the rhythms. And there's more to it: every culture starts to attach certain kinds of music to events — coming of age ceremonies, weddings, births, funerals. Again, a soundtrack for life activities. (This communal connecting gets exploited by the commercial music business.)

The older this agnostic secular humanist got, the more poetic he became. So please allow me this: I feel that the universe has a musical reason for why seashells spiral the way they do; why a beehive ends up with spiralling layers. (A scientist might say, "No, Mr. Poet, it's physics." Mr. Poet replies, "Your physics is but a factor in the metaphysics of my music.") It's music that makes the planet revolve around the sun in a fixed time frame and spin on its axis just so. Music makes the seasons come and go with regularity, as the moon waxes and wanes. I feel music in ocean waves and clouds in the sky, in the wind whistling through the evergreens on my property line, and in the way the rainwater drips from the edge of my roof. I sense music in the way snowflakes crystallize; in the symmetry of leaves and flowers and butterfly wings. I believe that birds sing because they are also unconsciously happy to be alive as they are involved in mating rituals, and because they are marking territory, as the sun rises. Living things chirp and whistle and howl and sing so that they can find each other — to create a sense of community. To celebrate, propagate, and investigate. Humans whistle in the dark when they're walking through graveyards to dispel their fear.

The universe says you're alive; you have instincts and emotions; *you need music.*

It's practically impossible to divorce the creator from the creation: to separate the cultural experience from the creator. Music doesn't exist in a vacuum. Whether originally commercial or intellectual, or perhaps simply a more organic kind of visceral, physical raison d'être, music ends up existing because somebody had a motive.

Music created for an intellectual or academic motive should never enjoy the status of being any more valuable than one made for a commercial reason. For a few decades, I walked the halls of academia and can say in all honesty that academic intellectuals all have their own motives, too, often just as cold-blooded or suspect (from an egotistical or exploitational perspective) in their own way as any blatantly commercial or industrial motive might be. It's hard to divorce ego from almost any human activity, no matter how high-minded — whether it's spiritual, religious, charitable, whatever.

Making a Transcendent Moment

There is both a joyful pleasure and an infinite challenge in the making of music. When one is engaged in music, it's as if time stands still. Of course, it's not true. It's even more of an absurd paradox when you realize that one of music's fundamental elements is rhythm, and it requires time as a component shared with other performers and listeners. But on a larger scale, in the river of history, music's moment of performance is when the accumulated knowledge of the past meets the potential of the future (all that possible hope, faith, and love; all that intellectual curiosity and the delicious human physical senses and emotional connectivity). Music has a presence, an immediacy, as it floats through the air. Artists of all stripes — actors, musicians, painters, yoga teachers, and transcendental meditation gurus! — talk intensely about being "in the moment," so that the moment becomes a searing, truthful, insightful chunk of *something* that celebrates being alive and hooked into the cosmos. Every time a musician performs, they have an opportunity to shed their earthly limitations and become an instrument for the music — to (try to) lose all self-consciousness and sublimate one's ego to the free spirit of the music and what it requires.

As Wilde's epigraph at this chapter's beginning suggests, music-making is its own flight of fancy: it defies gravity, defies mortality, and dreams out loud. It takes the past and the future and delivers it in a transcendent moment.

Music has an ineffable quality: its intangible nature makes it perhaps the most abstract of all arts, as it gives an audience the opportunity to alter, affect, and reinterpret the very essence of what the composer and performer intended. Active listening is vital to the life of the music, and the music does not arrive at its most complete state *until* an active listening audience has been engaged. Every listen moves the essence of a work.

When I wrote the song "State of Grace" (with Dave Dunlop), I did not fully realize that it would become a soundtrack for my brother's struggle with cancer; only tangentially did it have this quality as we worked it up. It was a song that my brother listened to over and over in his last few months of life. According to my brother's wishes, with everyone gathered in the church, before anything was said, his funeral ceremony began with the recording of that song. I sat there listening — in some respects, hearing it new again, different; my perspective completely altered. It destroyed me, emotionally. At the same time, I smiled through my tears, because I knew once again that music had delivered a profound moment in my life — a life blessed with many truly profound moments.

We are mortal, but our ignorance and wonder, our imagination, and our shortcomings are infinite. We dream and often cannot find any meaning in these surreal thoughts. And yet they are there, and they hint at the bigger picture, the universal gestalt. Tribes of humans gravitate toward music that enchants, intoxicates, beguiles, mesmerizes; it speaks to our bodies on a molecular level. Do we understand that? Not fully (yet). Music already plays a role in reaching autistic children. Maybe, someday, it will do even more. It has to do with the way our brains are wired, but we don't fully understand that yet.

Truly great performers are driven by a sense of something much greater than the sum of the parts. The adoration of fans and the admiration of peers are parts of the equation because music surely needs an audience, or listeners, in order to complete and justify its artistic existence (just as a painting requires eyeballs). A peer group brings other dynamics into play — a collegial kind of fraternity, a community that has its own intimacy. For who knows better the challenges and the sacrifices, the highs and lows, the prices paid? It also fosters competition — because someone in the peer group pushes the envelope of technique, or creates something beguiling that you simply must try to match or top — and this brings out your best. But in my opinion, neither adoration nor admiration provides the prime motivation. I think artists are driven by their own restless, hungry spirit. In a way, it's a bit of a curse, because they're never satisfied. In another way, it's a blessing, because it's never about destinations anyway; it's about the journey, the process. And that may be the biggest part of it: artists love process, like explorers and discoverers. An artist is driven by a quest for truth — for the moments that resonate in your soul, which say, This is what life is all about. They search for the meaning of life, or the face of God, knowing full well it's only glimpsed in tiny flashes, in cosmic insights that align the outer universe with the inner one, and knowing that these moments shift, change, and mutate — unknowable or unrecognizable until they find themselves in one, only to lose it as soon as they begin to sense it.

Some artists are tinkerers — having to take apart the cuckoo clock to see how it works. Dustin Hoffman once said he admired people who could just enjoy a sunset, because he instead wonders how best to shoot it, what lens is best, what angle captures it best, what f stop to use, et cetera. Artists can be like that: obsessive-compulsive, attention-deficit-disordered, free-associating more than average. Enthralled with something, they can stick with it and lose track of time, forgetting to eat or go to the bathroom, addicted to the quirks and quarks in the subatomic particles that make up the cuckoo clock. Wired this way, they don't need an audience or peers. They need a production advance (or a research grant) and a studio (or a science lab) and freedom to chase that muse.

Great virtuosi are like athletes in that they enjoy the physical sensation of their game. They enjoy the coordination, the satisfying accomplishment of a well-executed turn of phrase, a particularly demanding technique that they nail (like a figure skater landing a quad jump). They enjoy the test, the high-wire thrill of risk with reward — the fact that they can do this and, like a magician, make the impossible trick appear to be the simplest of all things. Maybe a showman enjoys watching himself in the mirror almost as much as performing in front of a crowd, because the enjoyment is in the turn of the trick, not necessarily the ovation of the crowd that follows. An artist might be driven by an addiction to the psychological flow state, becoming one with the instrument, the music — sacrificing, sublimating, lost inside the process. There is no bodily awareness, no mental consciousness; there is only the music, and you have become it in the moment. The average person can get lost in thought or in a daydream. But what if that feeling was not free-floating, but felt like you were humming, flowing, wired into the juice of life itself, plugged into the cosmos? (And then to be able to get an audience to applaud you for that parlour trick?)

I strongly suspect that many musicians end up on drugs and booze because they've experienced the incredible high of this flow state and want to duplicate and sustain it for prolonged periods.

An audience can assist in conjuring a flow state, because it raises the stakes with its own unique energy that amplifies the power of the music floating ephemerally in the air, transporting, communicating, illuminating, and charging the emotions and the intellect, filling the body with sensation. It's powerful — and dangerous because when the gig is over, the need for that high might remain, like a chemical need. Adoring and admiring the work itself, artists understand those dynamics are part of the formula and part of the reward and curse. They enjoy the communion with other players, composers, and arrangers — and yes, with audiences. They enjoy the process with humility and reverence, a deep abiding respect for the work, because it is inevitably a beautiful mystery to be able to put a gift to work and have it pay back more interest than they imagined was possible.

If this sounds spiritual, I don't mean it's religious or supernatural: it's extraordinarily human, an achievement of the human spirit. I think great players enjoy the way it feels to exercise their spirit. That exercise is extraordinarily rare. This can remind the artist, all in a blinding moment, that life is a gift, time is a gift, and gifts make you feel unworthy and humbled by the magnitude of the moment.

Music offers, but it cannot dictate, because the listener has freedom to interpret, so the composer and performer cannot prescribe the interpretation. Music is also ephemeral, shape-shifting, and adaptable, so maybe you think you get it, and then you age and perceive from a different vantage point and realize that the music has taken on new shades of meaning. This is the same for both listener and maker — yet another amazing quality about the stuff. We get it in the moment, but then the moment is gone. And if that moment was wonderful (an incredible source of dopamine for our brain), we long for that moment again. We'd love to sustain it, recreate it. Thus, nostalgia.

I didn't only make music for an audience, to get a paycheque or become popular; I made it for myself, too, trying to figure things out. Ever since I started writing songs, I did it partly because I wanted to carve into the school desk (the park bench, the summer cabin wall) "Rik Was Here." As I aged, that shallow, egotistical ambition evolved into servicing the goals of music-making. Yet even in my full, adult realization that creativity was my religion, songs remained my most natural vehicle for self-expression, creating a record of my existence, perspective, and personality.

In the end, I pursued a creative life because the process itself was at the heart of it. I felt honour- and duty-bound to try to get better at it: improve, evolve, make the world a slightly better place by writing slightly better songs. My purpose is inextricably rolled up into my productivity.

In the same way one can stand in a forest and get a sense of the universe, or see the way the clouds and sky touch the ocean across the horizon, or stare up into the starry sky, music brings me to that place where I celebrate a spiritual communion for the gift of life. As I often struggled to express in words as I thanked an audience for the opportunity to have shared the magic power with them, it was never about the sex and drugs or money or glory; it was always about the rock and roll.

Music is like the universe of mother nature — it all connects, doesn't it? When you learn even one little thing in isolation, you can also get the sense of how it's connected into the spiritual infinite. Even with my own little humble music ideas, I could get an inkling of a relation to something that stretched far beyond my tiny, finite humility.

I've always liked the architecture of classical music, its purity and integrity. I like this about all kinds of music, but classical music is where it started for me. I've always liked musicians who can really play, and classical players have chops. Jazz players often possess an even wider range of techniques. Rock and roll players and folk players sometimes have great chops, but that's not really what those styles are all about.

Classical style is based on performance of a composition. It has a formality to it that I appreciate, a vibe it gives off, that a sacred, spiritual quality of the music should be respected. The musicians have tremendous discipline. Jazz has some of this, too, but because it often relies heavily on sections where the musician's performance is improvised, it gives performers personal latitude with a wider policy on harmonic creativity. It also (often) leans on a rhythm section whereas classical musicians are most often tied to notes written on pages, relying on a conductor to glue it together. In pop styles of rock, country, folk, soul, rhythm and blues, rap, and hip-hop, the latitude allows for attitude, which (for my taste) perhaps too often overrules both respect for the material and a reliance on chops. Popular styles are more about hormones, fun and games, fashion, youth culture, and building wee tribes that are exclusive social clubs.

I taught college courses in a liberal arts program. *Liberal*, to me, was the operative word. I was also heavily invested in work ethic. If a creative person is fully embracing their unique spirituality and consciousness — their intellect and their response to their emotions, their empathy, their intuition, their reason — then I have faith in that process. The work is sacred.

Music can speak to people in many ways. When it speaks to me, it sometimes does so on an emotional level, sometimes physical, sometimes intellectual — sometimes all three at once. I suspect many folks can relate to what Leonard Bernstein was talking about in the following quotation about listening to Beethoven:

> Form is only an empty word, a shell, without the gift of inevitability . . . Beethoven broke all the rules, and turned out pieces of breathtaking rightness. Rightness — that's the word! When you

get the feeling that whatever note succeeds the last is the only possible note that can rightly happen in that instant, that context . . . There is something that checks throughout, that follows its own law consistently — something we can trust, that will never let us down.

Inevitability and rightness are concepts I buy into and tried to teach. His phrase "its own law consistently" seems to describe subjectivity. Composers and songwriters try to tap a piece into a universal kind of flow, so that it speaks its own language with its own syntax, its own logic, and an audience will say, Yeah, that was satisfying. That was right.

Now I have also had a lot of experience with students and collaborators who are only too willing to play contrarian. There are folks who think it's a deeper, stronger kind of artistic commitment to reject others' notions of inevitability, who take an almost perverse pleasure in being pointedly weird and abstract to mess with people's general sense of accepted rightness. I don't buy into that *if* it's just for its own sake. However, a further wrinkle to this is that writers and composers often talk about the element of surprise: how the arrival of the unexpected in the flow of the work provides the most compelling element of all. This can be true; after hearing it again and again, it becomes evident that the surprise was, in fact, the best choice, and now any other choice does not satisfy the notion of rightness. The surprise element is the very thing that gives the composition its unique quality. That's a perversity I accept: to avoid the banal and the boring, and to excite creative potential.

Additionally (but similarly), composers talk about happy accidents, when something unintended makes its way into the work. They leave it in, and it survives, and it often becomes the most compelling feature of what they have. Like a genetic mutation that contributes to evolution, somehow a happy accident can lead to a better piece of work.

It's a remarkable thing about music that it can satisfy the masses and yet — sometimes — also simply speak to one person, who connects to the flow so that it feels personal, subjective, unique, in that moment to that person. Many music educators admit that in music, there's no right or wrong. There's only good or bad. And good or bad is in the ear, eye, mind, heart, and soul of the beholder in that moment in time.

So, when you have a moment and it's all yours, it's lovely, ain't it? Highly addictive.

The Dynamics of Music Consumption

You can experience music as a live concert; as a private listening experience, interacting with a recording; or as a broadcast performance over airwaves.

When you're at a concert, you are sharing in a public communion. It's self-evident and all around you. The energy of the crowd makes the moment even more special. The performer is right there in the same space, sharing the same electric air. It's the energy of being alive and connected in very real, human terms.

When you're listening to a recording, it's usually much more of a private kind of ritual or ceremony — just you connecting to the music. The private connection can be intense but perhaps not as dynamic as a public concert, in that there's simply not as much live humanity to amplify the communion.

When you listen to the radio, *broadcast* describes its dynamics. The music is being cast broadly out on the airwaves, adding an element of human imagination to the communion. You are perhaps experiencing it privately, as you would listening to a recording. But you can't hit rewind to listen again, or lift the turntable needle and go back to review. Listening to a broadcast puts you in the theatre of the mind, a bit of the dream theatre, if you will. Who else might be listening at this very moment? Have I joined in a nation as we all experience this same moment in our own little corners of the universe, as this song is being played in coffee shops, shoe stores in malls, a boombox on a construction site, or in a warehouse where shift workers are doing their jobs? You're hearing the song, but you're also feeling its public scope, the weight and size of its auditory existence in the marketplace (wherever that may be imagined to be). That's waxing poetic, but music is such a unique and valuable human thing because it provides these different communal dynamics, this fusion of the private and personal with the public and communal, with the universe. The cosmic reduces into the moment. Each person's moment is private, unique, and yet shared, connecting humans with humans. And then the moment passes, and the vibrations that filled the airwaves are gone. And that moment can never come again. The arrow of time guarantees one-way passage with no going back; the musical moment was as private and unique as everyone's own perception of it. This quality of music makes it rare and special.

Art doesn't really imitate life. If it did, much of it would be shitty because lots of life sucks and gets boring and depressing. Art must enhance life: feel bigger than life; make a spectacle of itself. It doesn't have to do all these things all the time, but it must do some of them. It must feel deeper, more profound. It must speak to the ages. It must provoke, entertain, and satisfy emotionally, sensually; it thrills, mystifies, or reduces you to tears of joy or laughter or grief. It shocks; it comforts. It must enhance life for a large-enough segment of the public to keep that art alive, making life worthwhile for a decent-sized demographic of the public. It must speak to that demographic's spirit and heart and soul and mind in a way that nothing else can.

But what about market clout? Everyone's entitled to their own discriminating taste, so what matters to a ten-year-old has the same artistic equivalency as a Picasso show at the museum or a Beethoven symphony concert or a Metallica gig. Ah, but tastes change. People grow up, age. Cultures shift. If the music still stands up, well, then pop indeed had some art in it. The eventual consequences of art determine whether the artist managed to beat life at its own game, creating something that speaks beyond the pop-bang-whiz, the instant fizz of the moment.

There's a difference between the technical theory and harmony of a schooled musician and the extra stuff it takes to develop an artist. An artist digging deep speaks with an emotional and mental quality that won't necessarily come from sight-reading music, or doing the harmonic analysis necessary to improvise over the changes of "Giant Steps." A well-rounded life is critical to artistic process. Jimi Hendrix couldn't read music or improvise over the changes of "Giant Steps" (or even "Autumn Leaves"), but sometimes a person's gifts aren't packaged within accepted convention. Which is why noodling around is important too. Making music is supposed to be about having fun, as well as exploring and digging deep emotionally and intellectually. That range doesn't necessarily come from a degree in a college program (although that can't hurt — as long as it doesn't come with a set of blinders). Students need to be given opportunities for emotional and intellectual growth outside the boundaries of institutional authority. Where will they learn about, for example, love? Social justice? Families and friendships are often best positioned to do that, but it could be that artists are wired to keep taking it from wherever they can find it.

Songs that live beyond the life of the writer contain things that speak to the human condition, to the universal questions. The reason that paintings, plays, novels, poems, and music remain masterpieces that speak to human beings, centuries after their creators' own personal ego, is that they weren't (principally, most of the time) painting or writing about their egos. Ego was in service to the work, to the process, to the art. That's why it's great art. Songs that principally feature the ego of the writer might not age very well; they might become purely of historical interest after the writer passes (and maybe not even then, if there were contemporaries who had more to recommend them to history). For all the strutting and caterwauling, the singers of rock bands need to put something of more significance into their writing and recording if they want to generate a legacy.

How does one surrender the ego to what seems to be a greater good, a higher purpose, a purpose of benefit to the family, friends, the community, the environment, the planet, the universe? How does one leave the campsite better than they found it?

Those are good questions. That's strong motivation to start writing some songs.

Musicianship: The Mindset of a Musician's Musician

Musician's musicians put the music ahead of their own ambitions to be popular or commercially successful. They chase the art that pulls, like the north star, on their craft. Many of them don't give much of their atten-tion to popular songs that speak to the average person; they prefer songs that allow them to pursue the instant improvisation of complex musical ideas. They want to explore harmonically to see what will happen. The vehicle is often a standard — a well-known song from the past shared as a common structure, a leaping-off point, for the ensemble. Or perhaps a new, complex, beautiful arrangement, a unique rendering of the musical potential that a vehicle allows or suggests — an exploration of harmony and one's own technique; an opportunity to express something original, even if the song becomes submerged architecture.

Some hear musician's musician, and think virtuoso. They think of insanely advanced chops — John Coltrane or Keith Jarrett. I also put some songwriters on the musician's musician list, even though a songwriter is less likely to be thought of that way by the general public: Paul McCartney, Sting, Paul Simon, James Taylor, Joni Mitchell, Donald Fagen, Billy Joel, Brian Wilson. In my songwriting course at the college, I would also focus units on Woody Guthrie, Hank Williams, Darrell Scott, John Dowland, Stephen Sondheim, Johnny Mercer, Bob Dylan, and Leonard Cohen. Their ideas put them up in the constellation, too, alongside band leaders and arrangers like Count Basie and Sir Duke. And what about bands? Ensembles can do something truly unique, like Rush, Dream Theater, the Beatles. Most pro musicians, everywhere, recognize the huge accomplish-ments of musicians-as-ensemble. To my mind, they qualify as musician's musicians, although they choose the setting of their unique ensembles to do what they do. In my youth, I used to love prog bands — Yes, Gentle Giant, King Crimson, Genesis — and thought of the musicians in bands like these as musician's musicians because they were such strong conceptu-alists. (The Beatles, then Deep Purple, set me up for that, I think, and Led Zeppelin followed along in the development.)

As time passed, I became less interested in progressive structures and arrangements, and I started gravitating back toward simpler construc-tions: songs that had coherence by attempting to deal with one human topic at a time. A relatable story. I now feel that a musician's musician demonstrates an independence and transparency in their artistry.

My list of musician's musicians still leans toward jazz musicians, because they tend to have the strongest palette of musical comprehension and a skill set of techniques, which allow them the broadest range of choices — even if they ultimately choose to work a fairly narrow scope.

To me, Pat Metheny and Tommy Emmanuel are both musician's musicians. Metheny functions on levels of art and craft that Emmanuel would never attempt; it's simply not in Emmanuel's chosen repertoire or wheelhouse — and vice versa. Emmanuel reaches almost any audience with what he does and, as a one-man band, with such accessible joy and passion in his performances. Often more cerebral, Metheny leans toward intellectual jazz. Emmanuel, more a showbiz entertainer, favours the access found in melody. (Emmanuel's body is a drummer's, a dancer's.) Very different artists and musicians, but they both rank almost equally on my personal list of musician's musicians, and both right near the top. (A bonus of my life as a working musician, I had the rare opportunity and great thrill to meet both men, shake their hands, and thank them personally for their inspirational music-making.)

Performance: A Willing Surrender to the Moment

Music performers are like athletes in the sense that the best are involved 100 percent in the play — immersed in what they need to do. There's no question that an audience can help: it enhances what's at stake in the play, which can add to the high-wire pressure and to the reward. A good performer welcomes that pressure, relishing the poetry of the moment. The challenge is always there: to have the poetic moment play out properly. And then the moment will flow instantaneously into the next, and the next, until the play is over. The idea is to focus on exactly what is required to optimize the moment for the sake of the play, for the sake of the game.

Focusing on the crowd sets the wrong priority. Performers train to block out the inconsequential, so that they can maximize the music (the consequential) in the moment. They flow from one moment to the next until the musical sequence is finished. They acknowledge applause: smile, bow. That is the showbiz part of the game (and one can maximize that stuff too — a poetry of a different kind). But the real heart of the game is getting to the soul of the music and bringing it to life. That's a relationship between the performer and the gear (the instrument), the sound, and the composition. Working conditions play in, and an audience is part of that and can change the parameters. An away crowd is not the same as a home crowd; a crowd that got in for free is not the same as one where everyone in the room is a fan. But, regardless of conditions, the job is to play — to prioritize the things that can make it happen, working inside one's self and working with the music, maintaining its own set of challenges. Performers choose their priorities of consequence. If they only choose to focus on the crowd, they are likely doomed to fail.

This would be true of any performer: actor, dancer, athlete, artist, writer. The mindset is about a psychology where the ego willingly gets out of the way, so that the psychological flow of the moment can happen. (Mihaly Czikzentmihalyi offers foundational work on the psychology of flow — of being outside yourself and inside the process of the creative work.) Inside out, outside in. It's the work that matters.

Facing infinity is the challenge of good art. If that doesn't make you humble, nothin' will. The gift of life is made manifest in sharing — the giving, not the taking. As Thomas Edison said, "We do not know one millionth of one percent about anything." Knowledge like that keeps you humble. And yet we can tap into it: the play can work. How joyous is that?

Composition versus Improvisation

How much play do you want in your playing? And how much sober seriousness do you want in your recreation? Serious play is the appeal that jazz music has at its highest level. Intellectually and emotionally, jazz artists can respond to stimuli (another musician's suggestion, an intellectual thought written down in a chart, a seemingly random idea that pops into their head) and go off on a journey of discovery. To them, the intellectual and emotional payoff lies out there somewhere on that trip (boldly going where perhaps no one has gone before — or, at least, no one on this bandstand, tonight, so far).

Some performing musicians are not comfortable at all if the ballpark isn't completely defined. They want the chalk lines laid out, so that everyone knows where foul territory is; they want a fence that will define a home run; they want to have studied the rule book, with umpires doing their jobs, so the game goes according to the rules. To them, the intellectual and emotional payoff lies in the execution that occurs within the definitions — that the game has been respected and the material has been shown in its best defined and refined glory. (Members of a symphony orchestra require highly structured organization.)

There are also some folks who want the music to happen with absolutely no surprises at all. They don't even want a game; they want the play to follow a script. They prefer a novel, a movie, a play in the theatre. They want to know exactly how each story will be told and how each story will end. To them, the intellectual and emotional payoff lies in honouring the script in intricate detail: the original composition and recording has been recaptured and reanimated, with exacting precision and every detail thoroughly considered. Heavy script addicts want to remain comfortable within their skill set. They do what they do; they don't want to try to do anything else.

Some artists talk in a very proprietary way about "my music." It's not *the* music; it's *my* music. It's individualized, stylized, the exclusive domain of this musician: they don't see it as transferable or translatable. This dynamic also raises the issue between the songwriter type of musician and the musician's musician. This also raises the political dynamic, doesn't it? Some musicians are very liberal in their approach. Others are extremely conservative, very right wing.

Balance

I tend to be big on balance with a comprehensive approach to art and craft: you want some liberal process happening to open up the potential, and you need some conservative stuff going on (like work ethic) in order to give it substance and depth. To keep a clock balanced and running on time, the pendulum needs to swing freely and evenly both ways. The works require some tension.

I stressed values and qualities to student musicians. Jamming and improvising can work, but for how long and to how many? Musicians may love to blow, but that doesn't change the fact that most people in any potential audience still marvel at a well-written song that's well arranged into a well-produced performance.

There's no substitute for talent. But a fantastically talented basketball team that freewheels and improvises is going to end up losing, more often than not, against a team that has worked hard to develop discipline and character, and to run a team game with set plays, defensive alignments, et cetera. (Defence can't freewheel.) Talent utilizes its intelligence to figure out what really works for success, instead of hoping spontaneous genius might show up from time to time.

It's good to seek balance between the spontaneous and the deliberate: try to find new ways to play to your strengths and challenge yourself and your audience, stretching everyone's expectations. There's also a balance to be struck between a respect for the musical piece and the delivery — the performance in the moment. For an audience, a truly satisfying performance finds that balance.

We live and learn from mistakes (if we're smart). That means balancing our premeditation, as well as our post-game analysis and debriefing. This helps us modify our spontaneity, so that the next time we take a shot at some run and gun freewheeling, we might make some wiser, tastier, spontaneous choices.

Artist? Musician? *Craftsman*

One of the strategies in my life as a performer was that I tended to play things that I was good at; I didn't try to become a musician who exploits a total technical ability. I simply didn't have either the mental discipline or the physical chops. There were certain things I could do well, so I wrote music that I could handle. An interviewer once referred to Roger Waters as a musician, which Waters denied. The interviewer countered, "You're one of the most famous musicians in the world!" Waters explained that musicians were people who could play a sheet of music you dropped in front of them. He said he wasn't capable of that; he could only play what he'd written, imagined, and figured out.

That's true of a lot of rock and rollers and singer-songwriters. We're *artists*: good at what we generate personally but out of our depth when trying to play anyone else's idea of music. Now I may not go as far as Waters did, but I'd say I was about halfway there. I could still sit in and jam with some musicians, communicating on a decent level. But I could never sit in with jazz musicians and play standards because I don't have that repertoire memorized and I don't know the playbook of jazz, the harmonic language and facility that allows people to improvise over those changes. Some folks pay me lovely compliments about my abilities, but I think of myself as more of a craftsman than a virtuoso, with the hands and brain to prove it.

Practice doesn't make perfect. Perfect may not even exist — for, like beauty, it's only in the eye of the beholder. But good practice makes for positive preparation. And if you're positively prepared, you've put the odds in your favour for a successful outcome. With the odds in your favour, you can relax. You might find that you can relax enough to lose yourself in the moment, experiencing what psychologists call the flow state.

Good practice is great preparation. This is not a magic secret; this is just common sense (so uncommon these days). Practice raises all the various facets of the enterprise, so that when it comes to performance, one has mastered the repetitive physical motor-memory learning. One's hands obey the patterns in order to deliver the goods. Which is to say, all musicians need to practise and rehearse, to develop familiarity with the repertoire. One develops a comprehensive facility — to write what they write, play what they play, sing what they sing. When they find their voice, it's a liquid, self-assured, authoritative flow of music. It's not just about a technical ability: the speed of digits, the flexing of muscular testosterone. It ain't just physical. It's also mental and spiritual. The motor skills part becomes almost the least of the equation. Maybe you think it's about fashion and haircuts (and fame and glory). It won't be about that after a lot of good practice. It will be about what comes from, and speaks to, the heart and soul. It's what we keep working on, and we can always use more practice.

Is it hard to do if your guitar sound is crappy? Yes, it is — but that's why there are soundchecks and pedalboards with all kinds of terrific pre-sets. (Like I said, positive preparation.) Is it harder to do if you have a sore throat and spent too much time talking the night before at a party where the stereo was cranked up? Yes. So, if you want to do a good show, use your common sense, and you can be well prepared for success.

Let the Music Tell You Where It Wants to Go

With music students, I'd often ask, Where's the third dimension? The one where the range of your humanity lives, where music speaks across lines of technical prowess, where the song speaks? What's making this thing transcendent?

Soloing guitarists often indulge in qwerty snakes and ladders (like a typist with a complete command of the keyboard, blazing up and down the scales, faster, faster!). There are lots of notes roaring by, as if the idea is never breathe, never slow down, just keep going, keep firing away. Like a person possessed, they keep moving from one idea to another to another to another, till no one can possibly understand the language they're speaking, never mind what they're trying to say — except that everyone gets this message: "Look at me! Marvel at how crazy and awesome I can get!"

There's a time and place for Olympic virtuosity — technical and physical brilliance for its own sake as performance art. But let's not confuse it with music that connects, communicates, and communes with a wider audience. Open the doors of your artistic house, and invite me in. That's very different than bragging about the impressive features of your castle.

Sometimes music students at the college would mistake the writing of great musical parts — interesting charts, clever arrangements — as songwriting. They might mistake a great recording for a great song, or virtuosity for universality. Virtuosity is universal when it marries itself to musicality. Virtuosity without musicality is an empty athletic exercise.

Provocation, Novelty, and What Money Can't Buy

The work of a responsible artist strikes the listener as substantial but also provocative; it's novel but also works in a historical context. Substance means depth and quality. It means you offer up something that money can't buy; the value of your gifts goes beyond a commercial transaction. Provocation means you make people think: you get people to react emotionally. Novelty can be provocative, too, but too much concentration on novelty can make work shallow. Still you want enough novelty to make the work challenging and exciting. Good music acknowledges the fact that we stand on the shoulders of giants who have gone before us, which generously allows us a good look at the horizon to see what we're aiming for up there in the future.

The Importance of Arranging

I write music in the hope that the material will somehow communicate and connect — but it's unpredictable. Different people connect in different ways, depending on circumstances. On its way to a listener from a creator, music goes through several developmental stages. Each stage requires imagination.

It's not just a question of writing or production. (The sound of what you're recording is hugely important.) What glues things together is arrangement, a critical aspect of figuring out the puzzle. Like renovation contractors and interior decorators, the genius of arrangement in music can impart sophistication and magical qualities. Quincy Jones and Burt Bacharach studied arranging with Nadia Boulanger. They are both great writers and producers, but their ability to imagine music with scale and scope — their arranging — sets them apart as unique creative artists on a very high level.

Arranging enhances the accessibility of the writing's intentions. It dresses up Cinderella for the ball.

Tweaking the Formula

When Triumph did its reunion gigs, we tuned down a full step (for vocal range). Sometimes the tension of the strings felt a bit too loose and wiggly, which required adjustment. But adjustment is a way of life for human beings as they age. Failure to adjust dooms a crotchety old geezer to angry bitterness.

Over the years, everything I performed evolved, so every song I played was eventually different than written and kept getting tweaked with every performance. A song is never static. There's always an evolutionary imperative at work.

The Ephemeral Challenge of Finding Your Way to the Heart of the Performance

The great challenge of musical performance is right in this current moment, where the song is. How do you find something deep and true and real in the moment and make it evident for most of an audience?

As a young man, the rocket fuel was often ego-based — ambition, cockiness, self-confidence. As an older man, it was sometimes harder to find the juice of the moment. Sometimes not, because there had been decades of stagecraft, tons of wisdom and experience, so sometimes confidence came from another motor-memory place, a place that remembered the heart of the song because I'd visited it so many times before.

The music itself bears its own truth; it's just hard to get to that place, sometimes. (Sometimes the monitor mix sucks; sometimes the lights are blinding; sometimes the equipment goes down. Grin, Rikky, and bear it.)

The lovely thing about music is its abstract nature: rhythm, melody, and harmony at its fundamental core, and at any given point you can surrender yourself to any sliver of detail. But the music itself has its own profundity, aside from the meaning in any given lyric. And then there are other musicians on stage, and sometimes the moment is one of pure play — and any deeper meaning is inconsequential.

This can happen with an audience, too — a surpassingly beautiful thing when a moment of communion occurs — and so the moment has transcended all, including the literal meaning of a lyric or even the prosody of all the moving parts. It has elevated to a kind of spiritual plane, and now the abstraction (very real) is a spiritual one, with the music simply functioning as a catalyst.

Maybe an artist's best work is when they have removed themselves from the equation (the process), stopped worrying so much about their navel lint, and simply become a lightning rod, a conduit, for something the universe is offering. At the same time, a career in commercial music is now so often about the images of lightning rods — the cult of personality, the personality machinery that delivers the content. Content is now so uniformly packaged in demographic delivery systems that Marshall McLuhan's clairvoyance becomes apparent: the medium is the message. The universe increasingly seems to be offering us an endless stream of digital exposure to the navel lint of lightning rods. I continue to ask myself, What's in the work, the process, that comes from *beyond* the medium's message?

What are the sounds we can hear that come from beyond the noise of the marketplace?

EXPERIENCES — CHOICES

I am not what happened to me, I am what I choose to become.

— CARL GUSTAV JUNG

I always liked to draw pictures and write stories. I liked to sing. When I got my first guitar and learned a few chords, the first thing I did was write a song. The creative challenge of coordinating melody with chords, the story of the lyric, its rhyme, and phrasing was like solving a puzzle, and I enjoyed word games.

The inescapable British Invasion combined music, hormones, acting grown-up and cool and intellectual with being physical and playing — wrapping it up in a package.

On a psychological level, the path of a creative life seemed to be a way to cheat death a little bit — not like being an Evel Knievel daredevil, just a "Kilroy was here" value. Writing songs and making music seemed to create a meaningful legacy with honesty and truth in it. Life seemed messy and full of injustice — so much heartbreak and disappointment.

But music had a purity and a kind of righteousness that sparked me (and still does). Music gets me outside and beyond myself.

The guitar was a natural partner for me, complementing my own physical tendencies (left-handedness playing right, singing in a high tenor range). My relationship to the guitar keeps inspiring me, as the very nature of guitar arises through emotionally expressive tactile contact — touching, caressing, manipulating, striking, pushing and pulling and bending strings. Music-making ranges from imposing one's will on a set of circumstances to sublimating it in surrender to a higher purpose, waiting in the music itself. Either way, I find it compelling.

One of my earliest memories is of an early summer sunny Saturday morning. Still a young boy, maybe six, with the personal freedom to be my own boss and make my own breakfast, I remember enjoying a thick layer of strawberry jam on a piece of buttered toast so much that I made myself another (which seemed wicked and selfish), and then I took it outside (gasp!) and stood in the narrow walkway between our house and the neighbour's in the warm sunshine. I enjoyed that piece of toast, giddy with the sweet feeling of Saturday morning freedom, of establishing this unprecedented, decadent menu for myself and eating it in this oddly exotic private location. Life could not possibly get any better than this: that's how it felt. Simple. Quirky. Dizzying.

That man is the richest whose pleasures are the cheapest.
— HENRY DAVID THOREAU, 1856

I once nearly drowned. One late autumn — I might have been five or six — my family was visiting a relative's cottage that we intended to rent the next summer. I was on my hands and knees at the end of a dock, leaning on a boat roller, looking down at some fish in maybe six feet of clear cold Pigeon Lake water. The roller rolled (as it was designed to do) and in I went, wearing heavy brown leather shoes, lined corduroy pants, a thick wool sweater-jacket that my mom had knitted. I couldn't swim a stroke. I was trying to claw my way back to the surface, but I was sinking (and freaking). My dad came running, grabbed my jacket and shirt at the scruff of the neck, and hauled me up and out, dripping, coughing, shivering, crying. I was humiliated — plus the only dry extra clothes in the cottage ended up being women's pyjamas. A little later in life, I did learn how to swim, but I've never enjoyed it.

I'm not great with left-brain calculations, information storage and retrieval. But my brain never fogs up when I'm flowing along, creating. I'm okay at two things: motivated single-minded focus and brainstorming free-association. I'm not a nuts-and-bolts kind of thinker — not mathematical or scientific — just organic.

With my right-brained preferences for music, art, and English, I loved the social aspects of school far more than the classrooms. After grade six, I majored in gym, lunch, after-school activities, and field trips: drawing for the school paper, doing the morning announcements on the PA, performing at talent night, and playing on school teams. I thrived on the showbiz of school, not the business of education. Somewhat ironically, I ended up a part-time college teacher for a few decades.

I encouraged students to develop methods and techniques to think for themselves — figure out what was inside them and make their own choices. If they wanted, I provided some consultation on how to marry dreams to the reality of unique gifts and talents, along with the caution that the journey of self-discovery is never-ending. The world's a much different place than when I was a young man. Writing this book has reinforced my curiosity and wonder, reminding me that I'm really more of a student than a guidance counsellor.

To grasp my whole story, you need context. In the entry-level music biz climate of Southern Ontario in the mid-'70s, the boomer demographic's sonic explosions reverberated everywhere. The Canadian government had committed to Canadian content rules in '71, a system in which broadcasters were forced to observe the development and nurturing of homegrown product. That same year, the Ontario provincial government lowered the legal drinking age to eighteen. This generated a very active scene with a lot of potential for professional advancement: dozens of bars and taverns now featured live entertainment, looking to attract younger clientele. Almost every high school in the province had the budget for monthly dances or concerts, providing a secondary level for fledgling bands to find paycheques. Radio was doubling its impact through FM's album-oriented rock format that expanded upon the pop hit parades of AM. It was also a kind of golden age in a city like Toronto: national and international touring acts played multiact shows for summer festivals and municipal fairs. Universities, community centres, YMCAs, parks departments, even churches looked to have bands provide a draw for their events. As the hippie movement settled into urban commercial enterprise, there were clothing retailers, salons, head shops, music stores, and a small bonanza of coffee houses, drop-in centres, as well as folk, blues, and jazz festivals that fed the scene, giving young musicians a network for word-of-mouth vitality and exposure. Toronto's vibrant scene gave birth to R & B bands, folk artists in the coffee houses of Yorkville, and rock bands influenced by the British Invasion, West Coast psychedelia, and the proximal influence of Chicago blues, Motown soul, and New York jazz. Toronto's eclectic roots had fertile musical soil. CHUM-FM radio switched to a progressive rock format in 1968, and by 1977, CILQ-FM (Q107) became a competitive force with the superstar format that Lee Abrams had made widely successful in the U.S. starting in 1971.

Given that environment, the ambitions of my instincts were encouraged.

On my website forum, I was once asked, "In private you lean toward the negative whereas in public you are Mr. Positivity. Why is that?"

In private, the audience of one is me. And I can be hard on myself: I know all my secrets, all my weaknesses, failings, fears, doubts. I suffer from anxiety. Whereas in public, I've been a performer ever since the adults in my life forced me to confront my fears through performance of one kind or another. My duality was born young. The private person is insecure and knows it, deep down. But if the public person can find his brave face and perform, remaining in control of his marketable skills, he can hide away his insecurity behind a mask. I used to be quick: I could outrun my demons. Then I aged and lost a lot of my fancy moves.

"Do you feel that privately you do not deserve to be positive, or you feel guilty about being positive?"

It's not so much a question of being undeserving or guilty. In private, positivity seems to be unrealistic. The private Rik is ruled by modesty and humility. It always seemed to me that being realistic about life was being mentally prepared for worst-case scenarios. Boy Scout training (which I did) teaches you how to tie knots, apply bandages and tourniquets, and learn semaphore, because someday you might be a soldier and need to dig a latrine for yourself.

I was taken to Sunday school as far back as I can remember. I was taught that God is watching. Religious education boils down to guilt and performance. By the time I was twelve, the hard-wired performer had traded God and Jesus for teachers, principals, coaches — then music and the guitar.

Losing my religion cost me a large portion of my mother's approval. But performance solidified my identity. Rebelling against my parents, getting cocky, growing my hair, going to band rehearsals, necking with girls — God wasn't smiting me for having impure thoughts. Grandparents were dying, and there weren't any holy angelic visits or any evidence of an afterlife. God evaporated in Vietnam war protests and flower power. I began questioning authority like crazy, since it was clear that power was often cruel and self-serving. I had become a rebellious, smart-mouthed class clown — a cocky punk. And the dichotomy was set for life: the public persona that performed and the anxious private skeptic. Positive was for showbiz. Doubt was for private indulgence and deeper considerations.

Then I was in a band that called itself Triumph and came up with a song called "Hold On" — as if I'd arrived at a theme song for what I thought the band could stand for, positive inspiration and motivation for our fans. Once that had been established, I felt a responsibility to remain true to it and try to service it.

In my last few years of touring, I was struggling to keep up the public Mr. Positive facade, which is why I eventually had to quit my shrinking prospects in showbiz. I needed to reassess where my creativity was going to lead me. I didn't want to become negative in my work, but I couldn't deny that my personal world was changing, as the world itself was undergoing dramatic shifts in social and political culture. I couldn't maintain the same positive public outlook. I needed some time and space to rebalance myself, both personally and privately and as an artist.

My generation encountered a gap between our elders and ourselves — a failure to communicate. In my own golden years, I recognized my own great divide: over there, the supremely arrogant confidence and idealism of my youth; here, a mix of cynicism, skepticism, and wisdom riddled with doubt in the humbling decline of my corporeal swagger. My own children are now middle-aged. That's humbling. For a few decades, I got to know every cohort of college musicians: in between us was the tsunami of digital technology; the rapacious, voracious onslaught of bits and bytes in its constantly shape-shifting forms (let's call 'em market forces). In the end, I shrug, because there's a lot that I simply don't get. In keeping with my crotchety senior citizen status, I don't really care all that much anymore either.

Time brings along gaps that fill up with all kinds of things: culture wars, recessions, technology, pandemics, governments led by conservative autocrats. My personal balance between public and private, positive and negative, feels healthier if I try to keep my past, present, and future in balance. It's a tall order, and creative work keeps me humble.

One of my favourite old photographs is of a sunny weekday spring morning in 1975. I was twenty-two years old, still living at home but playing in Act III, a bar band, so hardly ever around the house. I had played a gig the night before, staying up all night and returning home as the sun was coming up and the birds were chirping. Ready for bed but hungry. My mom and dad were having their breakfast before Dad left for work. He was in his suit and tie, and I was wearing a shabby old red robe. The sash was long lost, so an old brown belt held it closed. I'd been touring for several weeks, so I had this scruffy patchy beard and mustache. I looked like a bum — and my dad was looking all shiny and spiffy. My mom thought this was hilarious, so she grabbed her little camera and made us pose at the top of our front porch steps on 94 Abbott Avenue. I couldn't resist camping up the moment, so I pulled the robe open a bit to show off some leg, like a showgirl, just to mock and scandalize my mom a bit and to create even more of a contrast between us — him, looking like a conservative banker, and me, looking like some counterculture cross-dressing hippie.

The Biggest Fourteen-Hour Roller-Coaster Ride of My Life

In the fall of 1984, somewhere around the end of October, my wife came to me with tears in her eyes on a Sunday evening. She was pregnant for the second time; we hadn't told anyone yet, as she was only in the first trimester. But something bad had just happened in the bathroom, and she was sobbing. "Something's wrong. I think I just lost the baby. There was a lot of blood." We drove to the emergency department of our local Mississauga hospital, but since it was a Sunday evening, there wasn't an obstetrician, gynecologist, or ultrasound technician present. The ER doctor said that from what Jeannette had described, and from the way things looked, it was likely that she had indeed experienced a spontaneous miscarriage. A definitive determination could only be made the following morning with an ultrasound. We went home, feeling lower than low — grieving the loss of an unborn child. In the morning when we returned to the hospital, for some reason that made no sense to me, the nurse said I was not allowed to accompany my wife into the examination room. So, I sat in a waiting area, numb and lost in a miserable sadness. After a prolonged period, Jeannette emerged, walking toward me across the lobby. I thought I could see the hint of a smile on her face. I asked, "So, the baby's okay, then?"

She said, "Well, we did lose one baby, actually. But there are still *two* in there."

Whaaat?

Flipped from the depth of sorrow to the height of joy — how many human beings experience something like this in their lives? We stood there hugging, and it was almost impossible to grasp. We'd lost a baby. Then we found out that she was carrying twins. It was incredible.

Jeannette carried those babies full term: not identical, they were born about five minutes apart — first Cassandra Leigh, at six pounds, fourteen ounces, a squalling birthmarked mess of a kid who had put up with her sister on top of her for nine months; then Ashley Erin, at seven pounds, four ounces, a perfect blue-skinned unblemished baby who required some vigorous rubbing and suctioning to get going, since she'd had a pretty comfortable ride for such a long time, then slid down a freshly blazed pathway out into the world. It was one of the most surreal adventures of my life: a double dose of infinite love, compounded by the fierce infinite love that I felt for my wife, this superwoman who went through a truly heroic labour to naturally deliver two beautiful healthy babies. Plus we had a three-year-old daughter back at home, waiting to become a big sister. I could never have anticipated the surpassing joy, gratitude, and wonder that these miracles bestowed. I had no idea of what we were embarking upon, but experience delivered a fulfilling lifetime of trying to be a husband and a father to this family. I was willing to go for it: I had the blind faith of a thirty-two-year-old rock star. That faith would be tested.

What's in a Name?

When I was a little boy, I was always Ricky to my family and neighbours. When I started school, teachers and classmates called me Richard, which was my public, social name. The diminutive form required the paying of dues: don't try to make me your little friend before you earn the right.

Along came sports and jockdom. Like the army, it was about last names. I was Emmett to baseball, football, and track teammates. Then my reputation grew to the point that I got a nickname. Rocket Richard was a famous Canadian hockey player, and Rik Weiditch, the bass player in our high school basement band, started calling me Rocket — maybe because of playing fast guitar licks, maybe because I was a football and track jock. Anyway, the nickname stuck. My younger brother loved hearing other guys calling me by my nickname, so he started calling me Rocket. When I joined Triumph, the other guys preferred my nickname to any of my given names, and when Mike Levine misspelled my name as R-i-k on the first Canadian Triumph album credits, I adopted Weiditch's spelling. I had myself a very slight, sly pseudonym — a label to inhabit, which gave me showbiz licence. "Making a name for yourself" had started out early for me: once I had the misspelled Rik, R-i-k the Rocket became a subtle cartoony brand — part of my showbiz mask.

When Jeannette is getting serious with me or I'm in trouble, she calls me Richard.

After a while, I told my college students to call me Uncle Rikky (as Randy Cooke, my nephew from another auntie, the drummer, sideman, and full-on force of nature, had labelled me many years before) — the advice-giving, cheque-signing, pedantic, didactic figure I'd become to the boys in the band.

The only people who call me Rocket now are Jeannette, Mike Levine, and Gil Moore. If I ever make it into an old-age home, the nurses will check my registration, call me Richard, and I'll know I'm in trouble.

Baseball

The start of spring training kindles a school-boy thrill inside me — spring is imminent, bringing the joy of baseball, a game that encompasses the pleasures of summer, the glory of autumn.

There's something sacred and spiritual about baseball. I still have the cheap little trophy for MVP in a Kiwanis-YMCA baseball league from the summer I turned eleven, on a team called the Dodgers. My game plan was usually to bunt for a single, then steal second, third, and home. The L.A. Dodgers won the World Series against New York Yankees in '63, then Minnesota in '65. As much as I loved and hated the damn Yankees, I loved the Dodgers more, with the leftie Koufax and my main man, Maury Wills, swiping 104 bases in '62.

In the early '90s, my brother Russell and I played in a men's softball league in Mississauga and had a blast. My dad was the third base coach for a few seasons, and in '93 we won the league championship. Then I started coaching baseball for my kids starting around '94, for a decade. I've been to Fenway (incredibly memorable July 4 weekend), Busch Stadium (goosebumps, awesome), stood at home plate in Comerica Park in Detroit in 2011, and sang the anthem for one of my son Brendan's college games. B-man played NCAA Division 1 on scholarship at Central Michigan;

his mother and I had countless proud moments watching him play as a Lorne Park Indian, Mississauga North Tiger, Ontario Blue Jay, Lorne Park Spartan, Central Michigan Chippewa, and a Mississauga Twin.

Stealing Home

Friday afternoon, June 17, 2005: it's the provincial high school baseball championships in the cavernous, closed-roof, washed-out surreal light of the Rogers Centre in Toronto. I have enjoyed lots of personal highlights and career-related stuff, but nothing compares to family events. On this great day, my brother Russell was there with his father-in-law, and my dad was there. (Russell had been an accomplished ballplayer in his day, and my dad played competitively during the Second World War years as well.) Two out of three daughters got off work to be there, cheering for the Lorne Park Spartans, their old alma mater, in row eleven beside their mom and dad. Their little brother, not so little anymore, had just turned seventeen earlier in the week. He was about to deliver a highlight for the scrapbooks and an early Father's Day present.

In the top half of the first inning, the Spartans ace starting pitcher seemed disinterested and unengaged, as their opponents, the rival Loyola Warriors, got off to a two-run lead. In the bottom of that inning, against a leftie pitcher (whom he knew well as an elite-league club teammate), my son worked a walk, stole second base, then got balked over to third. Before another pitch was thrown, I watched him take a long walking lead. I grabbed my brother's arm beside me and started to rise from my seat, saying, "He's gonna go!" And he did! Stealing home, with a head-first slide in a cloud of dirt; the home plate umpire threw his arms out wide — *safe*! What an incredible rush. The third base dugout (and the sparse families surrounding it) erupted. The next batter singled through the infield, and the game was suddenly tied. Out on the field I watched my son, in the swarm of his teammates, get right in his starting pitcher's face and deliver a message that could only have been about getting a fresh start and playing to win. The tone of leadership was set: the Warriors' mojo was shattered. The Spartans pitcher found his A game and shut 'em down the rest of the way, and the Lorne Park Spartans went on to win the Prentice Cup 6–2 — a thrilling highlight of my life.

Brendan and I went on a bucket-list trip to Chicago's Wrigley Field in September 2019 and caught a pennant stretch game between the rival Cubs and Cardinals. It was an incredible weekend. We saw the Mighty Blue Kings play the Green Mill (Al Capone's old fave hangout), and Brendan snapped a pic of me outside the old Aragon Ballroom, where Triumph played four times. (One of the dudes in a crowd pouring out of a heavy metal show saw me posing and razzed me as an "old man.") We took the official Wrigley tour — that's one storied ballpark. The game itself see-sawed, featured a short deluge in the seventh inning, and then the Cards beat the Cubs 9–8 on two home runs off two consecutive pitches from the highest-paid reliever in the major leagues.

I got invited out just after dawn on September 18, 2005, by Network pal and promoter Matt Belfield to stand on the pitching mound of historic Centennial Field in Burlington, Vermont, facing the oldest wood bleachers in North America. The sun was making a feeble attempt to break through after a rainy night, so the atmosphere made the moment even a bit more magical. After a few minutes, the harried university coaches were prepping that mound and the batters' boxes with Rapid Dry for their upcoming practice.

There's a field in London, Ontario, (now called Labatt Memorial Park) that sits on a hallowed piece of ground; it was an active organized baseball field in 1877, the oldest (organized) ball diamond in the world. In August 2013, Brendan was playing there, and (following my gentle request) during pre-game warmups, he put some of his uncle Russell's ashes in centrefield, just out past second base.

In high school football, I started out as a wingback, halfback, inside receiver, with a few gadget plays so that I could run reverses and some off-tackle stuff. In my first two years, I also played some defensive back. As I got older, I moved out to wide receiver. I was always the kick-return guy. In my senior year, I was the guy in the cast on the sideline, with a torn ACL that didn't get fixed until I was forty-six. (It didn't last. I got about seven years before it popped again and have lived with the arthritis settling in ever since.)

The 1987 NHL Awards offered me a gig as a presenter, which led to a little sight gag with Lanny McDonald, where I slapped on a phony big red mustache and we presented the Vezina Trophy to Ron Hextall. The voiceover introduction was provided by the legendary Alex Trebek. (Trebek said my name!) After the ceremony, people paid to be seated with celebs at a charity banquet in the convention centre ballroom. Our celeb table had some construction company owners and their young sons all in tuxes; on my right, my wife; on my left, ex-*Playboy* model and B-movie film star Shannon Tweed (originally from Newfoundland and wife of Gene Simmons of Kiss). Our table was right beside the Howe dynasty: Gordie, his wife Colleen, and their two sons, Marty and Mark, with their wives. Ms. Tweed made a lively dinner guest to be sure (my wife seemed less impressed) as the parade of autograph seekers continued almost unabated throughout the courses of the dinner — a good-natured part of the deal. By dessert, I couldn't resist the opportunity to grab the legendary Mr. Hockey's autograph for my dad. Howe was completely indifferent; maybe it was my '87 mullet hairdo. The event provided the shallowest of connectivity to Trebek, McDonald, Hextall, Tweed, and Howe — an epic night of Canadian celebrity tingle.

In December 1999, our daughter Shannon cooked up a big surprise at the local high school's Christmas concert music night. She was a senior at Lorne Park Secondary School (heading toward a music education degree in university), and our twin daughters Ashley (trumpet) and Cassandra (clarinet) were in grade nine in the junior stage band. Shannon enlisted her friends from the rhythm section of the jazz ensemble; wrote out a score of charts for the junior horns, woodwinds, and percussion; held extra secret rehearsals in our basement studio; and, as an early Christmas gift for me, conducted her arrangement of "Let the Light (Shine on Me)" from the Triumph *Surveillance* album. I had no inkling, sitting in the third row of the gymnatorium with my parents, surrounded by the other parents and grandparents from our neighbourhood. For me, the emotional intensity was profound. The performance? Well, it was a junior high school stage band, after all, so there was a fair bit of squawking clams, funky rhythm, and some frightening intonation — all beside the point, because it was a glorious, joyful noise. How many people get to hear an arrangement of one of their own songs, scored and conducted by one of their own kids, featuring two more of them playing? My heart felt like it was going to burst, having my very own mini *Mr. Holland's Opus* right there in the high school gym.

On the original master recording of "Let the Light," I'd used a portable Nagra recorder to capture Ashley and Cassandra as almost-three-year-olds giggling as I tickled them under a blanket tent in our living room. As the song is fading out, you can hear their laughter mixed into the music.

Let the light that shines in your eyes shine on me / Let it shine forever
Let the light shine on me / We can build a dream together / now.

Where the Spirit Resides

While on a weeklong tourist holiday in New York City in July 2001 to celebrate our twenty-fifth anniversary, Jeannette and I dined at a restaurant under the Brooklyn Bridge on the East River; took a boat ride round Manhattan on July 4th; and renewed our vows in Trinity Church deep in Lower Manhattan, exchanging simple fifteenth-century poesy rings we'd bought uptown at the museum store, inscribed "vous et nul autre." We also had a memorable dinner at the top of the World Trade Center.

Eight weeks later, the twin towers were gone, destroyed by violent terror. Trinity Church was a triage center for smoke and dust victims.

In the wake of this horror, somehow I still held a sense of good faith in the future, confident in New York's (and the Western world's) resurrection.

That's because of the poesy ring on my finger: a symbol that reminds me of my deep resolution that the spirit of love and good faith can never be extinguished. The emotion in human hearts and the knowledge in our minds is too beautiful and profound for evil to destroy. The best parts of human nature will survive and thrive. Evil fails inevitably because it cannot comprehend that good faith, in beauty and love, will always resurrect and overcome. For all my cynicism and skepticism, I still believe this, even in the darkest of times.

GIG STORIES

I may not have ended up where I intended to go,
but I think I have ended up where I intended to be.

— DOUGLAS ADAMS

Jams with Legendary Musicians

I enjoyed all of them but also — always — found them a little bit terrifying and intimidating.

Playing with Ed Bickert was one of the highlights of my career. There's a photo of us on stage together at the Night of a Thousand Guitars event at the Phoenix Concert Theatre in downtown Toronto on June 15, 1987. He's pulling a Jack Benny reaction because the (largely male) crowd of guitarists that night would not stop cheering for him. It's one of my favourite concert photos of all time. We also did a little duo gig together to support Rhombus Media's Canadian Guitar Festival movie premiere.

Beyond Borders was a cover feature and flexi-disc insert project that I pitched early in '87 to the editors of *Guitar Player* magazine (which carried my monthly column). It came out in July of that year. The concept was to feature an all-Canadian guitar quartet playing a wide range of styles, and I suggested the lineup: for jazz, Ed Bickert; for classical, Liona Boyd; and for a stylistic hodgepodge of everything else, Alex Lifeson and me. After getting a green light, I sketched out a composition of sections that gave each guitarist an opportunity to play to their strengths. There were some presession meetings, then a few days in the Metalworks, capturing each player's signature performances. No one made a penny, but it was a dream-come-true kind of project — purely done for the love of guitar. The opportunity to work closely with Liona, Ed, and Alex was a very satisfying, fulfilling experience.

During the making of that Beyond Borders project, I gently joshed Ed about the treble knob on his little Roland Cube amp being turned all the way off, and how he'd also back off the tone knob on his Telly. He replied that while Eddie Van Halen had his own signature "brown sound," he referred to his own personal guitar tone as "Scarborough Dark" — a reference to where he lived (though he was originally from Manitoba). The poetic metaphor has a cool ring to it. After Ed passed away in February 2019, as a tribute to Ed's classic guitar tone, I commissioned a road-worn replica build of a modified Telecaster — a Bickert Deluxe. The guitar's bridge plate is engraved with the phrase "Scarborough Dark."

June 14, 2001 — WNED Presents the Buffalo Niagara Guitar Festival. Jamming "On Broadway" with George Benson on the stage of the Tralf nightclub was totally mind-blowing, and I was somewhere out and up on cloud nine. I'd read that Don Boswell, the executive promoter of the event (and the president of WNED-TV, the main sponsor), loved the idea of getting guitarists up on stage jamming together. So, I sent word through management that George's *Breezin'* LP had been the soundtrack to my 1976 honeymoon (a true story), and since George was playing that same night up the street at Shea's Theatre (and his show would be over by 10:30 or so, but I didn't go on till after eleven), he might want to come on over and join me on stage for my encore. As the story goes, George's road manager subsequently found a note from Don Boswell stapled to the Benson paycheque that night, relating the backstory, with Don's personal request for George to give serious consideration toward a bit of late-night jamming.

Anybody who knows anything about George Benson knows that he's a wonderful human being, and totally fearless about jamming because *no one* on this planet can blow like George. He's ready, willing, and able to cut anyone's grass, anytime, anywhere.

So, we're heading out of our concert set and toward the encore, when my stage manager slips a note onto the stage in front of me that says "George is here!" I come back out for the encore and ask the crowd to please welcome "the man, the legend, the one and only, Mr. George Benson!" Two massive bodyguards, the size of NFL defensive ends, start walking George across the back of the club toward the stage, and my cheeky keyboard player Marty Anderson starts bopping the intro vamp to "On Broadway." In a few seconds, I'm standing there and thinking, Oh wow, that's *George Benson* standing right there beside me! He's winking at me! I was like a giddy little school boy, with no presence of mind whatsoever. Cellphones were flashing; a giant TV camera suddenly emerged on someone's shoulder at the lip of the stage. It was surreal — a fantasy dream come true. I have no memory of how or what I played, but I'm sure it was terrible. But George? Loosey-goosey from a hot night's work, he smoked the joint. He buried me. And it was glorious.

The *In Session* Shows with Bruce Cockburn and Ian Thomas

One of the things about my music career in the Triumph years was that I didn't really get to work with other music business people very often. I was off playing on tours, working in studios, writing in solitude; it's an insulating bubble world unless you're a schmoozer type, which I never was. The first time I did the TV shoot for *In Session*, in the spring of 1983, was more than a little intimidating, partly because Bruce Cockburn is such an accomplished artist — a wonderful singer, songwriter, and guitarist but also a quiet, intense guy. We used his sidemen for the show, so he had a comfort level, but I was stretching to play with those top musicians — Bob DiSalle, Jon Goldsmith, and Fergus Marsh. It was a very new experience for me. We did a nice duet on "Nuages," a Django Reinhardt tune, and I enjoyed playing dobro slide on Bruce's instrumental "Deer Dancing Round a Broken Mirror." His music has a wonderful clarity, and his creativity embraces a fearless poetic quality that I greatly admire. All in all, a very unique and memorable experience.

The producers extended a second invitation, five years later, to visit the Hamilton CHCH-TV studio again on December 3, 1988 — and I paired up with my friend Ian Thomas. This *In Session* was the polar opposite of the first: the backup band were mostly musicians I knew, and my pal Ian has the outgoing personality of a *Monty Python* comedian. We did some great, crazy stuff: a cover version of "You Shook Me," and the Kinks' "You Really Got Me," plus a few of our own hits. He also regaled me with an on-camera monologue about why studio speakers have tweeters, which had something to do with torturing budgies. I provided the laugh track.

The P.R.O. Trifecta — Pavlo, Oscar Lopez, and myself — were invited out east to play a headline show at Stanfest in Canso, Nova Scotia, on July 3 and 4, 2010. The mainstage gig was forgettable due to the cold wet windy weather. But I got to sit in on an afternoon workshop with Jerry Jeff Walker, and as he played one of his more recent love songs, I noodled little fills here and there. When a natural solo moment came, he gave me a little nod, and I tried to be as tasteful and complementary to his established melody as I could. When I finished, he caught my eye again and gave me a wink and a tip of his cowboy hat (which cued a warm round of applause). That *totally* made my weekend: a musical moment between a Canuck rock and roller and the man who wrote "Mr. Bojangles," the tall folkie in his trademark Stetson.

I jammed on stage with Sammy Hagar and Ted Nugent in 1983 at the Texxas World Music Festival in the Cotton Bowl in Dallas on June 18 and in the Houston Astrodome on June 19. Ted and Sammy are both take-no-prisoners rockers, heart and soul. We jammed out on Led

Zeppelin's "Whole Lotta Love," so it was a totally straightforward power riffin' thing. On the first night in Dallas, those two pulled off some big stage-coverage, track-meet choreography during the soloing, with me standing around watching. So, on the second night at the Astrodome, I decided to show what I'd learned from the masters and jumped the cue for a bit of stage sprinting of my own (so they'd have to come chasing after me). Afterwards, Ted and I shared an elevator up to the corporate suite, where he frowned at me and growled, "Man, you stole my move!" Then he grinned down and said, "That was *cool*."

March 8, 1985: Steve Vai and I jammed at a workshop at the Guitar Institute of Technology in L.A., which was amazing because his playing was off the charts, and I was perfectly content to host a moment where my special guest gave the room of guitar players (including me) a few free rides on his carnival midway. Vai was hanging out at the school (apparently not all that uncommon in those days), and I invited him up on stage to blow. Afterwards, we hung together for a bit, and he offered to drive me to soundcheck, so I sent the limo home, climbed into a VW Bug with his publicist, and they dropped me off for soundcheck at the Sports Arena. Vai is a sincere and unaffected human being of depth, connected to a staggering range of artistic and technical chops and intellectual musicianship. He has no ass, however, because he just keeps playing it off, over and over again.

In the same vein, I also loved the opportunities I had to play with Steve Morse. Steve is just an unbelievable guitar talent: he won best overall guitarist in *Guitar Player* magazine so many years in a row that they finally had to create a Hall of Fame and retire him into it. The Night of a Thousand Guitars in June 1987 was an amazing night. Steve and I also made a trip over to MuchMusic to play live on air there. He'd flown his own plane up to Toronto, spending a few days as our house guest so he could write and record on the *Surveillance* album at the Metalworks studio — another highlight in my life. There were dozens of great memories created that week.

One time I sat in a green room with acoustic fingerstyle legend Don Ross, at an Alan Frew and Friends charity benefit show at Oakville's Centre for the Performing Arts, as Don played human juke box, showcasing an amazing memory, dredging up the changes and arrangements of old pop tunes. It was a ton of fun scuffling around behind Don, as he played obscure requests for a room full of classic rock musicians and vocalists.

That night I got to perform "Lookin' Out for #1" on stage with Randy Bachman — another thrill of a lifetime. I'd seen Randy perform with the Guess Who in 1968 at the Canadian National Exhibition; the Automotive Building had been converted into a psychedelic experience called Time Being. I'd just turned fifteen, but I can recall being inspired watching Randy play, thinking, Someday, maybe I could do that. Eleven years later, Triumph headlined at the CNE Grandstand. And almost forty years later, there I was sitting across from a living legend, trading licks.

Speaking of legends: having Bucky Pizzarelli as the opening act to my set at the Iridium in New York in December 2011 was one of the coolest highlights of that year. I chatted with him backstage for a while and got some fantastic pictures. It was very inspiring to hear Bucky still ripping it up at his age, and he did it clean as a whistle, without reverb, on flat wound La Bella strings with a seventh string tuned to a low A! When Bucky walked into that club, it made the whole Iridium thing work for me. Les Paul had passed away, but I got a full measure of an important chapter of American guitar history, because of Bucky.

The US Festival Heavy Metal Day

It was an amazing thrill to fly in and out by helicopter on Sunday, May 29, 1983. That was a first. (We got to do it again at the American Rock Festival in Kalamazoo, Michigan, on May 27, 1984.)

It was over 90 degrees in the shade, but I had a pretty good gig that day. The evidence lives on YouTube. It was also a cool thing to find out, via the Banger Films documentary on Triumph, that a young John 5 found the televised guitar solo on MTV influential and memorable. All

I knew was the cameras were closer than the crowd, and they outnumbered the band members and crew, so it seemed logical to play to them.

One of the ironic things about this event, in the career of Triumph: we were almost always critically dismissed as a band that was all about our stage production, lacking in musical substance. But there we were, in broad daylight, smack dab in the middle of an afternoon with six of the heaviest, biggest rock acts of the era on the bill, with no light show, no special effects. We played after Ozzy and Judas Priest and before the Scorpions. In the aftermath, consensus was that Triumph had held its own, if not carried the day. That's because we had some pretty good songs — and it felt like a measure of poetic justice. I watched some of the Scorps (who were great), then took the chopper back to the hotel. I had no interest in the big backstage bash.

Celebrity Encounters

I'd have to single out Chet Atkins as a man who made a huge impression on me, without being intimidating. He seemed so self-possessed, so calm and respectful, intelligent, and intuitive. After I met him and sat and talked for a while in his office in the RCA Building in Nashville in 1979, I was convinced that the term "country gentleman" was perfect for him. As a young man signed to RCA Records, I walked away thinking, This is the kind of person I should strive to emulate.

As we were leaving his office, he asked if I wanted anything else signed. I noticed that he had a few promo copies of his latest *First Nashville Guitar Quartet* album, featuring Chet Atkins with Liona Boyd, John Knowles, and John Pell, on the floor leaning up against the wall. I asked if I could be so bold as to get one of those autographed. I have it up in my studio. The inscription says, "To Rik — Thanks for wanting this. Chet."

I sang the anthems in 1991 at a Toronto Argonauts football game where I got to meet Wayne Gretzky and John Candy, who were part owners of the team at the time. As far as the spotlight goes, I'm not keen on schmoozing or star-chasing. But Wayne and John were gentlemen who had the same qualities as Chet. In showbiz, you meet lots of people, and these people made totally positive first impressions, when many celebs fail to do so.

Presenting the Most Promising New Female Vocalist award at the Junos in 1985, Véronique Béliveau and I announced the winner, and k.d. lang came roaring down the centre aisle of the auditorium, wearing a wedding dress and veil with cowboy boots. She struck her trademark pose, a half bow with her arms widespread and one leg kicking up behind her. Right in front of our podium, we got the very full (unintended, rear) effect of the crinolines and boots that were a part of the whole shtick. Like pretty much everyone in that hall that night, I was stunned, in full-blown admiration of her cheeky anticipation of victory — to have changed into the costume in advance, to be waiting at the doors at the back of the hall for the announcement. What if they didn't call her name? Ah, but they did — preparation met opportunity, and she came sailing down the aisle to declare herself, making a larger-than-life splash — a publicist's dream come true.

I got a call around '92 from a lawyer who represented Tom Scholz of Boston, asking if I wanted to fly down to Logan Airport and spend an afternoon with Tom in his famous home studio, to see if we might hit it off, to work together. I mistakenly assumed that Tom was looking for a new creative partner to write new songs. After spending the day, singing parts on recordings, going out for a pleasant dinner, the lawyer called me back a day or two later and said, "Congratulations, you've got the gig. Tom wants to hire you for the upcoming summer tour." And I said, "Wait, what? This isn't about doing any co-writing, or participating in the making of the next Boston album?" The lawyer said, "Well, no, the album's already in the can, and we're just auditioning singers to take out on tour. But why not go out on the road and see where things lead?" I wasn't interested in being a touring sideman singing lead vocals. I said thanks, but no thanks.

An Asia offer came through John Kalodner at Geffen Records, who had taken a pass on signing my *Absolutely* solo album. Geffen was putting out an Asia *Then & Now* greatest hits CD around 1991, and the band was looking for a sideman to do a few outdoor things to launch the release. He must have mentioned me to the band. I talked to both John Wetton and Carl Palmer at separate times on the phone, but I simply wasn't interested in being a sideman for some European festivals, and it just didn't feel like it was going to be long-term.

A Damn Yankees conversation came from their manager, Bud Prager, in New York, who said something was coming together where I might fit in great. Then I got a call from Jack Blades (Night Ranger) — a terrific guy, full of energy, and genuinely excited about this project that was going to have Tommy Shaw and Ted Nugent in it. I'd met Ted years before and even jammed on stage with him; everyone knows that Ted is larger than life. I also hold Tommy in high regard as a total package musician, singer, songwriter, and guitarist. I thanked Jack, told him he already had an overabundance of guitar talent, plus I wasn't looking to join a band again, so I was just going to keep chasing my own humble little solo thing. I'm not even sure that it had been branded Damn Yankees yet, but what would they have made of a Crazy Canuck?

I got to meet Bun E. Carlos of Cheap Trick at a charity gig we did in Chicago at the House of Blues with Jim Peterik's World Stage show. I love Jimbo and sat in as a guest on several different kinds of gigs with him and his band over the years. There were some memorable nights with Mike Reno of Loverboy, Bobby Kimball of Toto, Don Barnes of 38 Special, Kelly Keagy and Jack Blades of Night Ranger, and Jimi Jamison of Survivor. Bun E. had some great stories. He told one about being invited by John Lennon himself to take part in a Sunday recording session in New York but turned it down, because, before heading back out on the road for a bunch of Cheap Trick dates, he needed to get back to the Chicago area on his day off to do his laundry. On that very Sunday, Lennon cut "Beautiful Boy."

On April 20, 2011, I sang the U.S. anthem before an exhibition game that my son's Central Michigan Chippewas baseball team played against the University of Michigan Spartans at Comerica Park in Detroit. Before I got introduced, as we waited in the tunnel, the umpires asked me to go out and sing "Fight the Good Fight." Sorry, I told 'em, not in the contract. I was nervous, it was cold, and damn, does an anthem ever fly by in a hurry. Before you know it, it's over and everyone is much more concerned with "Play ball" — why shouldn't they be? Our son got on base and came around to score a run, but the Chips lost the game 3–1. When we were crossing back into Windsor at the tunnel customs post, Jeannette was asked if she had anything to declare. She said, "No. Only our sadness."

Receiving the Queen's Silver Jubilee Medal

Modest humility seemed to be a common trait amongst the other thirteen people who were awarded this distinction that evening of July 24, 2012. It was a lovely bit of community, and nice to know that music and the arts ranked up there with other kinds of social and charitable activity linked to financial and political movers and shakers. We sang three verses of "God Save the Queen." I knew the words of the first verse; the rest, I'd never heard before. No disrespect intended, but the second verse lyrics struck me as hilarious:

> O Lord our God arise / Scatter her enemies / And make
> them fall;
> Confound their politics / Frustrate their knavish tricks /
> On Thee our hopes we fix,
> God, save us all!

"Confound their politics / Frustrate their knavish tricks" — what a couplet. I couldn't help myself. As these words were being sung all around me, I was thinking of a grand-gesture champion named Freddie Mercury.

Big Nick

I met Big Nick Misetic through Gil and Mike. As the promoter and buyer for his high school, booking shows for local rock bands, he knew Gil. When Triumph first started, Nick already held a lot of odd jobs around the Toronto scene. An imposing big bear of a guy, he'd been a high school football lineman, then trained as a bouncer, with knowledge in security takedowns. If it came to it, he could use his fists but was kind-hearted and had been described as "the soul of discretion." He worked part-time as a radio disc jockey, a limo driver, and as security for Concert Productions International. His limo-driving led him to bodyguard gigs for big rock stars when they came to town, including the Stones and Elton John. His presence was intimidating. No one ever tried anything when Nick was around, and as Triumph rose to prominence, we became good friends. He'd visit the house to hang out, smoke joints, and shoot snooker. We'd go shopping together, and he'd be at my side for local promo events. Jeannette would set a place for him at dinner often, and he'd hold court at our parties, backyard barbecues, big sports events on TV. From '77 through '82, Nick was like a member of our family. But he was also lonely and wanted to be admired and respected for more than his intimidating size. This lack of self-esteem led to a lot of drug use, then abuse; running up debts from a crack habit as the drugs took over, he lost his status around town and visited less and less. After I left Triumph, he'd become desperate.

In his work as a DJ, he often did graveyard shifts, taking the slots that no one else wanted to work, like on New Year's. He told me stories more than once about callers on that shift and how he'd often talk to suicidal people. On New Year's Eve of '89, Nick took his own life with an overdose. Although I never saw it, apparently he'd left a note asking for me to play at his funeral. But his estranged family's ceremony was held in a Greek Orthodox church, where music isn't part of the service. I could never have made it through anything, anyways; I was devastated.

But I resolved to write and record a piece that would try to capture the brilliance of Jeff Beck, whom we both admired and listened to all the time. As a former altar boy, Nick believed in a better plane of existence, free from the sorrow he had in his mortal body. I tried to write and play to his sense of hope. Many midnights, for many years, as the national flagship radio station Q107 ended its broadcasting day across its network, they would play a little bit of "Passage (For Big Nick)," a fitting epitaph for my friend.

The Greasy Chicken Story

One evening I was out with Jeannette, running late, grocery shopping. By the end of a tiring day, we were pushing our overladen carts toward the checkout. (With four kids and boyfriends gathering on weekends, there were always a lot of groceries.) Jeannette asked, "What are we gonna do about dinner tonight?" Too tired for cooking, she said, "Just run back over to the deli counter and grab one of those barbecued chickens."

I head over as she unloads the carts. There's only one chicken left. I grab it and a pack of potato wedges. Heading back toward the checkout, I realize that the container is cracked, leaking chicken grease through the bag, all over my hands. Damn. Suddenly a guy comes around the end gable of an aisle and nearly bumps into me. His face opens in astonishment.

"Oh my gawd!" he says. His eyes quickly scan the store to the left and right — checking for an entourage, or a camera crew, or maybe anyone else who can confirm what he can hardly believe. "You're Rik EMMETT!"

"Yes, I am," I respond.

"Oh my gawd. Man, do you know what you are?" My worried look makes him realize that he's created the wrong impression: that he might be an unhinged stalker. "No! No, man — YOU ARE A LEGEND! Ohmigod, a true legend!"

I humbly smile, shift into my polite thanks routine. Meanwhile the chicken bag is making my hands very hot, wet, and greasy; I'm uncomfortable and in a hurry. But the guy doesn't pick up on this.

"No, dude. I saw you when I was a teenager in 1978 . . ." Blah, blah, blah. As he rambles, he realizes his own life story is not endearing. But he can't allow this moment to pass without an interview. "So, anyhow. Wow. So, what the heck is a legend doing here, of all places?" he asks.

"Um, shopping. Getting a barbecue chicken actually," I reply. "Yeah, listen, man, my wife's waiting over at the checkout and I'm in a bit of a hurry and . . ."

"No, no, that's cool. I don't even need an autograph or anything. But before you go, can I just shake your hand?"

What can I say? With a smile on my face, I grip the dude's hand, pump it a few times, and say, "Nice to meet you! Take care now!" and leave without looking back.

At the checkout, Jeannette says, "Where the hell have you been?"

"Oh, just playing legend," I reply.

"What's THAT?!" she says, pointing at the greasy, messy, stained bag, as I reach for a plastic bag to wrap it in.

"The last barbecue chicken left," I say. "In a cracked container."

And that's how it was with my life. One moment, fantasy figure; the next, an incompetent annoyance to my wife.

The winter NAMM in California is an intense beehive of humanity and a bit of a carny freak show. It can get a bit overwhelming with so many people, so much noise and talking over a very high noise floor. In the early winter of 2006, it was a bit surreal to be a guest at the Dean Guitars booth, standing in front of a fifteen-foot poster of myself from 1981 with a video screen in the background looping footage of a spandex-panted flying-V guy doing the '81 tour strut, my name up on a giant pixel board with the Triumph logo. The autograph lineup never stopped; they had to cut it off. I was at a table with Rudolf Schenker (Scorpions), Leslie West (Mountain), Kerry Livgren (Kansas), and Rusty Cooley. Dave Mustaine showed up for the next shift, and I got to say hi to him and his two teenaged sons. Mustaine enthusiastically sang the "Nature's Child" riff to me, saying it was one of the riffs he cut his teeth on as a young lad. "Huge fans" confronted me to share their stories: how they saw me at Long Beach Arena in '85, or the Santa Monica Civic Auditorium in '79, lots of talk about the '83 US Festival. Every third person asked if there was going to be a Triumph reunion.

I had another interesting California weekend in the fall of 2006. I flew to L.A. on a Saturday (marking assignments the whole trip) and went to a party on Weddington Street in Hollywood at the new Yamaha facilities that night. I got to jam with Nathan East and Patrice Rushen, which was a super-cool thrill. Having the opportunity to say hi and chat with Frank Gambale, Rick Marotta, and a bunch of other endorsee artists, plus the execs from Yamaha U.S. and Japan, made it all worth the trip. Then I hitched a ride back to the hotel with some fans who crashed the party (thank goodness), because my Yamaha rep decided to get into the tequila and go to a karaoke bar. Jet lag was catching up on me, as a drive that should only have taken fifteen minutes lasted over an hour because Universal City was having a Halloween bash for the kiddies and the Moms and Dads were all picking up their offspring. I flew back on Sunday, marking assignments the whole way back, and was back in class at the college on Monday. Long commute. I wrote this in my journal:

> What's the more authentic part of my life — the guy doing the L.A. music biz schmooze, or the guy marking and grading papers for the college courses he teaches? How many other folks attempt this straddling of realities? Do they pull mental hamstrings too?

———————

In the summer of 2013, I got a call from my local city councillor, Jim Tovey, with the lovely news that I'd be inducted into the local Mississauga Walk of Fame on September 7. Triumph also got inducted into the Mississauga Hall of Fame (different committee, different location, different plaque) the following weekend — back-to-back weekends of smiling, hugging, and handshaking. Any time my name elevates into the same category and club as Oscar Peterson, though, I'll gladly, humbly take it.

Fame is surreal, weird; "make a name for yourself." So now there are slab-of-granite historical proofs that it really happened. For all that, I never looked very far beyond the primary focus: write songs worthy of a community, play guitar and sing in order to earn a paycheque, and offer folks something beyond the stuff that money can buy. Fame? A by-product. Still, nice.

I met Oscar Peterson twice in my life: once in the mid-1980s at a Roland event, and once in the late '90s in the concourse of Pearson Airport.

He was in a wheelchair; when I approached to reintroduce myself and pay my respects, amazingly he looked me in the eye, smiled, and said, "Oh, hello Rik. Nice to see you again." (He must have recognized me from Yamaha endorsement materials, since he endorsed some of their products too.) What I loved about that moment was that he was so generous with his positive nature. He knew that recognizing and greeting me by name made my day (my week, my month). A class act and one of the planet's greatest musicians, ever.

February 8, 2013: there's a contractual obligation after-show meet-and-greet in an anteroom to a large ballroom in a classy hotel in St. John's, Newfoundland. The promoter has assigned a security guy, and I also have two of my own entourage keeping an eye out for me. But the over-crowded room generates too many distractions, and a very messy drunk guy comes right up to me, literally weeping to meet his childhood hero — but the moment turns awkward and a bit surreal. He holds out his arms and steps in to hug me, but as he does, he slides his hands up under my shirt onto my bare skin!

It *freaked* me out, but the room was so packed and hectic that my security was preoccupied. No one stepped in and rescued me, because they didn't even notice. I joked, laughed, and quickly pushed the guy away from me, and literally ran from the room through a back exit, jogged down a back hall to the elevators, sprinted to my room, and was overcome by a full-on panic attack.

That moment soured me on meet-and-greets and the weakness of security in public situations. I mean, even with good security, it's too easy for an unstable person to do a crazy thing. You can't plan for that. A weird side effect is shameful embarrassment. I'm hardly an A-level celebrity and certainly not a public figure like a politician, where security is a necessary concern. In my case, 99.9 percent of the time, an obsession with security seems like inappropriate overkill, or a symptom of an inflated vanity. Nevertheless the incident pushed me over an edge down a long, slippery slope that lasted for the six years that led to my retirement.

Canada Day Rehearsal with the Burlington Symphony

I got booked to play a few songs with my local Burlington Symphony on Canada Day 2017. The biggest thrill came the night before, in the rehearsal at the L.G. Branch Auditorium, a gymnatorium hooked up to the Mainway Arena. In that space, oh man, did the orchestra ever sound huge! (Natural reverberations!) As I walked into the room, schlepping my gear, the orchestra was rehearsing the bridge of "Hold On" under the baton of my friend Claudio Vena. On the original recording, it was all guitars, but in Peter Brennan's orchestral arrangement, it's all violins, woodwinds, and brass on the low chord tones — glorious! That was a goosebump moment. Did I ever imagine I'd get to hear an orchestra playing my music as a senior citizen?

As a young man, I was filled with ambition and wild dreams, so my hopes might have entertained the thought. I imagined I possessed the talent and will to be able to make it happen. Was I positive? No. I think I was probably much more of a pragmatist than that. I saw the darker sides of things and calculated minimum returns whenever I got the full wind of ego in my sails. It's important, I think, to maintain perspective. This wasn't the New York Philharmonic in Carnegie Hall, after all. Still it was an event to relish and enjoy, a week and a bit before I turned sixty-four. It probably won't happen again in my life: wonderful to have it happen at all.

The Walk of Fame Announcement Dinner

Our Juno Hall of Fame induction in 2009 was extraordinary validation, offering legitimacy from a music biz perspective, but the Walk of Fame in 2019 felt sweeter, as it had a wider, general-public kind of patriotic sweep, with such a huge honour roll of inductees. Fame is so surreal, anyways, that it's hard not to be ambivalent about it. But it's nice to be recognized for its scope — the charitable side of the work, the fact that fame got me invitations into academia and my role as an educator. Fame gave me more than adequate ways to provide for my family, and later in life, it included us in a club of such auspicious contributors to our national culture that it was quite humbling. The announcement gala dinner was good fun and had many celebrities in attendance. My wife got a selfie with the Property Brothers (who are incredibly nice guys), and the *Dragon's Den* table was chock-a-block with gazillionaires — as was the rest of the exclusive event, held in a giant glass conservatory on the Casa Loma grounds.

Triumph Fan-Fest 2019

This event was about bringing things all the way back, full circle. Sweden and Rocklahoma got us halfway there, but this was like going back to 1975 and searching for the karma of whatever made the three of us happen the way we did. There was a lot of forgiveness and relief in the air backstage, without too much of anything being said — just understood. There were hugs and tears. At its heart, it was an exercise in spiritual healing. It was everything we could have hoped for — more — beyond best hopes, profound. Captured by the Banger Films crew, it provided a climax for the documentary movie. It was very satisfying for Mike, Gil, and me — a crazy rush to surprise the crowd with our appearance and performance. I had family members there, and Kathy Wagner and Rick Wharton were in attendance, helping to coordinate the day's events. There had been stress and strain leading up to it — lots of rehearsals, meetings, and emails — and here I thought I'd retired. But after the subsequent weekend of Walk of Fame events, I was able to settle back into a normal kind of lifestyle again. Thank goodness for my chiropractor (and pharmacist).

My Walk of Fame Acceptance Speech

Typically Canadian, I guess, but I've never really trusted fame. Fashion in the marketplace can be so treacherous. But Triumph's always been able to count on the loyalty of hardcore fans, so that's where the band's hardcore gratitude belongs. And when it comes to awards and celebrations, I always need to thank my wife, Jeannette. Smartest thing I ever did was marry her, and forty-three years later, she's still helpin' me keep it real. And the best thing we ever did was raise four amazing people, and I'm so proud to have them all here tonight, sharing in this — Shannon, Cassandra, Ashley, and Brendan. Love you guys.

I also love music: it brought me wonderful opportunities, and it's always an infinite challenge. But as Van Morrison once said, "Music is spiritual. The music business is not." So credit and thanks go to my two partners, Gil and Mike, who invited me along on their quest for success. The fearless and cheerful ambition that they shared gave my spirit a safe haven. We laughed off the slings and arrows of outrageous fortune, and together we built a rock and roll machine that took us on a crazy ride that forged our brotherhood.

I believe that the spirit of creativity is the DNA in our national identity. And we have the Walk of Fame organization to thank for curating that legacy. For us to be included in that company is pyrotechnically mind-blowing. So, with great humility and deep gratitude — from the bottom of our Maple Leaf hearts — thank you.

It was amazing to be in a gigantic convention centre ballroom filled with successful, rich, fabulous people (not just recipients but the well-heeled patrons of the arts who support the charitable cause). The things common to all the Walk stars are their dedication to hard intense work, their belief in finding their passion, and pursuing it relentlessly. The other commonality in that room was the humility of Canadian superstars — the genuine overriding feeling of celebrating virtue and charity. There was very little cockiness. Ego is sublimated into passionate work. From Will Arnett to Mark Messier (who cried!) to a band that had the chutzpah to call itself Triumph — humble gratitude and self-effacing humour ruled the vibes. It was very cool to be a part of it.

Touring

The best-laid schemes o' Mice and Men / Gang aft agley.

— ROBERT BURNS, "TO A MOUSE" (1785)

Live gigs often require an ability to cope with the unexpected. Power failures, tornadoes, acts of Gawd, force majeure — I've experienced 'em all.

Those who toured with me might suppress laughter and roll eyes behind my back at this, but I wasn't that difficult to please. I never asked for foie gras and champagne; hot tea and fresh sandwiches were fine. I wanted the gear and the monitors to work properly. I wanted to be given an even fighting chance to maximize the music for paying customers. Riders were straightforward; promoters' production companies often were not.

The Background of Network Tour Dates

The Network program came into existence because fans online would ask, "When are you ever going to come to my neck of the woods and play a gig?" If they were serious, my marketing guy Rick Wharton supplied them with the paperwork and guidelines (and hand-holding) that could make that happen. It was a digital age evolution of old folkie living-room concerts, and I agreed to give it a shot when I read about how keyboardist Patrick Moraz (from the band Yes) had built a viable business model based on the concept. As the mainstream music business was leaving me behind, Network shows became an element in my indie career and touring portfolio.

The Dynamics of Crowd Reactions

There were memorable old Triumph gigs in markets like Calgary, Edmonton, Buffalo, Detroit, Chicago, San Antonio, L.A. — places where the band was always warmly welcomed and had good radio airplay, good reviews, good crowds. We struggled more for acceptance on the

Canadian West Coast, where we experienced good old Canadian regionalism. Triumph was almost always labelled a piece of phony hooey in Vancouver, the business turf of Western Canadian managers and agents. We also got this when we went to England in November 1980; Triumph got critically labelled as Kiss without makeup, lacking in substance (compared to the U.K.'s adoration of Rush). Ironically, Triumph was perceived from the beginning as a band of substance in California and in the Midwestern, Northeastern, and Southwestern U.S. But not in the Pacific Northwest, and — apart from Florida — we had very weak radio support in the Deep South and anything south of Washington, D.C. This regionalism became even more evident after I left Triumph and went out on my own. In regions where the evergreen songs of Triumph had received great airtime, I'd get decent offers to come and play. In markets and regions where radio had failed to break the curse of lousy reviews and mean-spirited word-of-mouth, there were never offers.

Superstitions and Performance Rituals

I didn't have any crazy preshow rituals of any importance. I did like to sip spring water, maybe have a cup of tea. I liked to feel organized — set lists written and posted, picks and water placed in the right locations. It was more a standard kind of prep as opposed to ritual, more Boy Scout than voodoo.

I maybe did a little stretching and some breathing, just to kind of relax and cope with the little butterflies. As I used to coach athletes, "Those butterflies are your friends. They can help you perform better." A bit of adrenalin was good. It showed I still cared. A lot of adrenalin was bad; it showed that I hadn't prepped properly.

I liked to be able to sit in a quiet private dressing room that was warm and well-lit with a decent mirror to clear my head and have a guitar to noodle on. No-brainer, right? My pre-gig ritual included checking to make sure my teeth were clean, hair was in place, fly up, and no toilet paper trailing on the heel of my shoe.

Two of my intermission rituals came along later in life (when my gigs started having intermissions). Sometimes I really felt the need to change my socks (maybe my underwear too). It was amazing how a change of socks could make me feel refreshed. I almost always had a sip or two of Gatorade or apple juice, then some hot tea to warm the old throat). Then I'd brush my teeth.

Post-Soundcheck Prep before Gigs

In the Triumph days, after late afternoon soundchecks, I never hung around the arena if I could help it. I'd go back to the hotel and grab a short nap. I'd usually fall asleep with the TV on quietly and a lot of the lights left on. That way, I'd always wake back up after about thirty or forty minutes. I'd show up maybe thirty minutes prior to curtain, get into my stage clothes, and fiddle a bit on a guitar, sing a few things, and sip room-temperature spring water.

I rarely interacted with opening acts or hung out in venue dressing rooms. I didn't even like being in the dressing room, since it was the Triumph command central management office. Once mobile phones came into existence, the other guys had priorities. So, I tried to keep my preshow dressing room time to a minimum.

We didn't warm up musically together, and we usually didn't listen to music before we went on. I might limber up my fingers a little bit, but mostly it was just a question of getting into stage clothes, getting the stage manager's call, walking to side stage, doing a few jumping jacks or bounces, stretches or leg-shakes (like I used to do as a sprinter, before getting into the blocks) to regulate my blood pumping as the intro tape would play, then — boom — the flashpots would go off and we were underway.

As I stood in the wings, waiting to go on, I'd just be trying to get my head clear and game-ready. Once the gig starts, and it's game on, a million things can go wrong, but the professional thing is to imagine that it's just natural gravity, set in motion, and all you need to do is ride it and look like you're enjoying it. And if it goes well, you do enjoy it. And if it goes poorly, you need to look like you enjoy it anyway.

A good crowd makes a difference; an anemic one makes the business a bit harder. But the show still requires business-as-usual, no matter the kind of crowd.

After shows I would have always preferred to be like Elvis and simply leave the building. I enjoyed the quiet private security of being back in my own hotel room. I liked to read books, magazines, and occasionally watch TV. I'd write, do some journaling, maybe noodle a bit on guitar. The prevailing priority — always — was to try to get a good night's sleep, because the next day was a travel day.

Performance Self-Preservation

I never smoked. I drink alcohol in very light moderation. People made jokes about what a boring straight guy I was, but the truth was I preserved my pipes well into my sixties. I didn't do special exercises, but I did take my time warming up to the heavy blasting. When I was young, my reputation was built in the high tenor range. As I aged, things got a bit darker and lower, and it became more about control, not power.

Singing the high hard belting head tones of the old classic repertoire would blow my cords out and make it harder to sing the next day with as much tonal quality or control.

Most of being a vocalist, night after night, is purely genetic. But for me, talking in high-noise environments (at a party, during a long car ride, or at a bar with background music playing at a high level) was a major vocal-cord killer. On stage, I sipped room-temperature spring water.

When I was coaching, especially one summer in 1997 when I was involved with both youth baseball and soccer, my pipes were badly shot all the time.

I matured as a vocal stylist as the pipes aged. There were days when I felt like it was more shreddy, not as stable as I'd like it to be. But in the end, for me, good vocal performance was just forgetting about everything and letting it fly from the bottom of my heart and soul (and the soles of my feet). If it had some edge on it, well, that would just have to be a part of the style and charm that night.

In one sense, I was able to do a much better job later in my career in solo and duo acoustic shows, because I could sing instead of straining to be heard over a rock band thundering away with monitors that simply couldn't compete. Rock singers almost always did themselves damage because they couldn't even hear their own pitch inside their own heads. Which is why in-ear monitors made such a huge impact for vocalists in live situations.

In any case, I always had lower-frequency noise and shred in my throat after singing for a while. In other words, my throat was more likely to head toward Rod Stewart territory after a few hours of work, no matter how much I wanted to sing in a pure tone. (Mike Levine used to refer to my octave-down undertone as Harvey, as in the invisible seven-foot pooka from the old Jimmy Stewart movie.) In this respect, the sound that comes out after a half hour of singing is based, very much, upon the gift of DNA.

Perhaps the biggest skill of all is the acting quality of singing: of imparting style and emotion to a lyric, losing every shred of self-consciousness, surrendering entirely to the music, convincing listeners that you're committed to the meaning and message of the song and you're not just some kind of grandstander, seeking attention through fancy licks. The complexity of this dramatic theatrical skill is why mature singers are often far more interesting than youthful ones, even if youthful ones have chops (pitch, stage presence, charisma) galore. It becomes a total package thing. But without the dramatic interpretive commitment, you don't have the chemistry that glues the package together.

Managing Expectations

A former agent of mine once said (quite accurately), "My job is to manage expectations. Buyers always want to get the talent cheap. Talent always wants to get paid more than they're probably worth. So, my gig is to manage expectations on both sides of the equation."

Fans show up with their hopes and expectations. As I sat backstage and wrote up a set list, I did my best to cover their expectations and manage my own physical resources wisely. As much as I loved and respected the expectations of any audience, in the end, I would always default to the Ricky Nelson "Garden Party" career maxim: "You can't please everyone, so you got to please yourself."

As a singer my life changed dramatically in 1989 because, up to then in Triumph, Gil and I alternated vocals in a live set, so I only sang half a show every night. When I went solo, I doubled my vocal workload at the age of thirty-six, placing a lot more expectations on my pipes. Post '88, I also had to do all interviews, and on stage, I was the emcee doing song intros and chatting up the crowd (and I never did that in Triumph). So that changed my tour dynamics.

Forty-some-odd years of generating set lists taught me that it was often better to stick to the program and give the customer exactly what they expected. Don't try to be too clever; don't try to reinvent the wheel; don't explain or justify. Just stand and deliver.

Aaron Copland's *What to Listen for in Music* had a profound influence on me. It talks about "la grande ligne"—the long line, the thread that runs throughout a piece of music, whether it's a song or a symphony. What's most important is the integrity of the thing, and it should not be compromised. The rub here is that a moment sometimes has its own integrity. So that dynamic could come into play: the integrity of the song versus the integrity of the moment. The best concert moments are when both are well serviced; the worst, when the performer fails to honour either.

Set List Construction

The applause of recognition that greets the start of hit songs gives a set list a nice little gust of wind in its sails, and the performer gets a wee jolt of positive energy. There are no substitutes for those lovely little jolts; they feed the unique, addictive quality of performance art and craft.

There were at least six or seven Triumph songs that showed up in most set lists. One or two new songs from a new album would enter the set and stay there for a while. Once you've picked one tune, it starts to preclude others because you don't want too much duplication of feel, style, or tempo back to back. By the same token, you don't want to create a sequence of songs that don't hang together somehow; they must have that house-of-cards thing, too, once you've got nine or ten going.

People forget that, back in the day, the Beatles headline sets were usually thirty to sixty minutes, absolute tops. Springsteen might have taken pride in three-hour marathon sets with six encores. I was never a marathon runner, always more of a sprinter.

In showbiz, there's an adage: always leave an audience wanting more. I agree with that, always have. Hit the sweet spot, just past the point where quantity won't improve quality. Give your best, but don't repeat. Leave everybody with strong memories of your best. As I matured as an artist and producer, I became a bigger believer in less is more.

Bad Gig Stories

I've played off flatbed trucks in farmers' fields, in the giant lobby of an office tower at lunch time, in an indoor horse barn riding ring (smelled *great*).

Triumph was the closer act at an outdoor event called Canada Jam back on August 26, 1978. The show kept falling further behind, and our encore ended at 3:55 a.m. By then the grounds were all muddy, and the air was nippy and damp. Most of the crowd had gone home hours before. But once we got on and I started running around under the lights, it was just like a dress rehearsal, playing into the darkness, so it wasn't so bad.

In 1988 Triumph played Spring Break on South Padre Island, down off Corpus Christi. The wind was whipping in off the Gulf so hard, the sand was stinging. Really bad for singing.

In the mid-2000s, my band played the Molson Indy pit area in Toronto after time trials. A summer rainstorm hit with hurricane-strength gusts of wind. I was playing a solo with my head down and then looked up across the large audience patio area. Plastic chairs and umbrellas were literally sliding sideways across my vision, like the scene in *The Wizard of Oz* where a cow goes flying by the window. We wrapped it up.

The Rik Emmett Band played outdoor summer shows twice in total downpours — once in Cobalt and once in Port Colborne. In both circumstances, the stages were covered but the audience (what was left of them, huddled under umbrellas out in completely muddy conditions) was soaked through. We braved the elements for the sake of those hardy people (and contractual obligation) but shortened the set, calling it quits when rain started flooding the stage, threatening to electrocute us.

One time we'd driven all the way down into the flat outback of Ohio for a biker rally, and a summer hurricane blew in. I never left the motel. We still got paid because the cancellation was an act of God.

One memorable New Year's Eve, I played outdoors in a park in Niagara Falls USA, as the wind and snow blew straight in, so that the overhead radiant heaters for the front man out singing at the mike line were useless. (The drummer was toasty, though.) I got hypothermia: at one point, I watched as the snow landed on my frozen, numb fingers on the guitar neck, where it began to accumulate in tiny drifts. Ah, good times.

Beyond a doubt, the weirdest gig I ever played was a private Halloween corporate duo gig in Chicago on October 29, 2016. It was a big-budget life celebration for a Wisconsin woman, widely adored, who had passed away. There were three things she loved most in life: Halloween, the Green Bay Packers, and Rik Emmett of Triumph. Every year on All Hallow's Eve she had apparently gone all out on decorations, costumes, and parties. It appeared to me that she likely had deep connections in both party-planning and perhaps the film and TV makeup community. Anyway, a corporate event space in west central Chicago was staged to look like a miniature Lambeau Field, with a huge scoreboard up behind the stage area. The room was decorated to the nines with tombstones, skeletons, spiderwebs, jack-o-lanterns, ghosts, and goblins. Since it was a Halloween costume party, invited guests showed up as ghoulies, horror movie characters, and all manner of walking dead. From the stage, the audience resembled an even more eccentric cast of Michael Jackson's "Thriller" video — a few had hatchets in their bloody skulls. They had spared no expense in paying tribute. The long narrow venue was entirely glass and modern granite surfaces; the front-of-house PA mixer was pushing Spinal Tap knobs to eleven. For an acoustic duo performance, it was *loud*.

The most surreal moment of the gig came during the finale, "Magic Power." The assembled started singing along, as a slideshow of the young woman's life played on the ersatz–Lambeau Field jumbotron behind the stage. The entire audience, emotionally overwhelmed by grief and loss, started crying. It was bizarre, surreal, to look out and see Beetlejuice, Lizzie Borden, zombies, devils, Jokers, hookers, pussy cats, and fallen angels in lingerie with their mascara pouring down their cheeks, singing "I'm young, I'm wild, and I'm free."

The most humbling gig in my life was a guitar clinic in Kingston, Ontario, booked as a conventional appearance on a late Saturday afternoon in a music store. But the owner had his own ambitious ideas, filling the retail space with inventory for their super blow-out sale. With no room left inside for a clinic stage or audience seating, they planned to have it outdoors on an erector-set portable stage, across the street in the giant parking lot of a grocery superstore. Unfortunately, the windy, rainy, cold weather did not cooperate; no problem, they went to plan B and moved it indoors to a coffee shop area on the grocery store's second-floor mezzanine, with a PA set up, all ready to go. "Trust us," they said, "it will be great. You'll love it." (Promoter words that sink an artist's heart.)

It was *not* great. The open mezzanine sat directly above the produce section. From my microphone position (no stage), I could simply turn my head and look over the railing right down at shoppers squeezing the lemons. Confused housewives stared up, wondering what the hell was going on up there. For the soundcheck, it took what felt like forever to get someone to turn off the store's piped-in background radio, but they never stopped making periodic PA announcements, even during my abbreviated set. ("Clean up on aisle four. Price check at register six.") The biggest bonus surprise was that the mezzanine level brought the proceedings that much closer to the continuous thundering rainstorm on the metal roof. The final insult added to injury was that the weather ensured that everyone assumed the event had been cancelled, so no one came. In attendance, there was me, the PA guy, a few sheepish folks from the music store, one teller on break, and the sixteen-year-old coffee shop girl in her hairnet. Afterwards, I got to enjoy the consolation of the long drive home, west on Highway 401, in the relentless heavy rain, all alone with my wounded pride.

Summer Mini Tour with Nazareth

In the mid-'90s, my band got asked to do an opening slot for a little summer tour that Nazareth did around Lake Ontario. My memories are a bit vague, but I think we might have played around Belleville, then maybe Peterborough, over to Ancaster, and down around the lake to Thorold.

The last evening, as we played the Front 54 club in Thorold, a mini-tornado ripped through the town while we were up on stage, and the power went out. No lights, no PA — only red emergency EXIT signs alit in the venue. I got my stage tech to bring me my acoustic guitar and shine his mag light on me, and I played an acoustic set for the crowd, while we waited for the power to be restored. The venue had a green room down off stage left, and in the glow of candles and flashlights, I could see that the Nazareth guys and some of their crew had come wandering out to watch the oddity of this little solo acoustic performance. Afterwards, when I came off stage, I finally got an opportunity to meet them, as they had pretty much kept to themselves, living on their tour bus. I ended up in conversation with Dan McCafferty (vocalist) and Jimmy Murrison (guitarist). This is the way I recall the conversation going down:

Rik comes down off-stage. In the candlelight and flashlights, Dan and Jimmy meet him, pints in hand.

Dan (in a very thick Scottish brogue): "Holy fuck! Tha' wuz grrreat, man. Yerrr like a rrreal fuckin' mew-zesh-un!"

Jimmy: "Aye. Nicely dunn, mate."

Dan (looks at Jimmy): "Ochhh . . . we're not like that, are we? Fuck, noo. We're not mew-zesh-uns. We're just (raises eyebrows, and shrugs) . . . *Naz-arreth!*"

I admired the band for their brotherhood. Before going on every night, they'd form a little circle side-stage (I'm not sure if it was a prayer, but you could tell it was a career-long pre-concert ritual), then go on, and do their thing. Another reason that I recall that side-stage conversation was that McCafferty described a recent hangover as "mon-youuu-ment-al." It was so Scottish, so rock and roll . . . it was *Naz-arreth!*

Planes and Trains and Automobiles: A Horror Story

November 9, 2006: due to bad winds, our plane got diverted from LaGuardia to Westchester County Airport. A bad accident had closed the George Washington Bridge, so there were no cabs taking fares into Manhattan, so we shared a cab ride with some teenaged girls over to the local train station, then took a commuter train (with our luggage and guitars) south into Manhattan. When we got off the train, it was six p.m. in Grand Central Station, and the humanity was flowing through that place like a raging river. Lugging suitcases and guitars through Grand Central Station was brutal. There was zero chance that Dave and I could hail a cab to get us over to the club, so our road manager Kathy Wagner had come over in a fancy black Town Car to rescue us from the sidewalk on the east side of Grand Central. We went right from the car, past the patrons, onto the club's stage for a quick soundcheck, then down into the basement for a snack, change of clothes, and back on stage to play the gig. That day took a few months off my lifespan.

I had a nice thing happen to me once on a flight back from Texas. I sat beside a middle-aged fellow (empty seat between us) who was listening to some groovin' music on his ear buds; we never chatted. When the plane landed, a different guy, from the seat in front of me — a younger man travelling with his wife and their young daughter — was retrieving stuff from the overhead compartment, and when I reached up and hauled down my guitar gig bag, he said, "Ahh, so you're the guitar player. I noticed it when I was putting our stuff up. So what do you have in there?"

"A Gibson Les Paul."

"I have one, too, at home."

"A Les Paul?"

And he said, "Oh, no, I meant a guitar. Mine's not anywhere near that nice. It's just a cheap one. Maybe that's why I don't play it very often." To which his family just kinda snorted. "Well, you must be a pro to be travelling with a nice guitar like that."

I smiled and said, "Yeah, I've been around a bit."

And the guy's attention returned to his family. Then the gent who had been sitting in my row with me leaned in conspiratorially and whispered, "He's too young to recognize who you are." And gave me a knowing smile. It was a nice moment. I'd been recognized by my row-mate, but on a three-hour flight, he'd never even tried to strike up a conversation. He'd given me privacy and space. I got the best of both worlds — the glow of being recognized, and the routine courtesy of an ordinary stranger.

Celebrity is a bit of a strange deal. Some folks think that you owe them good cheer and should accommodate their requests because you chose a life of being public property. Some folks seem to expect that you should be entertaining and witty and be on for them because you are an entertainer. Some folks get weird — shy, awkward, fumbling for words, or garbling sentences as they try to talk and dig for a pen and paper for an autograph. Some people are rude and demanding. But the best folks are pleasantly surprised, just normal, polite, and respectful. Happily for me, that was most folks, most of the time.

My most enjoyable gigs weren't big ones. Even the significance of Sweden Rocks and Rocklahoma with Triumph didn't really have the level of personal satisfaction I got from playing a good Troubs duo gig at Hugh's Room in Toronto, at the Coach House in San Juan Capistrano, or Poor David's Pub in Dallas. We'd feel the love up close and personal in Philly at the Tin Angel, for sure. Toward the end of my touring days, the City Winery venues and the Supper Club in Cleveland were truly great places to play. I enjoyed the intimate acoustic gigs in the folkie singer-songwriter venues, with the storytelling, because they had more latitude and less physical hardship. Rock band gigs paid better, of course, and gave better one-off commissions to agents, with paycheques to more sidemen (to whom I still felt loyalty). But at all gigs, I honoured the nostalgia of the evergreen soundtrack, which was what fans wanted. I have sweet memories of perfect summer nights at the Canal Days gigs in Tonawanda, New York, with the band playing great and the audience making us feel like superstars right from the first song. The reasons people support an artist for so many years are principally emotional ones. Emotion isn't reason, but it makes its own compelling reason.

I liked duo gigs — having someone to share the moments with and to play off. Big rock band gigs always felt like I was only using a very narrow part of my skill set — granted, the skills that got me widespread recognition — but not the most musical, not the most artistic, certainly not the most personal. A rhythm section gives one a bigger, wider safety net. I remember the very first Network solo show I played in Mike

Burdick's condo party room in New Britain, Connecticut, in 1998 — the sense of exhausted fulfillment when it was over, that I'd just done something requiring my complete commitment.

Through adversity comes character. Through humility comes perspective. From perspective comes a kind of wisdom that cultivates a forgiving spirit and a more universal humanity. I liked when shows had a human, community-oriented, positive life affirmation, like a charity tie-in. Local promoters would represent in real time the ideas in songs like "Never Surrender," "Fight," and "Magic." It wasn't Marvel Comics superhero stuff: just people choosing to remain true to the highest calling of an ordinary life, pushing and pulling and bending themselves out of shape to have a go at the extraordinary. It made a difference in my own life, too, and I was very grateful for that. As Bob Dylan put it, "You gotta serve somebody." I was in the service of the art and craft of music and in service to the folks who tied me to their charity work for education and health care. I was grateful to combine the service of my music-making with the service of charitable needs and public service.

When my partner in the Troubs, Dave Dunlop, lost his wife suddenly in the middle of 2016, it made our touring and recording heavy to get through. Yet he desperately wanted and needed a life preserver to keep him from drowning in the ocean of his grief, and even though the situation was shredding some of the faulty wiring in my own nervous system, there was no alternative but to support the needs of my friend.

Plus there was the contractual obligation of an album to deliver to the European label, Mascot/Provogue. All things considered, that *RES 9* project was a damn good way to cap off the rock recording artist part of my life.

After that, I was learning about self-preservation, figuring out how to say no. I gave notice at the college and never went back. I worked through anxiety, a case of shingles, vertigo (which never cleared up 100 percent), alopecia arietta (so I learned about artful combovers), and played out the run of live touring dates on the books through 2018. Honestly I don't miss any of it.

PERSPECTIVES

Digging through the Catalogue of My Back Pages

Work is love made visible.

— KALIL GIBRAN

I'm not really given to wandering through my own back pages, but I know the past is of interest to fans who supported my self-indulgences. So, here's a review of my discography since leaving Triumph. For handy reference, first let me list the discography of the ten Triumph albums that I played on. I won't revisit any of this catalogue — only list it.

1. *Triumph* (1976)
2. *Rock & Roll Machine* (1977)
3. *Just a Game* (1979)
4. *Progressions of Power* (1980)
5. *Allied Forces* (1981)
6. *Never Surrender* (1982)
7. *Thunder Seven* (1984)
8. *Stages* (live album with two studio cuts) (1985)

9. *The Sport of Kings* (1986)
10. *Surveillance* (1987)

Now on to my solo career. Settle in, gentle readers. There are nineteen projects. First the list. Then the retrospective thoughts.

1. *Absolutely* (1990)
2. *Ipso Facto* (1992)
3. *The Spiral Notebook* (1994)
4. *Ten Invitations from the Mistress of Mr. E.* (1997)
5. *Swing Shift* (1997)
6. *Raw Quartet* (1999)
7. *The Spirit of Christmas* (1999)
8. *Live at Berklee* (2000)
9. *Handiwork* (2002)
10. *Good Faith* (2003)
11. *Strung-Out Troubadours* (2006)
12. *Liberty Manifesto* (2007)
13. *Push & Pull* (2009)
14. *Trifecta* (2009)
15. *reCOVERy Room 9* (2011)
16. *Then Again . . .* (2012)
17. *Marco's Secret Songbook* (2012)
18. *RES 9* (2016)
19. *Folk Songs for the Farewell Bonfire* (2020)

Before we begin — an overview of the two major transitions.

After bouncing around in the fall of 1988, co-writing with established writers, and doing some demos for CBS/Epic (which they passed on), I made a production deal with Phase One Studios and produced my own album, subsequently striking a deal with the indie label Duke Street Records, distributed by MCA/Universal in Canada. As that first solo album, *Absolutely*, was coming out, a U.S. deal was struck with Charisma Records. My manager, Ross Munro, negotiated a worldwide publishing deal with Universal Music Publishing with a large advance. Disaster struck: Charisma declared bankruptcy just after release, and the future of the album swirled down the toilet — no U.S. sales, no publishing revenues, no mechanical royalties. The publishing advance went unrecouped. Out of the goodness of my heart, I let Universal have the publishing rights for the next project, *Ipso Facto*, for nothing. By then, the rock music biz had transitioned to Seattle grunge. At the time I didn't see it, but with 20/20 hindsight, an old fart like Emmett was never going to be mainstream again. *Ipso* died, and '94's *Spiral Notebook* was my final attempt to reinvent myself as a grown-up singer-songwriter. One ballad from that record did okay on Canadian radio, but — as so many artists can tell you — radio-airplay turntable hits don't automatically translate into sales.

There was no point in chasing vestiges of the mainstream, so in '96 I began making independent recordings in which I owned all the copyrights and publishing.

Now let's go digging through the catalogue of my back pages.

Absolutely

This album stands up okay for me overall. I'd assembled a band that opened the dimensions of the playing field, in an obvious attempt to establish myself as a solo artist with material that would never have been on a Triumph album. My lyric writing took more chances; I didn't have to accommodate the image of the band as perceived by others. After my years as a rock star, I was attempting to show some range, even a sense of humour — developing scope and personality.

The rhythm section of drummer Randy Cooke and bassist Chris Brockway enjoyed leeway to do their thing, and tracks like "Drive Time" and "Stand and Deliver" remain outstanding, high-quality work. Every track was cut to click, and my own time and feel as a musician took a quantum leap, trying to keep up to Randy and Chris.

In retrospect, there are too many digital keyboard tracks on *Abso*, although I still love the sample string stuff on "Saved by Love"— a great radio track. Before it went bankrupt, Charisma had serviced that song to U.S. AOR FM radio, and it charted well right out of the box. The tune even got bought for the closing credits of a Hollywood movie, *Problem*

Child 2, because the producer heard it on the radio, while driving down the Malibu coast.

I'm glad that I invited a woman into the jock culture of rock; Colleen Allen's presence and musicality made *Abso* a very different project than I'd ever been involved in before. She was fearless and professional, with a wonderfully generous talent. The background vocals and arrangements on this album were a big growth from my past, but the production mix and engineering is too much a product of the times — too complicated with too many different reverbs in the mix on everything (yikes).

During pre-production, there was pressure from management and industry sources to not wander too far away from the "front man of Triumph" image and public (commercial) appeal. That had come back from label people when we shopped demos, which is why the album cover photo ended up being a black Les Paul guitar slinger with big hair in a leather jacket. The music inside was far more eclectic than that image. Still the cover design stands the test of time — a clean graphic in classic black and white and red. I wish I'd kept that simplicity in my approach more often over my career. But that guy on the cover didn't realize how much baggage he was carrying. He lacked the guts to step all the way away from the past thrust upon him by his management, record company, publisher, even fans. So, the songs got gussied up in ways that tried to please everyone, in the language and currency of the rock culture at the time, instead of trying to simply remain true to the artistic heart of the song. "Live and learn" takes time.

After thirteen years inside the Triumph bubble, some co-writing with experienced outside writers gave me a sense of how that worked and what it felt like. It was as much an educational growth experience for me (as a recording artist, as a human being) as it was an attempt to make a commercially successful record album. Plus the personal pressure was immense. Jeannette and I now had our fourth child; I hadn't received a partnership paycheque from Triumph for my last two years in it, and the negotiations of extricating myself from the Triumph business partnership went beyond the beyond. Despite the smiling guy on the back cover, flipping his guitar behind his head (how did I ever have such a flat stomach?), my guts were twisted up in knots.

Middle Ground: A Song, a Philosophy

I did have my moments, in the wake of my split with Triumph, when I was struggling to remain a level-headed, reasonable, controlled person and not a slave to negative emotions. I had a few places where I would try to gather myself and seek balance — clean myself out and let the tension and unhappiness slide away. That's a place where one can take a deep breath and say to himself, Middle ground. Balance. Inner peace. Here. Now.

It's funny what ends up having legs musically. "Middle Ground" reclaimed its real acoustic folk character years after midi sequencing became passé. The ballad "When a Heart Breaks" also works as a simple acoustic guitar and vocal tune (and not the power ballad it is on this recording). The social commentary of "Big Lie" and "World of Wonder" sadly remains applicable today. A few choices now seem like novelty-chasing mistakes — "Smart, Fast, Mean, and Lucky" in particular. (Although the song did get claimed as a theme song by an American speed-skater in a profile piece on ABC-TV's 1992 Olympic coverage.)

"Passage (For Big Nick)" still moves me, as it's infused with my grief and sorrow, my love for a departed friend, and my take on his hope that a tortured spirit could find its way to peace. This track owes a huge and obvious stylistic debt to Jeff Beck, but it's also my own in its harmonic structure and the melody sitting on that chord progression.

The album went gold upon release in Canada, but Charisma's bankruptcy killed it in the U.S. before it had a chance. Future writer's earnings from publishing got lost forever in unrecouped balance statements from Universal.

Ipso Facto

This was three albums in one, a schizoid Sybil of a project. It's not really a misrepresentation of an always eclectic artist, but the tri-album repertoire was also imposed upon me by the forces of the time, and in the end I agreed to it. I hadn't learned how to say no yet.

The first version of the album I started working on began with a bunch of demos engineered by Greg Critchley, the drummer in my touring band. In-fighting and politics had made the *Absolutely* ensemble untenable, so I gave them all notice and went lean and mean with a quartet — Critch on drums, Tom Lewis on bass, and Richard Evans on keys. It was a pleasure to work with them. I'd mistakenly tried to treat the original Rik Emmett Band members as family, creating family expectations and demands. I needed something cleaner, more top-down, and more realistic than that — a benevolent dictatorship, enlightened leadership. The first demos were "Let Love Conquer All," "Dig a Little Deeper," "Heaven in Your Heart," "Can't Lie to Myself," and "Out of the Blue." When Universal, the major label distribution company, heard them, questions came back: why are these all such pleasant, mid-tempo R & B tunes and ballads? Where's the good old Rik Emmett hard rock we know and love? My first reaction was that these tunes have pop accessibility, and they're melodic and radio-friendly; they just need a corporate champion to believe in them.

I always felt that album projects were also about weird little B cuts, sleepers, acoustic guitar instrumentals — recording experiments that an artist should undertake to push his own envelope. That B part of the album was also well underway creatively — fingerstyle guitar pieces like "Lickity Bit" and "Transition," and sparse, artsy vocal tunes like "Woke Up This Morning" and "Calling St. Cecilia." Uh-oh. So I decided to satisfy Ross Munro, my manager; Duke Street Record's president, Andy Hermant; and head honcho Randy Lennox at MCA Canada/Universal, and I went back to the drawing board for a hard-rocking part C. That became "Straight Up," "Bang On," "Rainbow Man," "Meet You There," and "Do Me Good." (In the liner note 'thanks', sixteen names are affiliated with record labels — maybe not a good sign.)

I hate the artwork; worst package I ever agreed to. My age, reputation, and image were seen as negatives. My manager and the labels were all feeling the impact of Seattle grunge bumping MTV hair bands and corporate rock out of fashion at FM radio. Advisers thought it best if I didn't appear on the package. In the end, the photographer Chris Chapman was hired to shoot some portrait stuff to be used inside the sleeve. Two shots — one with my Pacifica 1220 electric and one with the AE-2000 jazz archtop — capture two personalities of the album. In the music biz developing outside my own process, none of it mattered.

Ipso facto means "by the fact of itself" — its very nature makes it self-defining. I was beginning to take a fuller ownership of who and what I was, as my inspirations moved me from style to style. The guitar songs on this record mined the legacies of Hendrix, Stevie Ray, Wes Montgomery, and Lonnie Johnson, along with the technical fretboard pyrotechnics of "Straight Up." I was moving away from the biz, as it was leaving me behind anyway. My songwriting was evolving: there were modulations written into "Let Love Conquer All" and "Dig a Little Deeper"; open tunings on the guitars for "Bang On," "Lickity Bit," and "Do Me Good." I was ignored by the mainstream; the wrong thing in the wrong place at the wrong time had become a career refrain. Never hip or cool before, I was maturing as a musician and artist and learning how to produce records inexpensively and on budget. I was writing like an adult, expressing myself as an artist, even if there wasn't a mass market for it or any champions in the media.

In this game of retrospective rear-view mirroring, I see the points where I pretty much had to keep slugging it out on my own — under the radar, working hard enough to provide for my family and survive. Ross Munro, Melinda Skinner, and Duke Street Records did the best they could, but *Ipso* was the album where survival became evident. Never a one-hit wonder, never an A-lister, I'd made a few left turns off the path everyone thought I'd been walking, and I decided that creative left turns were my thing now.

We could only make a very small regional distribution deal for the album in the U.S. and small deals in Europe and Japan. There was no major label deal, no big-time distribution. UMPG continues to hold the publishing rights for the thirty-six Duke Street Records songs of that era and has never made a single licensing deal of any kind for any of them, to this day.

The liner notes mention the bed track sessions for "Can't Lie," "Heaven," "Dig," and "Blue" being at Manta/Eastern on November 9 and 10, 1991. This was one of the most memorable, pleasurable recording sessions I ever did. I loved that studio — the first place I'd ever done album recording, playing on *Justin Paige* sessions in 1973. It was a beautiful, spacious room like the orchestra tracking rooms I've seen in photos of Abbey Road, or the old-school label studios in New York and L.A. We rented the space cheap, overnight, and started after dinner. The drummer Greg Critchley knew three of these tunes, because he'd engineered the demos — and my expectation was to get those three songs done ("Can't Lie," "Dig," and "Heaven"). But well before midnight arrived, the guys had already nailed the three tracks. With tons of time left over, did they want to try to capture one more song? I'd written "Out of the Blue" and — given the hour, the circumstances, and the fact that an organ and Leslie rig was sitting out on the studio floor — I decided to teach it to the guys. They scratched out little charts for themselves, and Richard Evans played a killer Hammond organ and Leslie part (which I kept as the master in its entirety). It was magical — everything I'd always imagined making records would be like. It's a midnight kind of song, anyways, and the mood it captured was just right. So the credit says November 9 and 10, but that's just because we ran past midnight. I drove home from that session feeling fulfilled, elated. It had been really satisfying — the kind of night that makes a recording artist feel like they made the right career decision.

Later, we overdubbed the lead guitar at 1:2:1 Studio, and Richard Evans put some great sampled string keyboard parts on that song. For the lead part, it was the last time I ever used my old Marshall fifty-watt head to make a recording. Squealing and feeding back like crazy, it was perfect for that track. Sadly neither Manta nor 1:2:1 exist anymore, with most studios coming and going faster than artists on the hit parade.

The Spiral Notebook

I turned a corner, leaving rock guitar heroism and the perfidy of the music biz behind me. I started using the voice of a songwriter, not the head-ripping histrionic belting of a rock band front man. There were great sessions for this (especially the week of bed tracking up at the Chalet Studio, near Uxbridge, where I hired a cook to come in and serve us lunch and dinner every day). This project showcased my working relationship with keyboard accompanist Marty Anderson — a very positive and productive experience. Looking back, this was my swan song to Duke Street and MCA/Universal — the mainstream of the biz had left me behind, so I was simply accepting my fate and evolving.

The Spiral Notebook has a lovely (very expensive) artwork package — Michael Wrycraft's design, and Andrew MacNaughtan's photography.

It glows with a burnished golden hue, like a blonde guitar finish; it's my fave package by far, even though "A Man Called Wrycraft" and Melinda Skinner (she worked for Duke Street and Ross down at 121 Logan Avenue) made me handwrite every lyric and credit. The first single and video was "Anything You Say" — completely ignored. The follow-up was the ballad "Let Me Be the One," which got airplay on soft B market radio stations in Canada. It got a promo bump from MCA sending out freebie CD singles to all the wedding DJs they could find registered across the country. The album sold poorly, and by 1995, my mainstream commercial irrelevance was evident. In the lyrics, you can hear me shrugging.

"Every ripple set in motion, spreading into mystery / Leaves me humble at the beauty of it all."

"I think I'll take a walk out in the desert air in the moonlight — there's a promise waiting there."

"Comin' around, and comin' of age / Comin' to terms with the bars of this cage."

"Here in the days of half-empty glasses, and the faithless nature of the deal / There's not enough justice, too much law: too many cathedrals and not enough god."

Marty Anderson was the pre-production engineer of the demos and did such a good job in his home studio in southeast Mississauga that we simply transferred many parts directly over from his gear to the master multitracks. He was also a valuable contributor to voicings in the arrangements, building textures. "The Longing" is one of my favourite tracks I've ever written and recorded (with gorgeous background vocals by Karen LeBlanc).

I was getting better at song prosody, learning new things about (artistic) economy. That was the big takeaway: I learned that, above all else, I'm a writer. No matter what the marketplace says, I write, and the consolation prize is content. I love process. Writing is 100 percent you — your heart and your head and your holy ghost. *Spiral Notebook* confirmed it.

Ten Invitations from the Mistress of Mr. E.

In '93, I turned forty. My wife got a large group of friends of mine to pool their dough, then my pal Ian Thomas pretended to be auditioning several high-end models of nylon string classical guitars for himself and wanted my expert input. One was a 1979 Laskin, and I told Ian that beautiful, rare beauty was *far* too much guitar for him. Guess which guitar showed up as a gift at my fortieth birthday party? I'd always wanted to make a classical guitar fingerstyle record, and I'd put pieces on lots of albums, but never found the time or discipline to compose a full album of repertoire.

By the end of the *Spiral Notebook* run, there was no point in chasing any kind of commercial pop thing again. By '95, there were no major label record deals for forty-two-year-old Canadian arena rock guys out there to be had. I started going back through old tapes and notebooks, looking for little bits of things that might lead to full-blown guitar pieces. The internet was growing; indie was where it was at. Our little humble post office box III had blossomed into a cool little support group (it was also something I shared with my retired parents; mostly, my mom was into it), and so I started thinking, Why not sell off a bunch of my guitar collection and the snooker table in my basement, open up that space, and start a digital recording studio? I could (finally) make the classical guitar record I'd always wanted to make, from way back in my twenties. Why wait? I hated to lose my beloved snooker table, but it only made sense to have my own studio and rehearsal space in the house. Why not simply be able to take a cup of tea downstairs? I started calling in favours left and right. My old friend Tony Daniels became a hugely supportive right-hand man. I traded studio gear to get Andrew Craig (an exceptional Toronto keyboard player, highly recommended by Randy Cooke) to help me out with arrangements, recording, and background tracking on a few of the tunes. My little solo classical guitar instrumental record got more involved.

The Duke Street era was over: my manager, Ross Munro, was transitioning over to his own Watch Music indie label concerns, and though we were still doing some business together, I was operating more on my own. My relationship with the Rik Emmett Network team of Rick "Spud" Wharton and Kathy Wagner, as agents and marketing managers, was developing. They became indispensable over the next few decades.

My inspirations for *Invitations* came from a wide variety of sources. One of the principal ones was an album from my youth by Andrés Segovia entitled *The Guitar and I*, which included a lot of the Sor and

Tarrega studies. (MCA had the entire Segovia collection on CD, and my faves were volumes three and five.)

I used the Laskin, as well as two Yamaha nylon string instruments, and "Seventh Circle" featured an AES-1500 jazz archtop through an effect that produced harmonized fourths and elevenths. It was a torturously hard album to make — composing the pieces, learning how to play them, how to work the computer and the midi gear, the digital recording machines, and a Yamaha O2R digital board. It was ambitious, but I had no deadline. I lacked both discipline and patience, but this period of my life taught me, the hard way. I had the indispensable engineering collaboration of an old childhood neighbourhood friend, Tony Daniels. The album came out first as "a project by the OHC"— the Open House Collective. (I had registered Open House as a business name for my indie record label.)

My career still rolled along with enough gigs as the guy formerly from Triumph — a heritage artist. I had to keep touring; my kids were all still in grade school. My wife was also taking on more responsibility in her job and making more money. But I still needed a manager and a few agents to keep finding classic rock band gigs (thank goodness I still had a decent following for club dates and outdoor summer shows in the U.S.). As I was drifting farther and farther out on my own, away from any traditional form of a career, I started to sell a decent number of CDs via mail order, as well as off the stage, at gigs.

As my experimental, eclectic nature was leading me to write in other styles of music, and work them up in my studio, Tony and I began to hatch a plan. Two other guitar styles I'd always wanted to showcase were archtop and smooth jazz, and blues-rock. So, the idea of a trilogy started to take shape. At first, I'd made a distribution deal with a local Toronto company called Joe Radio (for indies). But once the trilogy was up on the boards and released, I had a real little indie label going — and by 1998, EMI's president in Canada, Deane Cameron, with whom my wife had worked for seventeen years before, offered me a manufacturing and distribution label deal. I had a great working relationship with Jeanine Leech, who put together awesome-looking pro packages for me. Everything was low budget. EMI asked me to repackage the *Invitations* CD and put my face on the cover.

Invitations is one of my deepest personal albums. The tracks of solo fingerstyle guitar pieces stand up over time, especially since instrumentals are not as specific or literal as songs with lyrics. They remain a bit surreal, abstract, impressionistic, so they offer more emotional latitude. "Castle of Regret" was a difficult piece to learn to play. It feels sad and lonely to me: the ruins of a Spanish castle, the ghosts of classical licks I heard in Tarrega and Sor studies in my youth. It's at a high level of intensity, requiring physical, mental, and emotional concentration.

My mom really loved the *Invitations* album and played it a lot. When she passed away, "Secret Wishes" was played at her funeral service. Something emotionally powerful like that obviously changed my interpretive feel for the piece — but any music remains open to the subjective, interpretive nature of the individual, which is one of the reasons that I love it so much. When I first composed the piece, I can recall, vividly, sitting in my studio late one night and performing it for my brother Russ on an archtop, with echoes floating into long reverb. (That effect is an integral part of the music for me: the chords floating and drifting in space.) He was transported, moved, and told me afterwards that it was "perfect." I don't know about that, but I can tell you that of all the concerts I've ever done, nothing will ever top that private performance for one. He and I and the music were all of one in that moment. When people ask, "Do you prefer to play a small club or for a giant crowd?" I always remember that night in the basement studio with my brother, and I'm reminded that it's never about the size of the crowd. The chemistry of the moment is whether the crowd is with you, inside the song — and it can be a crowd of one. (Or one in tens of thousands.)

Nothing will ever have a greater impact on what that song can mean for me.

There's an elemental power, a simple kind of pure emotional expression in the construction. As for actual nuts and bolts, would I have ever composed "Secret Wishes" if I hadn't learned Paul McCartney's "Blackbird" when I was a teenager? No way. We are all products of our influences and shared human history; every time we open our mouths, every time we express ourselves, there are phrases and vocabulary that we learned rote from our parents, evidence revealed about our DNA, what tribe we came from, what neighbourhoods we lived in. Can "Secret

Wishes" also be universal wishes? I believe they can be, yes. One makes music and hopes that it will cross through space and resonate with other hearts and souls, touch them, move them.

In 2017, for my brother Rob's funeral, I put together a playlist for my wife's iPod and included "Souvenirs." I had written it as a tribute to my old mentor and teacher Peter Harris. Now when I hear it, I realize it captured something that was not all inside me. It's as if I channelled something else that belongs to Peter, or to a player like Pat Metheny. It makes me smile, because I surprised myself with that one.

For many years in my life, I'd been afraid to trust my ability to make music with the barest of pretense — with the minimum of bells and whistles. Professionally conditioned by a rock band with a giant light show and a massive PA, wardrobe, special effects, marketing, and promotion — there's all the freight that comes along with that. But the *Invitations* album proved something to me; it was pretty much just solo instrumental classical guitar pieces, period. I realized that the teenaged kid who lugged his acoustic guitar up to the coffee house at the local YMCA to try his hand at a few songs had been on a solid path. Then he got seduced off on another track. But one acoustic guitar in his hands, one song in his heart, that kid had been standing on the middle ground. He just wasn't old enough or experienced enough to know it at the time. He didn't have the context yet of trying out all the different roles behind a showbiz mask.

Swing Shift

I really enjoyed making this record. It's one of my all-time favourites, despite being one of the weaker-selling albums I ever put out. For my indie catalogue though, it earned me the most songwriting and publishing income, because songs like "Santa Fe Horizon," "Three Clouds," and "Key Chain" got airplay, and CBC Radio used "Key Chain" as a theme for a radio show, going in and out of programming breaks. I love writing and playing tunes like "Taste of Steel" and "Mr. Bebop." Those kind of songs ("Woke Up" from *Ipso* is also in this category; "Beacon Street Hotel" from *Good Faith*; "Blue Sky Train" from the *Bonfire Sessions*) make me feel like a complete kind of guitarist and performer.

"Taste of Steel" was my standard opening number for a while, when I first started doing solo shows back in 1999. It's a fun song to play (challenging, too, especially right off the bat) and showcases a different side of my playing and singing. When I'd first played the tune for my manager, Ross, he frowned and asked me what kind of artist I wanted to be, because repertoire in that style was never the kind of material that could make a guy climb to the toppermost of the poppermost. He was right — of course, it's old school, a musicianly kind of tune. My answer to him was to shrug and quote the cartoon character Popeye: "I am what I am, and that's all that I am." That fundamental philosophy governed the rest of my career.

"Key Chain" is a devilishly hard song to play, requiring unrelenting amounts of left-hand endurance. It's very satisfying to arrive at the end of the damn thing. When I need to test whether my chops are in shape, I attempt "Key Chain." "Santa Fe Horizon" is a favourite composition to play: moody and intense, but so pentatonic and linear in nature that it flows, easy-peasy. "Three Clouds" has the big flowing riff; that song took on a whole different vibe when it became a duo thing with Dave Dunlop, but the recording was how it came into the world (with me playing a keyboard part for the riff, all on the white keys). Sometimes song recordings are like baby pictures: the songs grow up and turn into very different adolescents and adults.

Speaking of which, the trilogy is music for grown-ups by a grown-up. There was a maturity in deciding to take on this project. They were boutique packaged, stylistically, but the range of styles was relatively easy to put together for me personally, because there was not a single thought about commercial viability, radio or market potential. This trilogy was just me doing an eclectic, self-indulgent, creative thing. Artistically it turned out to be the right thing to do at the right time. (Bit of a change, for my track record.)

Raw Quartet

The electric rock blues of *Raw Quartet* was a bit different. As we got better at operating the digital gear, we could get more involved with thicker and denser material — more tracks, more level, wider frequency range. We set Randy Cooke's drum kit out in my garage and ran a snake down into the basement. You can hear the roots of 2016's *RES 9* material forming all the way back on '98's *Raw Quartet*. It's maybe not as clean and sophisticated in terms of its recording, but we were doing the best we could with the gear we had. I wasn't rethinking anything, no second-guessing. We took things pretty much live off the floor and lived with the results. My favourite thing about this album is the guest musicians: Pat Kilbride, Peter Cardinali, and the famous Doctor Music, the late and great Doug "Doc" Riley. It was such an honour to have him on this record. I decided to write and sing more songs on this one — *Swing Shift* had three vocals, this one had nine. In a way, I came back around to the rock and roller guy I'd been as a teenager — the guy who went to school on blues and made it work in the various styles of music I ended up in. In hindsight, I could have spent more time and energy getting a wider range of vivid guitar sounds. But it was what it was, and it was a snapshot in time. No matter how much time and energy you put in, an album is only ever a snapshot from that point in time. You can look back and go, "Ohhh, that was a cool little mistake — and that was a great little bit of execution. And that makes me want to gag, and that doesn't even sound like me, so what was I thinking?"

Someday my great-grandchildren might listen to this stuff. Who knows what they might think? But I was determined to be creatively prolific and make recordings as part of my legacy. These three projects stand as the first ones I made without anybody leaning over my shoulder and second-guessing my decisions. The trilogy was my standard, 1996 to 1999. It was what it was — a lot of fun and a huge education.

It never would have happened without the engineering collaboration of a childhood pal from the hood, Tony Micallef Daniels, who enabled my self-indulgence. I love him like a crazy brother from another mother.

The Spirit of Christmas

Sam Reid and I sat on the board of the Songwriters Association of Canada together in the later 1990s, and we hit it off. As the keyboard player in Glass Tiger, with a kind of producer's melodic outlook, Sam has a clear view of how a recording might work (influenced by collaborations within his own band and with co-writer and producer Jim Vallance). A genial, instantly likeable kind of guy, he had his own little indie nature label, Willow Music (which also made Sam very good at sonic texture and atmosphere), and since I now had Open House/Rockit Sounds, we got to talking. (He had a distribution deal with EMI, which paved the way for me to step into my relationship with EMI as well.)

He'd always wanted to have a Christmas record for his catalogue, and I said, Me too. We decided on the spur of the moment (early fall) to put a CD together of all public domain stuff, so we wouldn't have to pay any mechanical royalties. That condition of ancient repertoire made it a bit more of a sombre and spiritual kind of collection, but I liked it. It took me back to my childhood in a way, which is a sweet thing about Christmas. Sam had a tiny studio in a boathouse on a river north of Newmarket, south of Lake Simcoe, so I started driving up there a few days a week for a while. No second-guessing: I'd write a chart arrangement with his consultation, and he'd lay down a map in the computer, and then I'd play some guitar, sing a few takes, and leave him to edit and mix. Boom bang. My thinking was evolving. After the trilogy, it was clear that sales were all front-end loaded, then fell off dramatically. The market was never going to catch on and get behind something. I had a loyal little cult following. The truth of running a small indie label is that it's analogous to a bakery, having to get fresh product onto the shelves every day. So even though the Christmas album came much too late in the game for 1999, at least we got 'er done, and each of us had a catalogue item for the next few years.

Live at Berklee

Live at Berklee is a documentary — the culmination of something Rick Wharton and I had started two years before, with the idea of Network promoters. The Rik Emmett Network began as a loose concept of a fan club, which led to a mailing list, then a website, which led to the initiative of amateur-promoter house concerts across the U.S. and Canada. *L@B* was recorded at the Network show of all Network shows — at Berklee College in Boston, no less, thanks to a partnership between two amateur-promoters,

Dan Bolton and Pete Chestna. I look back now and think about how much pressure I was putting on myself: write a few new things to include on the package, learn to perform them, bring along an electric guitar and use backing tracks, then execute a long show, completely solo. After I did this project, I downsized and simplified my gigs. I started using Marty Anderson on keyboard for a duo approach, which eventually evolved into Dave Dunlop on guitar since Marty's sound and lights business was becoming a priority for him and Dave was available more often.

The tracks on this package codified a few things. "Fandango," for example, was a butt-kicking shuffle (with an accelerando!) that worked as a fitting closer on any gig — workshop, clinic, etc. Big energy ending. Tony D. ran submixes of things like "Last Goodbye," so I could also play those solo, live to track. A brand-new song like "Melancholy Moon" was going to get shorter shrift than it probably deserved, given its absorption into such a large, busy package of stuff (there was *a lot* of storytelling on that album). But a live solo album (with a few new songs) was fresh baked goods, up on the indie webstore shelf.

Berklee happened on January 28 and 29, 2000. This was right around the time my mom's cancer caused complications for her. She had a heart attack that spring, and it became clear that even though the ovarian cancer was not directly killing her, her heart and lungs were not up to the fight. She'd had bronchiectasis since her adolescence, with two lobecto-mies in her lifetime. During the first (I was eight), the operation had failed, her lung collapsed, and she stopped breathing on the table for a bit, so they resuscitated her and sewed her back up without completing the procedure. The second time, I was eighteen, and the removal of the lower two lobes of her right lung was a success. As she aged, she was really functioning on only one lung; even then, it was partial.

Her decline and passing in October weighed heavily on me. In my disc-ography, there's a gap of a couple of years — not a lot of writing, rehearsing, practising. It was a deep loss: my mom had always been very supportive of my artistic side. Larger than our own losses, my dad was alone and didn't handle it well for a long time afterwards. Typical of men from his era, he'd never cooked or done laundry, never really had any hobbies other than reading the paper, making conservative investments, doing his banking and bookkeeping, and watching sports on TV. He had zero interest in music. My brother Russ and I established a support system for him, and Russ was the real champion at it, having Dad come out to his store, help stock shelves, and hang out for lunch. We started searching around for housekeeping, but my dad was resistant. It was an intense time of challenges, given the depth of my own mourning. Public ambition seemed unimportant.

I was also absorbed in my own nuclear family: my kids were seventeen, fourteen, and eleven. I was coaching baseball and two house-league soccer teams. My wife had become our main breadwinner. This was a time of chauffeuring and struggling to remain relevant to my teenaged daughters. They were far more distanced from me than they were from their mom. Looking back, I can see I was responsible for creating a lot of that distance, allowing it to build up. So, not all sunshine and flowers, positivity and inspiration or motivation.

There are realities to showbiz that defy the understanding of those of us who have been in it — never mind folks who are at a distance, as fans of whatever it is of mine that they like. There are realities that I was happy to ignore: the music business, as I had known it, was over. Retail sales bases had disappeared. Record company presidents, sales VPs, radio promo guys (keep going — promoters, rack job retail buyers, etc.) all knew it: jobs were evaporating as the business downsized and brick-and-mortar operations shut down.

I chose to go simple — eyes on the horizon. Things boiled down to two thoughts.

1. No matter how much we discuss the past, it won't change how it got me here. Because here I am.
2. What's the next song trying to tell me it wants to be? Let's go from here.

Handiwork and Good Faith

Handiwork and *Good Faith* were cut at the same time: *Handiwork* became the all-instrumental smooth jazz album — a transition between *Swing*

Shift and the *Troubs* and *Trifecta* projects that were in my future. The guitar pieces, "Two Jigs" and "Knuckleball Sandwich," got a fair bit of live play in my concerts, and "Libre Animado" became another CBC Radio bumper. *Good Faith* was the companion project, as the singer-songwriter collection, with all the vocal tracks from this creative period. My daughter Shannon played flute on the track "Way Back Home" — a milestone in my life. There was also a particularly good day in the Rec Room studio, with Jane Bunnett playing some wonderful soprano saxophone overdubs on "Ask" and "Unconditional Love."

Strung-Out Troubadours

After touring in duo shows for several years and developing a comfortable, brotherly kind of rapport, I formed a partnership record production deal with Dave Dunlop, who used his burgeoning little basement studio (Room 9) and production skills to co-write an album's worth of stuff so that we could have an album to sell at our duo gig shows, splitting the proceeds fifty-fifty. That worked out well. Not a windfall but steady money, building upon the tour business merch on offer.

Even more importantly, the stuff we wrote together gave me an opportunity to pursue material that had always interested me: simpler recordings, folk-roots settings, fingerstyle, acoustic. We proved that a record could be written and recorded, produced and released, without it taking months and months of an involved budget of pre-production, production, and post-production scheduling. One of the things about being prolific, keeping forward momentum and not spending a lot of time in retrospection, is that these old songs come back at me and I think, Wow, did we write that? How did we come up with that stuff?

My brother Russ got so sick with cancer during this period that I was in a bit of a daze. My baseball coaching was over, as my son, Brendan, had moved on to the Ontario Blue Jays organization, then off to the NCAA. Our girls were all grown and gone, university graduates (only Cassandra — Casey — the most unlikely one of the bunch, pursued post-graduate studies). Shannon was already teaching. Jeannette was climbing the corporate ladder in her company. When I listen to "State of Grace," "Faithful Stranger," and "Rainbow World," it's like I hear a version of myself that I hardly recognize: a guy who was finding his way around inside himself, working on instinct. That's something I never really ever got to do as a guy in a rock band with a record contract and audiences who arrived with expectations.

The Troubs first album is far from slick, but it's *real* — me and Dave, stark naked, nerves exposed. It was fun to make because it was so different, for me, in terms of process. "State of Grace" and "Dos Arroyos" give me great satisfaction from a legacy point of view. I developed more insight into work that stood on its own.

Live at Hugh's Room was another installment in trying to keep the internet webstore bakery stocked with fresh goods, even though the material was all older stuff — aside from the inclusion of a cover of Dylan's "All Along the Watchtower." Loyal long-time bassist Steve Skingley engineered the recording, and it started a decade-long tradition of a December gig before Christmas at Hugh's Room. It always felt a little like going home, back to my childhood neighbourhood.

Liberty Manifesto

I met drummer and vocalist Michael Shotton at a Jeans and Classics performance night in London, Ontario, at the Grand Theatre. As a vocalist with a high tenor range, his reputation preceded him. I knew he'd sung on a Boston album and been a member of Von Groove, scoring a big record deal back in the day. He invited me out to his studio, and one thing led to another until eventually we were collaborating on the progressive, heavy, melodic rock project that became *Liberty Manifesto*. This was a return to a style of writing and recording that I'd gravitated away from, but it was a blast working with Mike, who has an infinite amount of creative energy and who knows his way around Pro Tools. He talked me into playing bass on the whole album — another first for me. Life had shifted into a very different place: making a rock album became a welcome change of pace.

The smooth jazz radio format in Canada embraced a few of my solo indie tracks, then gave airplay to the Troubs. From polls that the smooth jazz stations ran online, I was named Guitarist of the Year in 2005, which led to some nice moments reuniting with George Benson backstage, and the thrill of having him present the award. The Troubs won the Duo of the Year award in 2007. It was nice of the radio stations to expand their definition of smooth jazz to include us. By 2009, Dave and I felt we needed to give that format a solid effort in our next studio attempt, thus *Push & Pull* got a bit more R & B and funky.

An insight from this retrospective: the more I shifted toward jazz, the more I felt I was heading toward a higher musical purpose, toward a more sophisticated, mature, grown-up, cool part of my musicianship. But, for sure, the more that shift happened, the more sales shifted away. This reinforces my notion that depth and substance are not very recreational for the average music consumer.

"Deeper Kind of Blue" is another installment in the long goodbye to my brother Russ. The blue sense of then versus now, it's a song of grieving over change and all that's gone forever, the moments that can never come again, gloriously spent and misspent youth, growing older and wiser, and feeling winter blue coming on. No cocky youthful spring in that step. One comes to terms and reckons, attempting to balance the give and take. Forgiveness, reconciliation, reckoning, reassessing — after a while, the high road is simply the only one that makes any sense. And choices made based on ego, pride, or out of self-righteousness — I'd trade every one of them if I could have just one more afternoon laughing and joking with Russ. But I can't. We both knew that winter blue was coming; it comes for us all, one day. My brother asked me to walk a humble road in his honour and make different choices.

I wrote the lyrics (with no music) for "Only Time Will Tell" and offered it to Dave to compose the music and sing. (That was a career first.) We had both ballads in our live touring show for the next two years, and they'd get polite applause — nothing like what came back from a crowd when we scorched through the instrumental "Red Hot."

Production values on this project grew by a quantum leap. Dave grew more confident in his Room 9. We had more trust in each other, in our writing, and in his independence. Jeanine Leech put together a really striking package that suited the content, helping define the pushing and pulling red and blueness of the music. Dave suggested we lift the album title from the first lyric of "Deeper Kind of Blue," which felt right: the push and pull between a creative duo.

Alas it sold less than other stuff. Unbeknownst to us, Canadian smooth jazz radio stations were struggling for listeners. The one in our region changed over to a new country format in 2011. Fickle winds of change had already been blowing, and Dave and I hadn't picked up on it.

Trifecta

P.R.O. — Pavlo, Rik, and Oscar Lopez — were all clients on the roster of Darcy Gregoire at the Agency Group. Somewhere between Darcy, Pavlo, and Oscar, the idea for a modest kind of Canadian guitar super-summit got pitched to me. (I think Pavlo was envisioning something along the lines of McLaughlin, de Lucía, and Di Meola.) In the summer of 2008, we got together to see if the concept could work. The idea was to write together, make an album, and go out on tour. I asked Michael Shotton to engineer and help produce the P.R.O. trio project. It was an exciting adventure, like an experimental train ride that might come off the tracks at any moment.

Pav is a self-made entrepreneur, and his Greek culture is his musical calling card; his guitar playing is very similar to bouzouki stylings. Oscar is originally from Chile and has a strong background in Latin and world folk music. They don't have much blues in their musical vocabularies, and their feel doesn't swing — but they both loved to step on the gas and go with their passions.

The street date for the *Trifecta* album was October 27, 2009. The project was a bit terrifying and thrilling. The 2010 winter travel was exhausting, at fifty-six years of age. But I trained to get myself in better shape before it happened, and I didn't have to sing every song, night after night after night, because it was mostly instrumental. Plus, aligning with Oscar's performance style, the trio played seated. The tour was also all-Canadian dates in soft-seat theatres, so it was very civilized with no border-crossings in the itinerary, no customs and immigration. That was lovely.

The P.R.O. Trio Launch:
From My Journal, January 2010

Quite a week out in Calgary, working out of the elegant Fairmont Palliser Hotel. With an extra suite that we used for rehearsals, there were seventeen interviews over three days; we also squeezed in five rehearsals. There were business dinners with prospective promoters on two nights. The highlights: eight a.m. *Breakfast Television* live performance of two songs on Wednesday January 13; "Fiesta" and "Redbird," peppy and lively for early morning. I was a bit shell-shocked, but office workers from the building provided a spontaneous, curious crowd. It felt pretty good as it went down. Thursday January 14, I cabbed over solo to Q107 for a half hour on air with Patti MacNeil and Terry DiMonte. It was great — Triumph talk, then they played a bit of "Fiesta" on air and raved. Terry's career goes back to FM stations in Winnipeg, then CHOM-FM in Montreal. His fave cut from the old days was "Young Enough to Cry" from *Just a Game*, which I hadn't heard in years. Like old-time radio — a jock played an album cut from a vinyl record, live on air! I asked them to turn the solo up in the control room. Back on air, I admitted it was the only session I'd ever done where I got high. The story: my old friend and bodyguard Big Nick Misetic had come by the studio to take promo photos of me with the gear and guitars that I was using on the album. By three a.m., I decided to have a puff or two, then went for that solo, before we called it a night. There's a lot of Page and Beck in there — nothing wrong with having some influences.

Rehearsing with Pav and Oscar was very different than anything I'd experienced. No doubt they saw me as type A, bossy, uptight, white-bread — but we have very different approaches to music-making. It was enlightening and energizing for me, for sure. They didn't write things down, working pretty much from memory, then motor memory, no music notation or charts, very little theory to inform the parts they played; they simply memorize them. It makes the process a longer one, somewhat like the oral tradition of a Romani ensemble. I think Oscar would have been happier if we did the whole thing by the seat of our pants. I tend to be, um, a bit more anal than that. So, we were teaching each other. It was great, but they could never convert me into the kind of wine lover that they both are.

They lived life a bit bigger than I do, but I think they appreciated the fact that they could count on me to give their angel wings an airport hangar when needed. It was quite a brotherhood with a dynamic energy. The live set for the tour shaped up; beyond the entire album itself, which would only give us about forty-five minutes or so of material, unstretched, the common ground we found for cover songs was "Let the Good Times Roll" (a feel-good twelve-bar right out of B.B. King's repertoire), tagging on to the end of "Jumpin' Django"; a Beatles medley with "Blackbird" (my feature), "Norwegian Wood" (Pav sang and played his sitar), and then Oscar's comic turn, singing "With a Little Help from My Friends" with the intro and a few of the call and response lines in Spanish. It was cheeky but curiously, organically, totally appropriate. The encore began with some passionate improvising on the old "Malagueña" themes, then morphed over into a heartfelt version of "While My Guitar Gently Weeps" to end the night.

I really enjoyed my role as the primary rhythm section (bass and drums, on guitar!), holding it down in the trio. Working with great sidemen had really improved that facet of my musicianship. Plus, of the three P.R.O. dudes, I was the one who knew progressions and voicings. The other guys were much more melody players (which suited their playing-by-ear nature). I felt like the Guitar George character in Mark Knopfler's "Sultans of Swing": "Check out Guitar George / he knows all the chords / he don't wanna make it cry or sing."

After shows, we headed almost directly to the lobby meet-and-greet lineup (Pavlo's philosophy).

I felt very comfortable performing on the tour, and the similarities and contrasts between the startup of this trio versus the one that started up in '75 was fascinating for me. In many ways, Pavlo was a Gil Moore figure: he kept the books, liked to be the designated driver, and his family provided the background support (his wife was the publicist, while his dad kept the CD inventory stored in his garage.)

The travelling was brutal. We started with nine shows in ten days, not exactly a piece of cake. But I didn't have to do much singing — one vocal in the first set, with backgrounds on two more, then only three lead vocals the rest of the way. And in our version of "Lay It," I modified the chorus and lowered the melody, which made that song a whole lot easier to handle night after night. So small adjustments kept happening to enable the workload.

I was reminded (yet again) of how tiring and grinding travelling is: packing and unpacking the car, humping the luggage and gear (guitars cannot be left in subzero conditions overnight), checking in and out of hotels, et cetera. Overall crowd reactions were warm and embracing; they loved the scope of the music and the antics of Oscar. The guitar playing was packaged within accessible songs. It's nice to be in an act where some of the strongest moments are also the quietest ones: those pin-drop moments are cool, especially for a guy who had made his reputation being in a rock band with explosions and fireworks. Acoustic circumstances are very intimate, which suits me down to the ground.

Tour-wise — no road manager, no advance man, no roadies, no sidemen: it was a lean, mean streamlined machine. I ended up stage managing and often was the guy literally rolling cables and packing stuff away at the end of the night, after the lobby meet-and-greet. But Pavlo was the workhorse: he did advancing, merch, and house setup and settlement. He'd be up before the sun and over to an ATM to do the banking. He drove everywhere and entered everything into his GPS, kept the books and bank accounts, booked flights and hotels, and his wife, Sandra, did an outstanding publicity job. Overall I really enjoyed the fact that I didn't have to shoulder the burden of leadership yet enjoyed all the benefits of being a full partner in a small business model.

It was almost like going back to my roots and being a jobbing player, while at the same time enjoying the prestige of being a bona fide headliner with Hall-of-Fame credentials for the skeptical. I enjoyed the ritual of getting dressed up in a nice shirt and eel-skin boots every night, slipping my pocket watch into my vest, and indulging in the simplicity of playing the whole night on one guitar (my Godin A6) without having to worry about backline amps and guitar changes. Canada is a beautiful country, despite the harshness of a cold February on the Prairies. We lucked out with weather with only one snowstorm to drive in, from St. Hyacinthe to Montreal. Otherwise it was clear, clean, smooth sailing, a real treat, to get to see the country from the shotgun bird-dog seat, touring at my age and stage. It was a full immersion experience of novelty value in the soft-seater subscription series world — fascinating. I looked forward to gigs with nowhere near the pressure of being the front man and leader of my own shows. That was very enjoyable: like playing second base, instead of the starting pitcher and player-manager.

The *Trifecta* project got a 2010 Juno nomination for Instrumental Album of the Year. I was pretty sure we wouldn't prevail against other artists in the category, who had political currency, being on the Arts & Crafts label. My pre-existing Illinois gig (for the Rik Emmett acoustic trio) prevented my attendance at the Juno festivities out in St. John's, Newfoundland. I recalled the disappointment back in the early to mid-'80s, year in and out, when Triumph nominations never led to a win. So I was not surprised when the *Trifecta* album did not win the Juno membership vote.

It's hard to capture the lightning of novelty in a bottle a second time: the payoff for that project had been the Canadian tour we finished in March 2010. Our agent could never book on that scale again, and there wasn't a viable plan for foreign territories (the U.S., the U.K., Europe, Australia, Asia). To go after those markets, we'd have to enter regional showcase lotteries, investing time and energy and hard-earned dollars to try to get the act noticed by the bookers of the soft-seater circuits in those territories. (For entry-level guarantees? Not my cuppa.) So I returned to my portfolio of optional activities: the Troubs duo with Dave Dunlop, part-time teaching at the college, and the occasional heritage band gig popping up because I was the guy from Triumph. By the spring of 2010, I simply wanted to relax a bit, take stock of my life, and let the river flow by for a while, contemplating options before I dove back in.

reCOVERy Room 9

Dave and I put together this CD of nine cover songs in order to have something new for our touring merch table, and to give ourselves some fresh material for our live set. Recording covers also saves the time and energy it takes to write originals, so production turns around faster. We made a few wild choices for this playlist, but some of the arrangements hold up well. Don Henley's "Boys of Summer" and Stevie Wonder's "Superstitious" both made the set list of almost every gig for a year or so.

Then Again . . .

Since *reCOVERy Room 9* had worked so well, we decided to go for the most obvious cover songs album of them all: the evergreen Triumph songs and guitar pieces that we were playing almost every night on stage, anyways. Cheating a tiny bit, we got Don Breithaupt to play some keys on a few tunes, but otherwise it was two guitars, my voice, and Dave singing harmonies. Unsurprisingly this was the bestselling indie album we ever made. The magic power of the music is a gift that keeps on giving.

Marco's Secret Songbook

This stands as a strange folly: I'd entertained the notion of a large-scale concept piece for years. After meeting Steve Howe of Yes purely by chance in a hotel restaurant in Seattle, I gave him a few of my CDs, and we exchanged contact info. Shortly thereafter, I was singing a role in a Robert Asselstine musical about Frankenstein in a showcase at Hamilton Place, where I essentially did my bit at the start of the production, sat backstage in my dressing room for seventy-five or eighty minutes, waiting to sing a little again right near the end, and then joined the lineup for the bows. As I sat backstage, I got a bit of a brainstorm (being in a musical fed the inspiration), began making notes, fleshing out a concept that I'd been contemplating for a while for a guitar duo. Meeting Howe, the role model of mine from the most conceptually progressive band on the planet, sparked what I thought was a fantastic book concept.

Here's the elevator pitch: two guitarist brothers rebel and leave their traditional musical family business, going off on their own separate world adventures, creating original compositions during their travels, then sharing them with each other, like musical postcards, until they finally reunite back at the family home. I emailed Steve and pitched it: he responded that he thought I'd gone off the deep end (said the co-writer of "Tales from Topographic Oceans"). *Right.* I apologized, tucked in my tail, and never bothered him again.

But the idea stuck with me. The adventuring duo became a singular explorer, named Marco (as in Polo). My old friend Tony Daniels (the voice of CBC television) became the voiceover narrator; another old associate and sideman Richard Evans provided incidental background underscoring, and I completed the only total concept album of my recording history, with engineering co-producer Michael Shotton taking the tracks into places I hadn't originally envisioned (as I wanted to keep it very sparse and acoustic, but Mike insisted on fleshing out arrangements and orchestration). In the end, it never registered a blip on anyone's radar. Maybe because other things (like the *Then Again* remake of Triumph songs) came along and overshadowed it.

RES 9

What led me toward making a rock album project in 2016? Quite simply, Mascot Records offered me a deal. My touring rock quartet had enjoyed being on a "Legends" classic rock cruise ship package two years running, so that undoubtedly played into my open-mindedness toward the offer. Ed van Zijl, the owner of Mascot Label Group, offered a solid budget to make a rock record that I could produce with 100 percent autonomy. So, I took my touring band into Metalworks, had Dave Dunlop and Steve Skingley help co-produce, with Matt DeMatteo in as an engineering co-producer, and we fashioned eleven songs into an album that tied up a lot of loose ends for me.

Having drummer Paul DeLong in my touring band for three or four years provided inspiration to give the ensemble a chance to build some new repertoire, instead of only playing old Triumph material. Dave and Steve had been growing their engineering and production chops, so I hired them to fulfill those roles on my new tunes.

I don't just write rock songs. I write jazz tunes, ballads, folk songs, waltzes. A question of stylistic production execution can give a (good) song any kind of stylistic twist that an active imagination might conjure. A rock ballpark was something that Mascot wanted, so I edited my song selection from my notebooks down to stuff that could work for that. Since '94, I'd made fifteen albums —fourteen of which were not rock. (The Airtime project, *Liberty Manifesto*, was the only conscientious attempt to get heavy.) Maybe it was a question of the pendulum swinging back in the direction it came from. I looked forward to revisiting something and giving it a fresh twist.

So, I surrendered my independence, signing a worldwide record deal with a label that had its own distribution: the masters, publishing, and (product-related) merchandising rights belonged 100 percent to a label again. I liked that the deal simplified life. I didn't have to try to play record company, distributor, and marketing and promo chief. I could get a paycheque for simply writing, recording, and producing. Mostly I did it because a label was demonstrating good faith: "We believe in you. Here's a budget. Make a rock record. Write, sing, and play." I thought, If I never see a royalty, will that be so bad? Most of the churn and grind is in selling it. If there's nothing at the back end of the deal, I'll catch a buzz from the front-end process.

The band for the Mascot/Provogue release was dubbed RESolution 9. R-E-S: Rik Emmett Solution. Nine? A cat gets nine lives, and in this case, a sixty-two-year-old man was making a rock comeback in his ninth inning. In Chinese culture, nine is considered a good number because it sounds the same as the word *long-lasting* (old rock star makes a comeback rock album). Nine is also strongly associated with the dragon, a symbol of magic and power (Rik Emmett: magic and power). My right-hand man Dave Dunlop also has a fixation with the number, as it's the name of his studio space (Room 9), the number on his men's league hockey sweater, and he played in a band called Full Nine, which was a cool name.

People saw it as classic, retro rock, and I didn't mind; I embraced it. The Triumph guys played on the final track, "Grand Parade." Alex Lifeson of Rush guested on two tracks, and James LaBrie of Dream Theater sang on two cuts. It was a project that satisfied any lingering doubts about who and what I was and defined who I had become.

And so we'll sing a song that laughs at fate / in a style
   that suits our kind
Put doubts aside, and hit our stride / marchin' unafraid /
   in this grand parade / of time.
. . . and so let's raise a glass to by-gone days / to the ghosts
   of auld lang syne
To fires that raged, and prices paid / in a game well-
   played / in the grand parade / of time.
Here's to the life we made / in this grand parade / of time.

Folk Songs for the Farewell Bonfire

I retired from the road, but I didn't retire from writing and creating music. After a few years, I'd stockpiled a bunch of songs and guitar pieces, and I decided to get Steve Skingley to come over to my new home studio and help me record a batch of the stuff in the same way that John Hammond had captured Bob Dylan on an album back in the early '60s — just guitar and vocal. That had been enough to stoke the fire within this eleven-year-old. Fifty years later, I put a batch of my own new songs (and six guitar pieces) down for posterity. I'm not sure if it was, or will continue to be, a farewell, but my horizons were shifting: I was interested in writing poetry for publication. I started thinking about a memoir. Then COVID came along and changed everybody's perspectives on a lot of things.

SONGWRITING

*It's not like you see songs approaching and invite them in.
It's not that easy. . . . You have to know and understand
something and then go past the vernacular.*

— BOB DYLAN, *Chronicles: Volume One*

I've done a fair bit of teaching about songwriting: read textbooks, done seminars, workshops, structured college course curriculum, and been in classrooms, trying to help songwriters develop. In any good writing, it's likely that something personal has been put at risk, made available to the listener. That subjectivity often leaves a writer vulnerable.

On Criticism, Critique, and Teaching Discriminating Taste

Criticism hurts more than it helps. Critique is different. If developing songwriters are made to feel that critique is constructive, their own subjectivity and discriminating taste is respected. I tried to be sensitive and diplomatic toward developing artists. Nurturing the development of their own opinions can help them realize and shape their own self-critique, so they don't swallow anyone else's whole.

Much of the time, I enjoyed teaching. (Marking and grading was a grinder.) When my passion showed, I hoped it demonstrated that song-writing's about exploiting emotion, intellect, and heart in combination. They didn't need to emulate my passion, only generate and manifest their own. I tried for simplicity — not a dictator, a facilitator. Like coaching, I made information available, looking to inspire, motivate. I preferred the term *resource leader* to that of *teacher*, because right and wrong become subjective ways for people to arrive at fulfilling work. I made suggestions, proposed shortcuts, offered the benefit of my experience — but always recommended seeking out other opinions and the benefit of other experiences, because everyone's perspective, everyone's career story in the music business, is unique.

The process is all about building up experience. Ideally we develop our own ability to critique ourselves. A resource leader might provide a bit of electricity, then encourage students to turn on the little lightbulbs above their noggins all by themselves. Some beautiful music can be made in the warmth of that light.

The Teaching and Learning of Music

Passion may not be something you can teach, but it can be demon-strated and made available. Peter Harris (my college guitar teacher and a mentor) once told me that you can't teach anything to someone if they aren't ready. But if someone is ready, you can spark a spiritual fire. And if aspiring musicians are to discover their passions, I think a crucial aspect of music is play. It's not just about studying and reading music and practising techniques. It must have some simple joy in it; a sense of accomplishment follows. You need to have fun. Every time you pick it up, some aspect of the session needs to be play. Creativity is also a big part of it as praise for creative acts gives a sense of identity. As soon as the metaphorical and allegorical wonder of music starts to dawn, passion can catch fire. Music doesn't even have to resemble anything conventional, as long as it's received with love, respect, admiration. When teachers demonstrate how and why music moves them, windows open for student artists to see their own motivation for creation: to move others, to share with them and enhance their lives, offering them joy.

Children learn how to love by being around people who are loving, how to be creative and passionate by being around people who aren't afraid to show and share their emotional spirit about art. The first step toward performance education might be awkward; it could be scary, and it's possible that it will not go well because of nerves. Encouragement is required: unconditional love — arms that will catch a stumble or fall, faces that will smile and reassure. The biggest thing is praise. Every performer needs fans, a sympathetic, willing audience. If self-expression is respected and praised, passion can blossom.

Songwriting Process

Most of my songs come from sitting with a guitar, pencil, and notebook and a small recording device handy. Occasionally jamming away on a guitar, I might come up with a riff I like and hit the record button on my iPhone (used to be my wee old-fashioned cassette recorder) and capture a seed that way. But odds are I'm singing and humming and putting a bit of melody on top of some harmonic content. For me, writing a song is rarely a linear process. Things come in chunks, then get moved around, like jigsaw puzzle pieces. It's not so much writing as it is rewriting. But at critical points in the process, writers must get themselves and their own egos out of the way of the song and start listening to what the song is trying to tell them it needs. The song dictates where it will go, what gets written into it. A writer is kind of like a radar dish, a conduit for the song. Some attribute this to a kind of spiritual or even religious experience. To me, it's more human and instinctive than that: a question of placing a much higher value on the work than your own self-aggrandizement. Certainly creativity has ego in it, but there comes a critical point in writing when the song takes over, and the writer exercises humility in the process.

Sometimes a song is in a hurry, coming through you in a rush; writers might say it's as if they channelled something that came from the universe and only used them to become worldly, describing it as an out-of-body experience. That's a rare occurrence for me, and the rush jobs aren't all that great. In my experience, quick works are below average (which is to say, hard to interpret the emotional meaning or to understand the form). It's more common that instinctive hurried songs are self-delusional, self-serving, or banal and cliché. Much more commonly, a writer's patience allows the work to arrive in its own good time. An acorn has an oak tree waiting inside it, but it takes a long haul of favourable conditions to allow the seed to germinate and sprout a few tender roots. It needs moisture, sunlight, and time. Usually a piece of work requires listening, scanning for the clues it offers as it morphs along in its process, trying to make itself evident, striving toward the universal, cutting through the noise.

Throughout this process, form and architecture are the creator's best friends. They give the work strength, flexibility, shape, and identity. Sometimes an idea arrives, and the creator has the (instant) instinct for a magnificent, fully grown realization but no real methodology or understanding of how to get from alpha to omega. Those points in between might require experimentation, research, exploration, a weighing of options. Because a song's ultimate characteristic is its integrity, the creative writer is consulting with the song itself for potential revisions (e.g., the tailoring of melody, harmony, or lyric for arrangement or production). Even if the song is at first secretive, songwriting requires faith that eventually the process will give it up. When it does, it seems obvious, as if there had never been any other choice possible. When the integrity of the work is talking to you, that's a very rewarding process.

Sometimes I have a tune in mind when I'm writing bits of lyrics, but more often, chunks of lyrics happen with only the rhythm and phrasing strongly suggested. Melody grows from the shape of the language of the line, and where the hard consonants and long vowels fall — again, phrasing.

All of the songs from *The Bonfire Sessions* were written lyrics first; the music came afterwards. On jazzier tunes, the style dictates that progress happens more organically; chords and melodies (and even some lyrics) are all part of an original creative stew. Usually I develop only a verse-chorus form, and when I'm somewhat satisfied with that, I'll start to flesh out the rest of the lyrics and the concept or story for the song. Often I'll then revisit the original verse and change it, if necessary, to suit the things that have happened during development.

As a song lyric forms in my head, I also usually have the groove and feel going, knowing how the phrasing will work before I pick up a guitar and start working out melodies and chord changes. They were likely floating back in the foggier regions of my brain, anyway.

Surviving Quality Assessment Review

Many beginnings of creative ideas turn stale as better ones come along, so weaker song ideas get left behind. Sometimes unworthiness becomes apparent when an idea gets revisited with a fresh, open mind. Sometimes I know a work is finished because it seems like anything I might do will only make it different but not necessarily better. Then it's either bound for sharing with the world or for the trash can. Other times, on a deadline or running out of budget, I might say to myself, It's only a Polaroid of where I am at this point in my life. It's not definitive by any means. I'll always have a chance to do something better tomorrow. Mollified by these rationalizations, I'd shrug and put it out.

Sometimes it's as good as it's ever going to get in my hands, and I know it. When I recorded guitar pieces like "Knuckleball Sandwich" or "Two Jigs," I played, edited, listened, and tried them again a week later and realized it will just have to do, for now. It won't achieve another level of development until I woodshed for a few months, or play the piece every day for a year. Inevitably pieces evolve from performance over time. But (as visited in many of my song lyrics) I continue to have a running battle with time in this life. I was never going to be the kind of artist who only puts out a record every decade. My ambition would love to put out new stuff every month — if only I could figure out how to maintain certain standards of quality, because I never had unlimited resources. Or budgets.

I hoped I could reduce my fear of releasing recordings for public consumption, that I could become more experimental and less self-conscious about process; become more prolific, more productive. Even if the recordings varied drastically in terms of audio quality or in terms of the execution of the performance, the flow was bound to be more liquid in a modern digital age.

Part of this was because of the integration and communication with fans and patrons; part was because I was influenced by young artists in an MP3 and filesharing, downloading age. You either get with the program or risk becoming a mastodon in a tar pit of your own past.

Process — Flow

At any given point in time, I might have the germs (seeds — however you might think of a nascent song or poem concept) of fifteen or twenty things in my notebooks, plus maybe another five or six that are already turning into full-blown ditties sprouting their arms and legs.

Some songs or poems never get fully written; some are still pretty good ideas (maybe) and might get fleshed out down the road for some other project. A lyric from one thing can morph into something else cooking up. Once the water's on the boil, any ingredients within grasp could be fair game.

Once I started to feel a collection of songs taking shape, with the pressure of having to get a new CD out, I'd focus in on the ten tracks that would give the package a rounded vibe, and I finished them. If there was any creative spillover, it would almost certainly take shape on a later collection.

In writing sessions, it usually takes me a few hours to get up to speed. It's still hit or miss, but at least I'm in the creative mode and can fish around with a liquid kind of flow. That's why I prefer a quiet, safe environment with no distractions and plenty of resource materials. After three or four hours, there's a law of diminishing returns. Might be wise to take a break.

I consider flow to be the most important part of creativity. When I improvise a solo, I don't want to be too conscientious about anything; I want to find out what the current offers and assess whether it's any good or not. During writing, there are eddies and dead ends. Then I try to switch streams and move to something else. I'll revisit the problem spot later, when my head is in a different space. It's a kind of single-minded focus: being in the daydream intensely, unconcerned about the surrounding day. Those moments of fantastic connectivity can be wonderful, when one good idea dovetails with another, then another, and you're on a roll. Not a wild one — the process is still somewhat careful, controlled, considered. For me, flow moments are rare and usually take a while to surface. Sometimes they turn out to be desert mirages: momentarily amazing but later, in a cooler state of mind, self-induced hallucinations that prove to have less value than originally imagined. So it's back to the drawing board. Rewardingly, sometimes the work stands up.

Lyrics vs. Poetry

Stephen Sondheim says a song lyric needs music and melody to become truly fulfilled: words that stand up on the page by themselves approach poetry. Poetry completes itself through words and language, whereas lyric is about rhythm, form, flow, and often brevity and repetition. In his book *Finishing the Hat*, Sondheim reveals the few principles he tries to adhere to (with varying degrees of success): content dictates form; less is more; God is in the details — all in the service of clarity. Some poetry has this in common with songwriting, but not all.

Good lyric writing often boils down to very specific criteria. Striving for memorability, lyrics often repeat phrases and forms, return to hooks, choruses, or refrains. Lyrics might seem a bit simple or corny, but the music rescues them from how they read on the page. Lyrics need to work with their song's phrasing and the energy of the harmonic and melodic constructions. Poems (sometimes) leave phrasing up to the reader and can certainly play with it, leaving more doubt and shadow in a reader's mind about the writer's intent. Poems can often be intentionally elliptical; songs are making more of an effort to be accessible.

Songwriting tries to make an impact on first listen — to be catchy, to say something powerfully, to tie into human emotion immediately. A song shouldn't require lengthy explanation or a listener to be following a lyric sheet in order to parse puns and wordplay. A question for song-writers to ask themselves is "Am I trying to make it hard on a listener or easy?" Radiohead quite intentionally makes their choices of integrity and accessibility, as does Disney for songs in films for general audiences. There is a wide range of different song integrities.

Song lyrics often boil down to simple kinds of morals or maxims; they're not usually trying to be philosophical analysis for a doctoral thesis. Often they're trying to reach a tribe of folks right where they live and reinforce something that's a truism in their lives. A poem can be ambitious and try to do several things all at once, whereas a good song is almost always trying to stick to one idea, one script.

Nuts and Bolts: The Craft of Art

Here's a big thing with song lyrics. Where do short notes go? How about long ones? Consonants and short vowels help tighten and shorten; open vowels allow a singer to hold longer open notes, slow a song down a bit, shine a spotlight on the fancy-pants singer. Acceleration and deceleration of form keeps reoccurring in song development. It's one of the big things that separates seasoned writers from those starting out.

A secret of songwriting (which is not a secret) is prosody: the marriage of rhythm to melody to harmony to mood to the phrasing and the choice of words. For me, sometimes, a moment in a song can change due to a well-placed consonant, or the right vowel extending just a tiny bit at the right time. (There are an infinite number of ways that song moments can change but usually only a very few choices that suit.) Choices depend on what the song has been building toward. (Let's call this development.) A critical aspect of songwriting is how songs breathe, and I'm not talking about tempo; I'm talking about form, architecture. Songs accelerate and decelerate in order to score emotional points with listeners.

Instinct can offer lots of good stuff, but experience teaches you that good commercial songs use crafty technique to get at the emotion and energy. Song lyrics and melodies speed up and slow down in order to give a song power points, highlights.

Songwriting usually isn't like *Star Trek*, where you boldly go where no one's gone before. There have been many generations of fantastic songwriters that you can learn from. It's a tradition that goes back to troubadours and minstrels. Knowledge of their work and process can help you determine your own personal voice — not lead you astray, confuse you, or make you unoriginal. You gain knowledge and learn techniques, then customize to suit your purpose.

Once a song is out there, it's open to interpretation. Still your copyright, it's no longer strictly your property, because it requires people to listen to it. And since songs traffic in emotion, people's emotions will inevitably bend the song to their will. Isn't a certain generosity of spirit one of the things that leads to writing songs in the first place?

Some song lyrics are intentionally written with ambiguity, even without a conscious, specific point. Others get written about something and over time take on meanings originally unintended. Muddy original intentions disappointed me as a writer because I felt I'd done a poor job of expressing the song's meaning. But maybe not if the emotional value of the song worked. But that's also just me. Some interpretations are surprisingly valid, and I learned to live with that. The song continues to say what it says and be what it is, even as it redefines itself over time. Sometimes a song reveals itself in layers; sometimes it remains opaque, open to different interpretations. Sometimes its mystery is its appeal. Songwriting can be many things to many people. Its range is one of the delightful things that makes me love it so much.

As writers continue to grow and gain experience, they build their allegiances to form. The discipline of rhythm and rhyme must prevail for lyricists because they marry their work to music: the groove, the beat, the instant flow that lyrics must provide. Sondheim teaches in *Finishing the Hat* that lyrics are meant to be sung, not read: "Poetry is an art of concision, lyrics of expansion . . . Music straitjackets a poem and prevents it from breathing on its own, whereas it liberates a lyric. Poetry doesn't need music; lyrics do."

Liberation — you need to write to a melody that you hear someone singing. Some syllables are long, some are short; some lines are spit out in anger, others cried out with tears falling. The drama of your lyrics comes alive when married to the rhythms and flow of music. You don't have to write it down and work it out with every word, phrase, or line you write; you can leave something to the listener's imagination, confident that the music gives that emotion the wings to fly into your listener's head and heart. Sondheim is saying that the sum of lyrics plus music can be greater than the parts. That's the kind of math I understand.

I've never been that keen on collaboration with more than two people, to be honest. I believe that art isn't democratic, and its craft even less so. While I made a career habit of jumping borders and boundaries and lines drawn in the sand — and often made jokes about the discriminating taste of jazz, classical, and folkie fanatics treading dangerously close to totalitarianism — the truth of an artistic, creative matter really does require committed passion about a single viewpoint. Too many cooks thin out the subjective art and craft. (That's just me. I note that many modern award-winning songwriting teams have anywhere from five to ten writers and producers; it's digital age collaboration.)

In songwriting workshops, I'd often come upon things in a song — a line or two of lyrics, say — and I would ask the student to unpack what the writing was trying to achieve. In therapy something seemingly insignificant can get unpacked, and a whole mess of stuff can get revealed. That level of investment — of packing — is a *big deal.* The dynamic of packing is what writers do. Unpacking is how the depth of creativity is revealed, as a storytelling, emotional, intellectual consistency exists throughout. There's an integrity to the (writer's) pack and the (listener's) unpack.

A song is given depth when the songwriter shines a spotlight on an iceberg tip, so that the listener can't really miss the significance: They recognize it and thus become aware of a massive iceberg below the surface. The writer doesn't announce and describe the iceberg in detail; that would get boring, and there's not enough time for that in a song. Better that the writer's implication leads the listener toward sensing it, feeling it, discovering it, and interpreting it.

I've alluded elsewhere to the influence of Aaron Copland's idea of the long line, a golden thread that runs through a work, making it consistent to its own sense. The creative, artistic mind works along that line. Weak ideas won't stand up to unpacking. You can unpack an onion and go through a lot of layers, but you end up with nothing but a lot of tears (and a mess on the floor). It's super difficult to unpack a diamond, because it's the hardest and most perfect, valuable thing to us carbon-based life forms — the most densely packed carbon we've got. It's the very heart of something great. People move mountains of rock and slag in order to get at it. (That's a lot of unpacking.) And then even when we have unearthed the diamond — beautiful, perfect — we still get the jeweller to cut it, shape it, fashion it so that it reveals its lustre and sparkle. It gets repacked, placed into a setting just so — to show it off and give it razzle dazzle. I'm always fascinated by creating, chasing long lines of thought — packing and unpacking.

———————

Some people say you can't teach songwriting — one either has the instinct and talent, or they don't. But there certainly is technique in it: form, structure, conventions. You wouldn't put much stock in a surgeon who said, "Oh, I'm self-taught, and I only go on my own instinct and intuition." Nope, I prefer the ones who studied from the fundamentals on up to the latest state-of-the-art advances in the shared pedagogy (the craft). I'm not discounting or dismissing instinct and intuition. I just prefer the catalogue of a writer who also studies the art and craft of form and who takes cues from the precedence of time-honoured standard repertoire.

Our lowly little acorn, lying on the ground, carries the dream — the potential — of a giant oak tree. It will require a long process of favourable growing conditions. How impatient are you? How focused can you remain on the potential dream? My work as a songwriting teacher was to try to direct students to become better listeners to what their songs were trying to tell them they needed, what they wanted to become. Like a song whisperer, a song detective, a sculptor who walks around the chunk of rock and keeps thinking in three dimensions and considers all perspectives. What's the rock telling you?

Is there some magic hoodoo in this? Yes. Are some people mystically gifted, more than others? Yes. But can you learn how to be a better detective if someone gives you an understanding of how to develop procedure at the crime scene, insight based on experience? Of course you can.

In Robert Hilburn's book on Paul Simon, Simon's creative approach is revealed as almost always based on his instinctive, inspirational evolutionary nudges. He preferred to start with music and develop the rhythmic foundation, using that to discover what words, phrases, and ideas might work. Then he'd wait for a story of lyric to develop, which is why sometimes his lyrics seem so abstruse and personal that they are almost poetic in nature, not very literal at all. But he did have a central inspirational concept at work all the time. He was observing an integrity in his approach that made his ideas gel.

There are all kinds of ways to write songs. You could start with a title; you could start with a lyric; you could start with a melody; you could start with a riff. But the next step is always going to be what you have that suggests a logical, satisfying, inspired way to go next. A common mistake of amateur writers is that they think they need another great idea, then another, and another, until their song is crammed full of ideas that don't rely upon one another. They don't exercise enough critical judgment to ensure that the original idea's integrity is being preserved, honouring the heart and soul of their first puzzle pieces — enhancing the integrity of their originality. It's why songs build to hooks that pay off, why good songs deliver strong energy and tell a good story that hangs together. This is song development. All good songs develop.

Hank Williams didn't (necessarily) do it the way Johnny Mercer did. Lennon and McCartney had different stylistic strengths than Bob Dylan. In class, I would use John Mayer, Bruno Mars, Taylor Swift, and Ed Sheeran for modern examples but also insist on the students considering Woody Guthrie, Bob Crewe, John Dowland. There are always things one can learn by opening pathways in the brain.

On my course outline, there were around twenty-five topics of song technique that I would deliver in eleven or twelve classes. These building blocks allowed students to work on developing their song-detective-whispering skills. Creativity is subjective, and everyone has their own pace, their own sense of this. Still there's a logic to the jigsaw puzzle process; pieces must fit together.

I can't stress the importance of rhythm enough. Rhythm is the machine *and* the ghost in the machine. It reigns supreme in all the component areas of songwriting: harmony, melody, and lyric are all governed by the rhythms of the idea. If you're stuck, my first guess is that consideration of rhythm — pace, groove, syncopation, feel — will help you find your next possible logical answer.

I always recommend to those who want to get serious about songwriting to check out Jack Perricone's *Melody in Songwriting* and Sheila Davis's *The Craft of Lyric Writing* as your fundamental texts in the field. Those books provided a lot of the basics that I used to build my own course outline.

I struggled to find words to describe to songwriting students what's happening in process when the sum ends up greater than the parts. A common poetic and lyric writing term is *prosody*, and by strict dictionary definition, it's perhaps not accurate but I used the word *prosody* for creative alchemy. The conceptual term might be *emergence*: when the combined power of things is greater than their individual component parts.

Songwriters' creations are like their beloved children — even the flawed can be loved for their own special quirks and unique features. My SOCAN catalogue currently has over five hundred titles in it. This year, I'll likely add another dozen or so. I'm proud of that catalogue: it's the undeniable evidence of my eclectic ambition in the range of styles it contains.

Once a song is up and taking baby steps, it has a character and a personality that needs to be considered. It's a mistake to make decisions based on the ego of the writer colouring the decision. (Perhaps untrue for performance considerations, but this relates simply to ushering compositions into the world.) I'm not suggesting that ego doesn't insinuate itself into the process, but, as much as possible, a writer should try to focus on the work at hand and let what's best for the song guide their creative choices. It's a little like being a parent: there's no perfection in the process, but the idea is to try to do what's best for the child and keep the child's best interests at heart.

Compromise and Collaboration

Compromise has big implications, because it is both internal and external, see-sawing and balancing itself in one of the fundamentals of life — give and take. How can one co-write without engaging in compromise? How does one create anything artistic without being fully aware of one's own limitations, one's own circumstances, one's budget or time commitments? These all generate compromises. On the path of a song making its way through pre-production, recording, and mixing, there are hundreds of choices and decisions made — and they seldom get made alone. There's usually someone else there — engineers, producers, musicians, managers, editors — smart, talented people with opinions that they'd appreciate getting the opportunity to express.

I tended to be a much more careful writer as I aged — probably also a function of circumstances. As a younger artist, I had more net-worked connections into the larger music business. As I got older, my own creative world shrunk along with my demographic commercial prospects. My circle became more private, insular. The things that I might have fought tooth and nail over in my earlier career gradually became conversations I was having with myself. The whole dynamic of compromise changed. The efforts from the last few decades of my life offer an unvarnished, uncompromising look at a bunch of work — a conscientious writer delivering a writer's work, compromised by limited budgets and resources. The irony is that nowhere near as many people were exposed to those works compared to the work of mine that corporate interests got people to listen to five decades before.

Which creative work had been more compromised?

Creative Process

Leonard Cohen would continue to rewrite songs that had already become well-known. Songs of my own, which I sang on stage for years, underwent evolutionary adjustments with prepositions dropped, phrases, melodies, and arrangements adjusted. Even the process of having audi-ences interpret songs changes them: if they've managed to survive for decades, they take on a nostalgic value and therefore newer shades of meaning never originally intended.

Duke Ellington was admired in part because he kept revisiting compositions and arrangements over the course of his life, changing them and creating new versions. Sir Duke had a desire to never let a song rest and always have his music becoming something else.

My experiences taught me that songs are never fixed and immutable. (Although I think plenty of songs can be changed without getting any better. You'll only succeed in making them different.) But, by and large, songs are only snapshots of something at a point in time. The song could morph, change, and take on a completely different character, a different collection of small details, different arrangements, so the song is never a static thing that's done. Mixes of recordings stay the same. But songs? They evolve.

Let the Music Do the Talking

I hardly ever start writing with an end goal in mind. I always develop an instinct for an end goal when I've formed a solid sense of what it is I'm working on and what shape it's pushing me toward.

It's hard work to make inspiration fit into disciplined structures. No single approach or formula is going to be foolproof and consistently successful. I don't focus on novelty very much, but there's no question that it's important. I tend to gravitate naturally to universal kinds of themes. In the end, of course, it's impossible to be objective about what I do. When I put an album out, I see it as the best work I could manage over a period — a series of snapshots of where I was at that point in time. But if you ask me ten years after the fact, I'll invariably see them differently.

It's hard to define what makes songs commercially successful. It's an alchemy of things: cultural zeitgeist, timing, accessibility, a record company spending a lot of money to expose the song to capture the public's imagination, more money to drive that song into the machinery of zeitgeist.

Songs are but one aspect of what constitutes a music career. Taken as a whole, an eclectic catalogue served me well (as much as I admired the pop craft that creates mainstream money-makers). I wasn't going to apologize for being eclectic or complain that I didn't make it deeper into the mainstream with big hits. I was grateful that I could sell enough records, doing it my own way and having it be my own thing, so that I could survive and get the chance to chase it again and again.

Writing songs can be seen as (at least partly) autobiographical, no matter what the song is or where the song ends up. They're also partly creative fiction, figments of the imagination. For me, even my fictional character–driven songs were semiautobiographical constructs, so I didn't have to stretch too far. (Marco, with his secret songbook, was a guitarist, after all. He wasn't, oh, a dentist from, say, Budapest.)

I'd never taken on a theatrical, long-form concept piece before *Marco*, which made that project different. I enjoyed different challenges from time to time, which gave the process a creative freshness. The bottom line is an instinctive choice: is the work good enough to deserve an opportunity to find an audience? In some ways, the answer to that always remained as grey as whether the song (and its creative process) was finished or not. Maybe this thought is relevant: many producers in the music business say that records are never finished. There only comes a time when they must get delivered.

Song Characteristics

A good song is often like a short story, maybe a screenplay synopsis. Plenty of good songs give birth to mini-movies that play inside people's heads; they are dramatic, evocative, metaphorical, and full of rich imagery that is compelling and emotionally engaging.

This characteristic drew me toward songwriting in the first place. One of the truly wonderful things about music is that everyone gets the opportunity to build their very own customized, personalized mini-movie inside their own head. It's open to interpretation.

No surprise then that I cursed the day that concept music videos became popular — because it's a form of tyranny regarding visualization. Everybody is subjected to the same sequence of images. Instead of leaving a song open to interpretation, it narrows it down, locking it in and requiring less of the listener's own involvement. Interpreting songs used to allow a much more active process for a listener. Then they were watching videos, then videos on YouTube, and music consumption became a much more passive activity. Imagination became victim first to the MTV lifestyle-marketing machine available 24/7, and then to the digital universe, which (like *Star Trek*'s Borg) seeks to assimilate everything in its path.

We live in an age where many feel a tremendous desire to multitask, with the internet beeping, buzzing, and dinging in their hot little hand. Can we successfully juggle even more things tomorrow? I wonder if simple isn't better. (That resonates like folks from my parents' generation saying that no one in my generation knew what good music was. They were both right and wrong. Just as I am now, I reckon.)

Transposing Pronouns

Nothing works more powerfully and directly than *I* and *you*. Transpose emotion through the choice of pronouns. Most of the broken-hearted love songs that I wrote came out of my imagination or from looking at someone else and writing about them — except I'd change the pronouns in the lyric.

The *she* in "Magic Power" — "she climbs into bed, pulls the covers overhead, and turns her little radio on" — was not at first a she, because it was a nine-year-old me. Women liked that song; it gave Triumph a wider audience.

Time: The Great Equalizer, the Story Clock

I used to write songs and make music that celebrated my youthful ambition and ego. Some of them followed me through my life, becoming an exercise in both nostalgia and irony. I used to be young and wild and free with lightning licks and athletic stage jumps — fading photographs in an album on a shelf. I used to play in a rock band that proposed to "tear the roof off" tonight. Now I fantasize about peace and quiet. My passion used to be an asset; now my sentimental heart can be a real liability. Now my creative resolve is to spend time wisely, in order to try to buy a bit more of it.

When my grandma turned eighty-three, my brother asked her what wisdom she might offer us about life. She thought about it, gathered herself, and with a sad frown said, "It all went too fast. It's not fair." In that awkward but oh-so-real moment, she seemed like a child who didn't want to have to go to bed. Time: the great equalizer.

I freely admit my obsession with the topic, and I'm not alone. In Daniel Levitin's bestselling book *The World in Six Songs*, the (debatable, but still very useful) six categories of all songs are friendship, joy, comfort, knowledge, religion, and love. All are given emotional resonance and poignancy via the ways they manage the element of time. And there are two reasons for that. One, we're all wired for stories, and stories play out on a timeline of the author's choosing. Two, every human being converts from child to adult, from innocence to maturity, when the realization of our mortality truly sinks in. The reality is that this world, as we know it and perceive it through our senses, is going to be the death of us. Our natural mortality colours everything we decide to do, everything we choose to attempt, because time is always ticking. How does a writer handle the element of time in the storyline? It's an ingredient in a lot of, maybe most, great songs.

Transcendence

Truly great examples of songwriting feature transcendence: the quality of the whole becoming greater than the sum of the parts, of something defying time and place. Long after we're dead and gone, people will hear some old songs and be drawn to them; their imagination will be captured by the relationship of melody to harmony to lyric to emotion. Maybe some imaginations only get captured when they can hear a cash register ring. Certainly many successful music executives believe good is when the numbers speak for themselves. But I prefer when a little number makes its way into my heart and soul, capturing my imagination from the inside out and not necessarily from the marketplace on in. Transcendence, for me, goes inside out, outside in.

Transcendence is something I measure in my deep spiritual places. Human nature can be translated into the coin of the realm, if that's what drives you. But for me in my senior years, songs are like invitations to visit the cathedral inside.

Storytelling

We're constantly surrounded by stories. People place faith in stories and draw strength from them. Everything in human social and cultural activity has a story, a narrative, a construct. Politics is a story, finance is a story, wars, religion, sports are all stories within stories. Music is no different. Our brains are wired for stories. Why? Because we want to figure things out; we want to believe there will be a happy ending, a purpose, and that it's not just random chaos — that we matter and can make a difference. Maybe an ear worm sticks with you, and you can't get rid of it until you've figured out its story. What is it trying to tell you? Maybe it makes even more sense if you flip it around: what is your story that you can divine from the song that's sticking with you?

The stories we live in can be the ones we choose. Maybe we get this short little dance on a blue ball circling the sun, and all we ever do is make-believe, trying to make some sense of it. I'll easily admit that my perspective on music may be self-delusional, in the way that some people believe in angels and demons or in the way that a child accepts the story of a tooth fairy.

Music makes sense to me. (Not all music, but lots of it.) Self-help in my life was deciding which stories I would invest myself in. Creativity makes sense: my guitars and my notebooks are my life companions. That's my story, an' I'm stickin' to it.

Night after night after night, I played "Lay It," "Hold On," "Fight," "Magic," "Ordinary Man," and "Suitcase Blues." There were always the Triumph guitar pieces and a few songs that came and went from set lists ("Somebody's Out There," "Never Surrender"), but those half-dozen evergreen tunes combined Triumph success with autobiographical milestones.

"Lay It on the Line" came first. I can't recall if the verse or the chorus arrived at the beginning of the process, but I do recall that the chorus progression felt like it climbed up, so I wanted the verses to feel like they were moving down. I had a cinematic kind of imagination for this (as I did with "Hold On"). I could hear the guitar overdub layers, the harmony vocals on the chorus. I knew the guitar solo would get built over a bridge harmonic construction (which I was borrowing from my guitar piece "Petite Etude," which came from the classic diatonic cycle of the baroque era, updated by jazzers on the standard "Autumn Leaves"). Domenic Troiano used to refer to the three power chords b6, b7, and Im as the "money chords," so I wasn't inventing the wheel here. Those chords were in the guitar solo of "Stairway," Hendrix's "Watchtower," and Rick Derringer's "Rock and Roll Hoochie Koo."

Here's a cute anecdote about this tune: I flew in to Illinois to be a guest artist with Jim Peterik's World Stage shows, and "Lay It" was going to be on the set list. His great guitarist, Mike Aquino, asked me about how the voicings in the intro went, showing me what he'd worked out, unsure if it was right. After thirty years or so, I had zero recollection of how I'd executed the arpeggiated part, so I had to get Mike to teach my own part back to me. I had to admit: it was devilishly clever. (No wonder I couldn't remember it.)

I like that the lyric is about a guy asking for honesty. The subject, the content, and the style that frames it up has worn well. And forty-five years down the road, it's still a pretty good title for a memoir.

Like "Lay It" and "Magic," the song "Hold On" starts with a slow, soft, half-time feeling, then kicks into stronger gears as it develops. I liked the idea of symphonic songs that Brian Wilson had originated. I love when arrangements build and shift the landscape. It was definitely album-oriented rock.

My songwriting notebook had the verse chord progression as the foundational idea — the hard twelve-string acoustic strumming E, B/E, D/E, A/E. In my head, I could hear the E5 power chord on electric guitar sustaining over the acoustic changes underneath. The intro idea came along when I went magpie-searching back through a folder and found a poem I'd written in high school entitled "Old Tune" — *"music holds the secret, to know it makes you whole."*

I had already been fooling around singing "hold on" over the busy strumming, imagining how easy it would be to harmonize those vowel sounds. The "holding" was now in the intro and the chorus, and the challenge arose in the execution of the lyric — hold on to what? The fact that the payoff of "dreams" ended up being a high lead vocal B (B5 on the piano) was less than ideal, because the human voice gets thin holding a high B like that. On the record, this got saved somewhat by having a violin pad entering and swelling to support it.

I also composed a long instrumental breakdown bridge for this song, with a kind of disco groove and an eight-bar chord progression loop of ||: E | D | C | D :|| that took its sweet time developing over twenty-eight bars; I envisioned building a wire choir of layered sustaining and controlled-feedback guitars. Fortunately I was working with English engineer Mike Jones, who had done work with Justin Hayward of the Moody Blues, layering guitars and bouncing tracks to create sonic textures. These kinds of creative indulgences reveal how I was coming into my own as a writer and recording artist, but a song pushing beyond the six-minute mark could work for the Beatles or Bob Dylan — not for an RCA rock band on its sophomore album stateside.

So, the label did a radio single edit, which got it on the *Billboard* chart. The tune never really worked well with the trio in live performance. We had to play it in St. Louis, where the tune had climbed to number one on the KSHE chart — but thereafter it dropped from the set except if I played it solo on acoustic twelve-string, as a folk song. (All of these evergreen songs scale down to acoustic folk delivery and still work. The campfire test is a strong indicator of whether or not a tune has what it takes.)

Writing "Fight the Good Fight"

Gil and I came up with the rhythmic outline of the main chord riff, then co-composed the chords for the music of the A verse and chorus, writing together in the Metalworks studio in late '80 or early '81. Then I ended up writing the main vocal melody, the B sections of the verse, plus two versions of lyrics for the song. Gil had composed a melody theme section sequence that I suggested we use as the intro and outro bookends, it just needed a little tweak to turn it around and loop the descending progression back to its home key. Gil wasn't initially keen on the song title and chorus, so there was a second version of the chorus, "Every Moment." Both versions received final mixes, and it came to a vote, with Mike and I preferring the idea of a rock anthem titled "Fight," but in the double chorus, at the end of the recording, the repeat chorus kept the introductory vocal lyric line, "Every moment of your lifetime" — the only place in the song's master mix where the hook line from *that* version survived.

The catalyst for the lyric was my aunt Joan's battle with cancer, but the context expands out to a more universal idea of fighting to find the best person inside, trying to survive all the crap that life chucks at us. Who are you? What do you believe? What will you choose to give your life meaning and purpose? The second verse references The Good Book, and the phrase "fight the good fight" derives from the writings of St. Paul in 1 Timothy 6:12 and 2 Timothy 4:7 of the New Testament. Many evangelical Christians have had strong positive feelings about this song, interpreting it as a Christian religious anthem. Raised in the United Church of Canada as a child, that background certainly contributed to my work as an artist and writer, but by the time I wrote this song, I'd long become a secular, agnostic humanist. The talk about faith and spirit, in the song lyric, comes back to self-empowerment, and being the master of your own destiny, arising from your own heart.

The Bible never actually talks about God helping those who help themselves; it's centered on God helping the helpless, and people having to surrender their own will to God's grace. Ancient Greek playwrights originated the notion of gods helping those who help themselves, and Benjamin Franklin popularized the phrase. In truth, the overriding moral and ethical philosophy projected in my lyric is closer to Franklin than

St. Paul — people should arrive at moral decisions within themselves and not have outside influences make this determination for them. My humanist values align quite comfortably with the ethics of something like "do unto others" (Matthew 7:12), or, as the song lyric itself suggests, "better to give than to receive" (Acts 20:35). Just for the record, Christianity didn't invent those ideas either — both are borrowed notions, a lot older than the religion that St. Paul built.

The lyric attempts to harmonize the morality of my own humanism with the religious beliefs of my aunt (and my mother), within the context of trying to determine what life is all about. It suggests that it's not about chasing money all the time, that the courage required to be honest with yourself is often not the easy way to go, and good things in this life often come at a cost that you must be willing to pay. The fight is constant, and the commitment requires consistent renewal. Maybe the lyric has been popular and effective because of the range of the "fight": from my aunt, who was fighting to survive (I subsequently also lost my mother and both of my brothers to cancer); to the fight that evangelicals perceive (and the song has been licensed in the past, for example, by NFL Films, for use behind footage of popular evangelical Christian football players); to the fight that an ordinary person encounters, every day, just trying to remain positive, summoning a smile for a stranger.

I was twenty-seven when I wrote that lyric. Now, as a senior citizen, life isn't as black and white as it was then. I see many more shades of grey — more perspectives, points of view, questions of degrees. What's good and righteous can change with time and with conditions. Life is far more complex than it was in 1981. I'd opt for an effort to lighten up, both on yourself and the other guy. Maybe I was always more of a lover than a fighter, deep down, but a younger man maybe feels like he has more to prove, and so is more passionate, and more naive. The good fight remains both a social, political, external one as well as an internal, ethical/moral one. But it's more of a constant, lifelong dialogue one has with oneself, and the choices and decisions one makes, based on circumstances and context. (But a song title like "Dialogue the Good Dialogue" doesn't really resonate, does it?)

The song still has legs. It wasn't just a pop confection that only had enough dimension to make a short impact on current commercial conditions: it's held up and helped to define what Triumph was, as a band. It helped us live up to our name, which mattered to me.

"Magic Power" was a love letter to radio. The story of the song, told many nights from the stage, begins with the gift of a transistor radio to nine-year-old Ricky. Sneaking that into bed at night, beneath my pillow, was like a passport to the universe. Later in my life it became an extraordinary gift to hear my own songs playing on the radio in distant cities, familiarizing folks to our songs.

In an early draft of the song, the second verse was autobiographical: "He climbs into bed, pulls the covers overhead, and turns his little radio on." Switching the pronoun to *she* gave the band crossover to new demographics. We weren't just a heavy metal band; we had a power pop song.

I have fond memories of working intensely with Mike Levine on this recording. He wanted the arrangement to get heavier, and the tune leaned on some Pete Townshend chording and the bright crunch of a Gibson Howard Roberts Fusion guitar. (The influence of "Who's Next" on our *Allied Forces* album is obvious.) I recall an afternoon where Mike was playing the Hammond B3 and Leslie parts for the song, and I was producing and arranging, forcing him to create all the growls and glisses that punctuate the energy of the song. Mike was not commonly an organist, so that session chewed his hands up. But, to me, a lot of the magic in that track came from those overdubs.

"Ordinary Man" could have lent its title to this memoir. It's almost certainly the most autobiographical tune I ever wrote in my Triumph years, and its lyrics keep reoccurring in this memoir. Whenever the business started twisting and torquing me, this was my default — *just do the best you can. Try to hold on to your blind and simple faith.*

I was not the kind of musician and songwriter who was usually satisfied with cowboy chords and straight minors or majors. I liked the atmosphere of altered chords and extensions; I loved their duplicity. (They felt more like a life soundtrack to me.) When I learned my first minor ninths as a young teenager, I felt like I'd discovered space travel. In "Ordinary," it's a bit of a tickle to me that the opening chords use an add eleven (which I used again in "Never Surrender") and the same Am9 voicing I'd used in the intro to "Lay It" (a voicing which shows up over and over in my compositions).

Triumph never performed this song live in concert. The album had already yielded "Magic" and "Fight" as evergreen tracks. But my fans knew this tune had a personal depth that tied listeners to the performer, one of the most important ingredients in evergreen.

The guitar solo on this recording took a long time to arrive at. I couldn't find the right vibe. Late in the session, I heard the guitar leaking back in the engineer's talkback mike from the control room. I asked Ed Stone, "Why does the guitar sound so different in the control room right now, when your mike is open, than it's sounding in my cans?" He replied, "That's not my talkback doing that. It's because your talkback mike is open, halfway down the room." I said, "Then keep my talkback mike open in my cans and blend it into the part going to tape!" He did — and the next pass was the keeper. The ambient sound inspired the performance.

With "Suitcase Blues," we were desperate for decent material to work up in pre-production in '77 and '78. We were always headed back out on the road, touring, trying to establish and break the band in new markets. I was not the kind of writer who limited my creativity to crafting pop hits. Because my approach to the guitar was eclectic, I was as likely to be taking a nylon string acoustic back to my hotel room to work out fingerstyle classical or jazz stuff as I was to come up with rock riffs. One tour weekend, I had a Joe Pass chord book out with me and was fiddling with a progression in it. I started to think about adding a bar or two, here and there, and inserting a bridge of my own. I came up with a typical tune for a band's third album: a road song. Except it was laidback old-school jazz blues. When I played it for Gil and Mike, they both loved the vibe of the tune and felt it made a great B-track statement, as a kind of "Her Majesty" addition at the end of the album, a little something out of left field.

I liked left field. It was my kind of place. "Suitcase" was the song at the end of the encore for the last two and a half decades of my life. I was a travelling musician, and it was the theme song from behind the mask, off stage, out of the spotlight. It took the unreal and made it real.

GUITAR, GUITAR, GUITAR

I play guitar because it lets me dream out loud.

— MICHAEL HEDGES

Nothing is more beautiful than a guitar. Except, possibly two.

— FREDERIC CHOPIN

A guitar can be a friend for life: a compass on a journey of self-discovery, a force field, a security blanket. It's been my passport; it gave me identity and keeps me sane and grounded. It also challenges me and kicks my ass, routinely.

On the guitar, I could write over my head (not too far to have to go, actually), then struggle to master the material. It's not just chops — what my hands were capable of doing at any given point in time. I'm talking about imagination. There's a mental and spiritual gymnastic ability at work in the performance of a piece of music. No one else can play it exactly like little old me, because my playing requires my rock and roll heart and my minstrel troubadour spirit in order to reach its full potential. When artists realize that subjective quality gives them an edge, that self-conviction provides a public voice, a profile, that differentiates them in the crowded, noisy marketplace. Some artists possess that quality quite naturally, instinctively;

others must work to find their way to it. But the goal remains: make who and what you are manifest in the things you're playing.

The Search for the Holy Grail

Once I was standing backstage with Neil Osborne, the lead singer of 54-40 — an intense, charismatic guy. At the time, he was playing a Telly missing a knob, no plastic cap on the pickup selector, front pickup sunk into the pickguard — a guitar essentially beat to crap. I said, "Hey, man, that's quite the axe." He replied, "Man, it's not an instrument to me. It's just a tool."

Which reminded me of a quote from Pete Townshend: "I don't polish the fuckin' thing. I just play it."

To some guitarists, one tool solves the problem nicely of getting their music across. In most cases, an acoustic works better for writing, and an electric of some description works better for performance (easier to play and more versatile). Think Bob Dylan, a man who lives for the song if ever there was one.

But as a guitarist develops more needs and wants — as a writer, as a recording artist, as a performer — they often find that one guitar can't cover all the territory their imagination runs around in. For live gigs, there's a showbiz element to this too. When a guitarist switches to a different axe, it's like a wardrobe change. It signals a different mood, attitude, landscape. In my days of having a guitar tech, I loved changing it up to better suit the song. But some guys leave it up to the music — and I can relate to that totally.

I once played a summer outdoor show on a bill with Cheap Trick, and Rick Nielsen used a different guitar for every song. Out of the giant main PA, all those different guitars pretty much sounded exactly alike — like the roar of his amp. But I'm sure there were guys in the audience going, "Wow! Now he's got a sunburst '58 Les Paul! Oh man! What a tone he's getting!"

Woody Guthrie's guitar had a saying written into its face: "This machine kills fascists." Pete Seeger's banjo had a more poetic inscription: "This machine surrounds hate and forces it to surrender." A guitar is iconic. It stands for something poetic, rebellious, beautiful. It's an instrument, sophisticated in the right hands. Yet it can also be dangerous, a weapon — a rock and roll machine. And relationships with guitars become addictive.

I am speaking from experience: throughout my entire adult life, I've been a guitar collector, blessed with endorsement relationships with companies generous enough with their creations to indulge my own custom experiments and natural curiosity for their products.

Let's speak to the abstract idea of a chameleon guitar: the Holy Grail guitar, the one guitar to rule them all. I propose that what makes us react to the sound of a human voice is that we're hearing a *unique* voice shaded by its own subtleties, fuelled by its own emotions, mind, and spirit. Authentic integrity is the thing that TV singing-contest judges encourage and reward, as the drama moves into later rounds.

We learn and flatter by imitation. But we cannot achieve greatness until we become masters of our own domain.

Over time, I realized that one chameleon guitar that can do it all is an impossibility. A guitar usually ends up being truly great because a combination of features gives it a wonderfully unique sound and tone. The greatest chameleon ever can't become a tiger or a giraffe; it can only change colour.

Another perspective on this is a player's own human nature. Some singular model of guitar might be able to cover the terrain for guitarists who never get restless for tones beyond the guitar in their hands. But some guitarists need a few dozen axes to cover the territory they hear in their head. I've always leaned toward the latter persuasion.

Still if we're going to talk Holy Grail, then here's a pretty good one: George Harrison played the lead guitar solo part in "Something" on the same red Gibson Les Paul that Clapton used to play "Guitar Gently Weeps." That's right in my wheelhouse. I could make do with that.

Sometimes new technology is cool, but classic simplicity is always a beautiful thing. The Fender Telecaster guitar is still very popular, even though the design hasn't changed much in sixty-odd years. Leo Fender got the design mostly right from the get-go — form followed function. Gibson figured something out with its Les Paul model in 1958. In six decades, technology has not been able to best either. (The front rack of my home collection has five Tellies and three Les Pauls. *Guitars, guitars, guitars.* My wife says, "You can only ever play one at a time." But I also played *doublenecks*.)

The Death of Guitar Solos

MTV started killing guitar solos in the back half of the '8os. Grunge began killing off flashy playing on progressive AOR FM radio, which coincided with the extinction of progressive A & R at record companies. Nirvana got signed to their first record deal in 1989. By then, energy had to come with attitude, the slacker combination of pop culture awareness blended with irony and self-loathing, anger, frustration, the recycling of hippie political mistrust — all that youthful rebellious testosterone funnelling into a post-punk reinvention of the wheel. Rock culture's song orientation combined with a record production focus. Nirvana captured the zeitgeist ("Here we are now, entertain us / I feel stupid and outrageous") as guitars started getting detuned. There was a counterculture rejection of nimble-fingered sophistication.

Another theory is that Eddie Van Halen pretty much gave birth to a style that couldn't get to another level, because any higher level was going to lose the mass market's capacity for imagination. Virtuosity eventually burns itself out, and the culture's pendulum starts heading the other way.

The advent of the digital age meant anyone and everyone could make recordings on their computers. They couldn't play like virtuoso musicians, but they figured out how to make riffy, hooky songs hang together and how to make recordings of those songs sound good. Thousands of bands (and tens of thousands of rappers) popped up every month, but very few featured guitar players who had woodshedded for a decade. Meanwhile rhythm sections became highly competent at laying down groove, trained to quantized click tracks under headphones since they wuz babies. Attitude sitting on top of programming spread like viral wildfire. Internet and cellphone technology compressed it for instant impact. Guitar solos? Too long, too complicated.

Now more than ever, we live in the age of music as wallpaper, as sound-bite, as soundtrack: accompaniment for video games or vegan dinners with white wine, atmosphere for cultural events with hundreds of curated channels on streaming services. Music as lifestyle boils virtuosity right out. With demographic slicing, the culture gets chopped up into tiny little pieces. Guitar soloing is now a subgenre of a subgenre, because it doesn't appeal to a big enough target demo. The numbers game in a multichannel universe, with expanding ranges of consumer choice, guarantees that virtuosity will always be an acquired taste for a small select group — not for mass consumption. They used to be, but guitar solos ain't pop anymore.

Napster launched in 1999, the death star of the mainstream record business as it had been known. We now have the technological ability to create great-sounding music without musicians: drums without drummers, bass lines without bassists, orchestras without university-trained players. It's a producer's age, not a musician's. Most modern audiences love the immediacy, vitality, and energy of performers carrying through on the energy of attitude and style. The guitar solo has been reduced to a two- or four-bar soundbite — a wee taste of nostalgia.

Since the mid-'90s, I've had acrylic nails applied to my right-hand fingernails. The great Canadian guitarist Don Ross turned me on to this. Every five weeks or so, I get them back-filled as my own nails grow in. Acrylic-coated nails changed my life, allowing me to become much more of a fingerstyle guitarist. My own nails were too thin and weak, tearing and breaking too easily — especially given the pounding and grinding of rock playing on steel strings. Acrylic nails gave me a shot at classical, folk, flamenco, and jazz right-hand techniques, allowing me to get a variation in tones.

When I met Chet Atkins at his RCA office in Nashville and offered my hand for a polite shake, he gave the fingers of my right hand a little squeeze by reaching and placing his left hand over top. The RCA promo rep who'd arranged the meeting and driven me over explained afterwards that Chet always protected his right-hand fingers, since they were at the heart of his legendary career.

When I recorded guitar pieces, often before I'd really mastered them, they contained clams and missed notes. (My internal clock has always pushed me to play so on top of the beat that I would often rush and get ahead of it.) I would do several takes. In the old "Petite Etude" and "Midsummer's Daydream" days, we would use a reel of quarter-inch tape and simply stop after a mistake, go back to a logical restart point, pick it up, and continue. Then the engineer would get out a razor blade and cut the tape to eliminate most of the big mistakes. If I knew a piece a bit better, I could play longer chunks and maybe even do multiple takes. Then we'd use longer pieces of better takes (say, a first verse from one take, a middle section from another take, etc.). Nowadays with Pro Tools, I will do a first take, counting it in (and usually playing to click or an unobtrusive drum loop pattern). Then I will use that same count to do at least three, maybe four takes and then move chunks around to build a master composite out of them. Even then, sometimes there's still a mistake in there. I might do a repair take and edit it in. But sometimes I opt to leave a mistake in. It's an honest expression of my limited humanity. A piece from me shouldn't feature perfection. I'll continue to revise them later, after I've really learned how to play the piece over and over — because a piece of music is never finished. It goes through many stages of existence, and one continues to refine and alter their approach to the repertoire they keep performing.

Playing great guitar parts is about listening — hearing the way you want it to sound in your head, and fixing that goal in your imagination; then listening to the notes that you play and adjusting your technique (and your gear) until you're matching the same sound, tone, or feel that's in your head. This requires tweaking — maybe a different position, a different fingering, all kinds of things — but in the final step, I can't really explain it. It's about being able to listen to the notes you create and just *be* those notes. Once you're playing, you don't really worry about hand position or technique or fingering or amp setting or anything. You just listen to the notes going out into the air and inhabit those notes. That's mostly how you get it to sound good.

Guitar Heroism

Playing some serious guitar, for the sake of guitar, is part of my thing. Guitar magazine readership and guitar record audiences had always been a male-dominated, relatively small demographic. There was an era in the late '60s and early '70s when guitar heroes were a big draw — Hendrix, Clapton, Page, Beck. Those guys got on the radar and never relinquished their positioning. Their media champions never stopped idolizing them because demographic numbers drove that. The guitar hero radar screen was comfortably populated. When a second generation of great guitarists (with even greater technical skills) came along, and some managed to make names for themselves, the business was already evolving away from guitar heroics, as grunge took over. The guitarists who did manage to get noticed were competing for a shrinking mainstream radar screen, and the ones who survived were either supernovas (Eddie Van Halen, Eric Johnson, Steve Vai, Joe Satriani, Yngwie Malmsteen, John Petrucci) or specialists with jaw-dropping prowess (Michael Hedges, Don Ross, Tommy Emmanuel, Tuck Andress).

As a guitarist, I never committed myself to any one stylistic approach to the exclusion of others. I was too much of a singer-songwriter with eclectic style-hopping tendencies to be in the competitive circle of guitar heroics. I was too acoustic and fingerstyle to be an electric guy, too hard-rock electric to be thought of as an acoustic fingerstyle guy. I ended up playing a hybrid of many styles. Nevertheless, electric blues guitar is probably my most comfortable, the one that comes to me most naturally in terms of feel. I'm a rocker, but I do like to play with a bit of swing.

Even though I was something of a jack of all trades style-wise, I managed to scrape into a few Halls of Fame, and stay creative into my golden years, so all good.

PHILOSOPHICAL ADVICE

Two things are infinite: the universe and human stupidity;
and I'm not sure about the universe.

— ALBERT EINSTEIN

- Be yourself — the best you staring back from the mirror for
  the rest of your days.
- Stop trying to force issues and thinking you always have
  something to prove. Slow down: let the truth come to you.
- Stop being so hard on yourself. Don't be your own worst
  enemy. Your best ally and friend should be yourself. Be
  self-empowering, not self-limiting. Give yourself permission
  to be great, to be creative, to be wonderful and excellent, to
  bypass fear and doubt to take on truth, wisdom, and beauty.
- Step outside of yourself. Imagine your work as something
  greater, wider, smarter, deeper than little old you could ever
  imagine. Let the work tell you what it's trying to become. Set
  your imagination free, so that you can channel the universal.
  Articulate your vision.

- Share secrets with people you love, because they can take some of the burden away.
- Truth sometimes hurts, but honesty is always the best policy because living with lies rots you from the inside out.
- Ambition and competitiveness, sure, but balance them with virtue — honesty and humility.
- Balance all things. Don't let things consume you.
- Beware the ego and your ideas of what constitutes discriminating taste.
- Be the person with the best work ethic, the strongest belief in delayed gratification, and the most discipline in comprehensive efforts. Make choices that person would choose. (Easy to preach, never easy to consistently deliver.) Develop your instincts to help your willpower recognize the best choices.
- Keep the work itself out ahead of the personality. The spiritual quality of the work is the end goal, not fame and fortune.
- Revel in the sheer beauty and wonder and infinite mystery of plurality. Keep parochial tribalism contained. Honour and value your perspective and respect for others.
- Offer to share your music. Don't dictate it. Work straight at an audience with respect, honesty, and truth. Don't work down at an audience, imagining that your taste and intellect is above the crowd. Don't work up: honour the balance and integrity of your equality, straight through the work, to your audience.
- A musical life has a rainbow of potential. At one end, it's very private, intimate — just you, your instrument, and the music. At the other end, it's a connection to an audience sharing in a moment, in powerful, spiritual communion. Surrender the ego to the rainbow: that's where the infinite potential for the music lives.
- Leadership doesn't come from the dog who barks the loudest. It comes from the dog who has the least fear, the best idea — the dog who naturally assumes responsibility when the pressure's on.

Showbiz has a fair bit of empty, going-through-the-motions, PR-spinning stuff. The dynamics of showbiz stir up a complicated stew. The longer I was in it, into middle age, the more complicated it got. Then I grew old, and things got simpler again. I could just let the work lead me forward, allowing other stuff to fall into place.

Occasionally I enjoyed doing something professionally unexpected. I got a bit of a charge from screwing with people's expectations and assumptions. That aligned with my aversion to pigeonholes, shoeboxes, and demographic typecasting.

There's no denying the power of music to conjure powerful feelings of nostalgia and transport us back to the past, where our future lay ahead of us and hope sprang eternal with a glorious array of choices and opportunities. But now — here in the present — I've grown old, and the past is gone. But it gets celebrated (the documentary, the Walk of Fame). Yet even in that affirmation and validation, there's a bit of melancholy, even measures of guilt and regret. Maybe you don't deserve this, a gremlin of imposter syndrome whispers inside. What makes you so special? So many worthy others never got this lucky taste. My brain has complicated humility defaults. Maybe that's Canadian. I don't get the coin of the realm without checking both sides.

I've done a lot of thinking (and writing) about time in my life. It always coloured my process. And music-making is a highly specialized kind of physical, technical skill. At some point, aging becomes an equal opportunity destroyer. Parts of the mind are still willing, but critical parts of the flesh have become weak. A Hall of Fame status also carries with it the melancholy and regret of the erosions of time. I felt I had to exercise humility to avoid looking like a buffoon who, for some twisted reason, wouldn't act his age.

I wouldn't want to create the impression of something false in my humility, something cooked in order to have modesty appear praiseworthy. This business of showing has always been a paradox and contradiction for me personally. My more natural instincts have always been toward the observer, the pilgrim. The high-wire stress and anxiety of performance was a life either thrust upon me, or one I defaulted into through reflex, with the talents I possessed. I reached an age and stage where I wanted to pursue a deeper spiritual path; the great divides and upheavals in our culture drew me toward different forms of both public and private expression. It's still a fascinating challenge.

Control Issues: The Marketplace

As an artist, I take pride in what I create. But my own original, genuine, personal connection to the work might not be what some consumers choose to make of it. Certainly audiences, listeners, fans, and critics all have a prerogative right to interpret the work in any way that they choose. (Or ignore it entirely.) But an artist doesn't always have to accept all the slings and arrows of outrageous fortune. Some artists learn, out of self-preservation, that criticism can be cruel and mean-spirited, and customers are not always right. An artist sometimes needs to hold true to the direction of their own inner compass. I could never completely disregard the noise of the marketplace and needed to take it into account. But it was still my account.

When I felt the awkward tension of these dynamics, I wanted to move along, get back to creation and away from the interpretations and consumption of the marketplace.

This speaks to control issues. At conception, an artist worth their salt is a control freak. Marketing moves dynamics beyond the artist's control. Live performance is also about control: an artist being able to deliver in the moment and build a community of consumption — one that they orchestrate, arrange, conduct, and deliver. One of the dangers of public display is that the expectations of others can generate a twisted bit of self-consciousness within the artist. Green rooms at awards shows are full of neurotics.

On Pessimism and Optimism

I choose to try to act out of love, not anger or fear. Some might say I'm a romantic; sometimes I'm chided for being cynical. But I would say I remain a hopeful citizen of the planet, having the faith to act out of optimism, not pessimism. When things get ugly, fear and anger raise my hackles, but in my creative work I try to push back against fearmongering

— even when it gets inside my own head and heart. Isn't that a part of the good fight?

On dark days, I'm a brother in the family of realists and pragmatists, trying not to degenerate into stoicism and cynicism, then descend into sarcasm and ironic pessimism. One step down and to the far left or right awaits misanthropy. Some people quite rightly deserve our fear and loathing, our distrust. And it requires strength of character to face hard truths, ugly reality. We then need even more strength to find a smile and sing a song for people who need it, to reassure us about life. I felt a sense of duty to seek an equilibrium in the music I offered to the world, because I thought there was an audience in need of it, and because I felt I owed it to them and to myself. I wrote songs and made music to try to make sense of my life, hoping it helped others to do the same.

My family often called me on my tendency to predict negative outcomes, looking for the (petty) smugness of being right when things turned out lousy. It certainly has truth in it, but it was also true that my coin had two sides, and I tried to balance my optimism and hope with what I considered to be healthy doses of realistic strategies for coping with bad outcomes.

Despite the armour of my pessimistic cynicism, I once wrote, "Only a fool takes a leap of faith on the strength of a butterfly's wing." I do leap; I *am* that kind of fool. I think it takes an even worse kind of fool to lose one's sense of delight in watching a baby smiling, gurgling, drooling, and shrieking in happiness like a pterodactyl simply because her belly's full and the world's a soft blanket with a bunch of colourful toys, surrounded by people with trusting smiles. Life can be simple. Curmudgeons make it complex. Our babies need somebody to watch out for them. We do it with never-ending hope, because babies can't do it for themselves yet. They need to learn how to be strong, because optimism requires more wisdom, passion, and balance than pessimism.

On Artistry

Jimi Hendrix was a great guitarist. His limitations as a musician made him the guitarist, singer, and writer that he was because he struggled against them and became creative within his quirks, tendencies, insecurities, and personal affectations. When someone says, "Genius. Maestro. He could play anything," humbly I say, "Not true." Genius blazes its own quirky path that it can't help but follow. It's eccentric, like absent-minded professors who wander out of the house without their pants on; they are by nature idiosyncratic.

This should give hope to every person who picks up an instrument, pen, or paint brush. The goal is to be the best you that you can be (as army recruiters and *American Idol* judges love to say). In art, only you get to figure out the best you every day, with every note, sentence, or brush stroke. The process never ends, and it never moves away from the subjective, either at inception or final perception by third parties.

Creativity is a process. We learn about the work through the doing; we learn about ourselves. It's in our nature to be competitive, but we may have become a culture that's far too contentious. Win immediately at all costs. (One of the music business class mantras relating to entrepreneurship was "Be First, Be Best, Be Different.") I understand how business is uber-competitive, and therefore these attitudes are important. But I also firmly believe that the business of art is not just about the result. Concerns of the heart and soul need a reflective phase. Like good whiskey, they require time to distill and mature. Yes, the idea of a pop song can happen like the bang of a firecracker. Some pop ideas can be executed quickly and happen in a sugar rush. But not every idea is a dash to the finish. Some ideas deserve a longer, deeper, more carefully considered process. And in the end, one had better learn to love artistic process, because it may be the only reward one gets. The marketplace may never recognize your work; you may never earn a living from it. But your work can give you joy.

Some musicians and writers act as if they will require stardom in order to fulfill their dreams. And we do live in this strange era of social media where so many seek a few nanoseconds of fame, instant celebrity. Follow me, me, me! But the process should be about the work: what it offers to an audience.

Did a younger me make this mistake sometimes? You bet. And aren't some pieces of work autobiographical in their very nature (as one writes a memoir)? Of course they are. But it's always a good check to step back from the work and ask yourself, Is this too much about me and not enough about the subject? How does the subject work in this world? They don't call 'em *works* for nothin'.

Overthinking and underthinking are both dangerous. Keep adjusting until the balance is right. Current events have knocked the social climate out of whack, so we need to work to try to restore it. The work — an act of good faith — is a constant, ongoing job.

The game of life comes at us in a lot of ways. Sometimes we get aggressive, press the issue, and take it to the game. But my prevailing attitude is that it's usually better to be patient and let the game come to you. Too many errors get made when we're trying to force it. On the other hand, too much passivity and maybe I end up too far inside my own head. Maybe my head gets stuck somewhere that turns me into a self-fulfilling pretzel. The exercise of a consistent, passionate work ethic, day in and day out, leads to a game-day performance taking care of itself. Once again there's a humility in that attitude — a respect for the game, the work, the process.

My Own Music Playing at Home

On social occasions, I get really distracted if music is playing loud enough for me to be able to distinguish chord changes, voice leading, et cetera. It's even worse if it's my own music. Everyone in my family knows that I don't enjoy having my music playing. I would almost never choose to have my own creations playing around the house.

I'm not someone who can multitask. When I watch TV, I'm engrossed by it and can't split focus to also carry on a conversation or do a crossword puzzle. When I listen to music, I don't do it in order to give myself a soundtrack for exercising or reading or housework. I'm aware of how music can enhance any of these activities for most folks, but if I'm sitting down to dinner, with family or company, I can only enjoy background music that's barely audible.

I realize this puts me in a minority, making me seem like a curmudgeon, but that's how my brain works. If the background music happens to be my own, that's worse. I really hated doing a meet-and-greet or attending a launch function where my new CD was cranked up loud. It made me want to leave the room, holding my hands over my ears.

I can close my eyes and hear music in my head. I can also make it up
— open my mouth and improvise it — and the possibilities are limitless.
Satisfying creative quality is rare, however. Substantial depth takes time
and energy aplenty, so there's always too much promise in the peace and
quiet of the moment for whatever fresh creative potential might be waiting just up the road ahead.

The Inner Critic

I try to be my own best friend, which is hard for my inner cynical critic to
allow, but I keep trying to love that curmudgeon, too, and forgive him his
trespasses. He's certainly an important member of the committee but will
never get to be the chairman with veto power. He thinks he's the smartest guy in the room, and that he's protecting my inner Whitmanesque
multitudes — but he's the killjoy, the most short-sighted dumbass at the
boardroom table. I forgive him. Speaking from experience gained from
frustration, abandonment, loss of trust, broken love — those aren't the
places to work from. I keep telling him to let go of all the baggage of
negative emotions he's lugging around in the here and now. Lighten up,
dude. Let it go.

Life Lessons

Obviously these are not graceful times. Yet the digital universe is
infinite. As a pilgrim on a path toward a more graceful life, somehow
I'm confident that science will advance our world, despite minority
factions that question facts and those who might prefer the use of a
guillotine to accepting the knowledge and wisdom of an elite. We're
on the right track with a healthy, balanced approach when we accept
change as inevitable and therefore seek to make changes that enhance
our lives and those around us. That's not a leftie plot: that's the high and
dry middle of the road.

It's also healthy to understand that any pecking order is not a per-
manent condition, which is to say wealth does not necessarily make

one wise. Wisdom does not necessarily make one powerful. Power does not necessarily make one righteous. Righteousness does not necessarily make one infallible and correct. Humility remains necessary.

Grace abides within the virtue of humility. My standard operational manual suggests a wrestling card of virtues versus vices: humility against pride, kindness against envy, abstinence against gluttony, chastity against lust, patience against anger, charity against greed, and diligence against sloth.

I have no idea how love survives the horrors of our inhumanity, our criminality, our perversions, our vice and sin — but somehow it does. It can. It will. I also have faith and place hope in love as the ultimate answer and best solution. Love can get twisted and perverse, and it can be used to manipulate and to coerce, but in the end, somehow, love finds a way to conquer all that shit too. I'm not religious; I cannot accept notions of an afterlife. But if you say God is love, I will say for us humans, on this little blue ball spinning around the sun, that feels right.

Issues of entitlement and accountability make the whole process of searching for grace trickier. There are issues of power here, of judgment, of semantics in the discussion. In my search for balance, along the road toward a graceful life, I choose to believe that cynicism and skepticism remain valuable tools, as I wouldn't want to get overly seduced by a fancy storyteller. My cynical nature remains skeptical of vain prophets of false gods.

Lately every system is running a deficit. Virtue and ethics are on the endangered list. It doesn't make for a great environment, does it?

We live in times when far too many people are not self-governing enough. They don't account for themselves before they start judging others. Too many people have expectations of their own entitlement, before they consider the entitlements of others. The Golden Rule — the ethic of reciprocity — requires a self-imposition before we start climbing up on soapboxes and shouting through our digital megaphones. I don't claim any entitlements that I wouldn't extend to my neighbour. We should hold ourselves accountable before we start sitting in judgment of each other. That, to me, is a step in the right direction along the path toward Graceland.

Time

Time is a constant theme and subtheme in my writing, one that I believe all conscientious writers must weigh as a factor in the depth of their storytelling, in one way or another. Time, neither cruel nor kind, is like Old Man River: it just keeps rolling along.

The longer we live, the more grief, horror, ignorance, and brutality we have endured. The closer time brings us to our own passing, the closer we are to the death of our perceptions, and end of our conscientious awareness of the beauty and glory of this sensual, emotional life. Ironically we humans find the exercising of this conflict entertaining. (Horror movies? Evel Knievel thrill rides?) Give us a good tickle right between the finite and infinite bones, and we become enthralled. In a pure, fundamental way, slave hollers led to blues — the soundtrack to the cruel hardness of life. Music makes the journey through time more tolerable, enjoyable even. What doesn't kill me makes me stronger!

Someone somewhere is always selling nostalgia for the good old days. Slow things down, turn back the clock. Remember when we weren't afraid to take on the world? Remember when everything seemed possible?

Meanwhile the timeline grinds on, relentless and unchanging, following its one-direction arrow. I'm not the prime minister or the secretary-general of the UN. I've never won a Grammy. What can little old me do to make today a better day for the people I encounter? I default to this: music is an attempt to establish common ground, balance. The pendulum keeps good time if it is balanced. Get creative: make music, write words that contribute balance on the timeline. I remind myself how uncommon common sense is, and I try to get back to common decency, common courtesy. Ordinary man.

A Musician's Life of Good Faith in His Garden

Consider the miracle of this world in this universe: fossils of life that existed 500 million years ago on tectonic plates that shifted across distances as wide as the ocean; the infinite glories of plants and animals, represented by the modest glories of flowers in my very own backyard;

the scent of sage and thyme in this corner of the garden, the lavender over there, the glory of the wisteria, as the warmth of the sun makes its way into my blood, my bones. Consider these miracles of air, water, earth, and fire that somehow keep the balance of our fragile ecosystem going; the mysterious wonders of gravity, sunlight, and oxygen.

Do the birds and insects get depressed by the unbearable weight of life, or do they simply take it as it comes and live it? I try to turn the complex into simple healing. Even when I'm struggling, I can still work on creative things and offer them to others. Whenever I descend into heartbreak and sadness, I remind myself that I can still choose to be kind, generous, open-minded, open-hearted. I can choose gentle wisdom instead of my anger, my frustration, my sorrow. Too often I come up short, but I resolve to rise back up from my failure and find my way back to the mysterious wonders of life's simple gifts.

The nature of loss is unfathomable, a black hole. How do we work with that? Offer love to others. Be a person of light, not darkness. Show kindness to strangers. Help build a world that works, and there are many people who can and will work with you — the fabric of a creative community.

We live, we lose. It's the way of life. But for those of us still around, still breathing, still able to make a joyful noise, we can find each other, offer each other something real, something true, something beautiful, something hopeful, faithful, and loving.

Every lesson I have learned
Every scar that I have earned
Taught me how to raise a joyful noise
So now for each and every voice
Denied their songs of choice
I must sing: I'm bound to sing.
And so — I sing.
Oh yes — I sing.
　　　　　　　　— *"I Sing," 2016*

When people give themselves away in good faith, yes, it's risky. But at work, at play (and play is my work), a demonstration of trust offered to relative strangers has the chance to be a beautiful thing. I always tried to infuse the music with something that money can't buy. I put myself at risk. To me, in the end, that's why people are willing to invest themselves in it. That's good faith.

The meek and humble, who thought they were going to inherit the earth, perhaps only inherited the wind. But the hunger for power is corrupting, so without irony, I'll put my faith in art. This ordinary man will continue to give myself away, with a blind and simple faith.

Creative art speaks more truth to me than any politician ever could. Mother Nature reminds me about values — humility and awe high on that list. I guess that's how I'm wired. Keeping my good faith in hope and love was my business model, and (cribbing from B.B. King here) I gave that away for free. You just had to pay me for my time and travel.

PORTRAIT OF THE ARTIST

Don't think about making art, just get it done. Let everyone else decide if it's good or bad, whether they love it or hate it. While they are deciding, make even more art.

— ANDY WARHOL

I magine how many times I've listened to a song before the public hears it for the first time — how many hours, days, weeks of my life have been spent deeply engrossed in writing, listening, analyzing; dissecting details of a song in rehearsal; recording, mixing, mastering. And it flows by in less than four minutes.

The job I started part-time at fifteen was an avocation I loved, and I wouldn't have wanted to do anything else. But I also had to try to keep it in perspective, so it wouldn't eat up the rest of my life. I required two separations of church and state — the first between the job as state and my life of family and friends as church. Those folks deserved that reverence, but as a younger man of ego and ambition, pushed by fears about financial security, I often struggled to find a balance.

The second was within the job itself, because I respected certain things about music as sacred, whereas the music business was like

Caesar's state, and I rendered unto it as such. I was a bit better at handling that throughout my life. In the final analysis, the distinctions of the balances I tried to bring to the work helped me keep on keeping on (and still do).

An old showbiz adage advises you to leave an audience wanting more. I've often felt that when it comes to commercial considerations of the attention span of any regular audience, a performer has more success bonding with their audience via a two-and-a-half-minute song than with a suite in twelve themes and variations. That's the songwriter in me. But I'm also a musician, and I love album-oriented music, especially the kind that allows for the excursive accommodation of solos or long sections of expository ensemble work.

I always felt that singing took precedence and pride of place over guitar playing (which is, after all, accompaniment, not the lead). There were some guitar parts that I simply couldn't play while singing. So, I would always prioritize getting the singing down, then figure out what I could manage effectively as accompaniment. Some singer-guitarists possess an astounding ability to roll along on a fingerpicking pattern, taking it for granted, while they engage in an ad lib spoken intro. I simply can't do it. I need to know, somewhere centred in my body, how I'm marrying the two elements together. I need to be able to feel it.

Who Am I? Who Have I Been?

Anyone who encountered my work could formulate their opinions, based on their own taste and preferences. But I wasn't only the guy who wrote and sang arena rock anthems or ballads, or the guy who blistered blues licks out of a Les Paul, or the guy who got his nails done at the salon so that he could play classical and jazz licks.

As an artist, I was an eclectic style-shifter. The range of songs was a main reason I wanted to be a songwriter. Over the course of my life, my catalogue characterized me, giving me my voice. It really wasn't the other way around.

In the early rock and roll machine days, things got done with gaffer tape and a lot of optimism. As we got bigger and more successful, older, wiser, the gear itself and the methodology became more sophisticated. It bears noting that after thirteen formative years in the machine, I quit, went through a transition, and spent about three decades playing mostly acoustic-based solo and duo gigs. No special effects, no production values. I was comfortable doing that. I might even say I came full circle and arrived back at my calling — where I'd started, playing acoustic solo when I was in high school.

I've had a lot of music go into these ears in my life. As I got older, I found myself craving solitude and the serenity of peace and quiet. It's just physiology — my ears tire more quickly now and are more sensitive, not as resilient (just like a lot of other body parts). The brain can't keep up with the volume of wide frequency ranges that contain harsh strident tones, big low end, and a mess load of decibels.

As I age, I don't love music any less but in more complex ways. I did find myself, from time to time, envious of the amateur musician or the straightforward fan of music, who could enjoy it without too much analysis. I tried to recall the pure, unadulterated joy of my youth — to be able to make music without all the theory and harmony knowledge, without the baggage of marketing, academic, philosophic, and career-related stuff that filled the head, polluting the stream of notes as it headed toward the soul. I understand why Picasso wanted to paint like a child with a primitive naïveté and abandon. I wanted to end the career in order to rediscover the joy of the hobby — to escape the tyranny of retail consumption, the bullying of market judgment, of economic and political validation. Throughout my life, I tried not to let that disqualify my humanity, my normalcy. I felt I needed to protect that perspective and to continue to make good work for its own sake, not for a voracious marketplace.

Accountability

While it's important to take an audience into consideration, I felt I must remain far more accountable to the music itself, to the creative work.

I'm also responsible to account to myself, and to that end, I also believe that entertainers should remain somewhat remote, inaccessible, with some mystique, which is a healthy thing for both one's mental health and career. Once you have a bit of notoriety, people are curious; they speculate. They want to get inside the process, to eavesdrop or spy — maybe even participate. This is human nature, part of the fuel that drives social media. I have little interest in feeding the beast, yet I understand the necessity of some limited access, equalized with some distancing. I didn't share all my life — I shared a part and tried to keep things in balance. Sometimes it got away from me. Maybe this memoir is helping me set some of the record straight and reclaim some equilibrium.

Smaller or Larger Venues?

I had no preference for size of audience or venue — only for the quality of the connection.

As I've written here, some of the more memorable performances in my life happened with an audience of one. The key ingredient is the focused intensity and the exchange of energy between the listeners in the audience and the performer in the moment.

A large crowd can give you awesome power surges — but in large venues, with follow-spots on full, you're often working to a kind of impersonal black void. Or in a daylight crowd like the US Festival, an impersonal sea of humanity set back behind the barricades, half a football field away. Big shows bring with them a big, long list of logistics, which can mean there's a lot more that can go wrong and become huge distractions.

In smaller places, with a little bit of spill light from behind, you can really get a sense of the house and see faces to make one-on-one connections. You can even step off mike and deliver material that the audience can get. There are still logistics, but there isn't as much potential for interference in the electric connection between the work and the listener.

From a personal, musical, artistic point of view, I did prefer the range of personal expression that a solo, duo, or even trio afforded. It allowed for more intimacy and less logistics. But now and again, it was also a treat to plug in, crank up, put in my earplugs, and tap into the energy of a larger ensemble, going back to that part of my roots.

I know some fans thought I was most myself when I strapped on an electric guitar and cranked it up, because that's how they got to know me first (and, in their minds, best). But they didn't know the high school kid who was learning to become a musician by performing solo acoustic at parties, campfires, coffeehouses as a folkie, or as a kid, singing in a choir. If they had first been exposed to me as the front man for a Jewish wedding band singing a *Fiddler on the Roof* medley during the dinner portion of the evening, they would have a different take on who I was and what I did.

I am a musician, addicted to the moment when the connection is completely alive — spiritually synchronized. It's a magical thing when it happens, so all the logistics get built up around the conjuring of that moment whether it was a crowd of one or one hundred thousand.

A live stage performance completes music in a way that no other experience can; rehearsals and recording sessions are different beasts. There's no substitute for a live audience in the here and now — that high-wire act with no net.

But in that here and now, there is also very much an element of "then again." Some of the crowd greets an old evergreen standard with warm applause — the obligatory dynamics of a Pavlovian response, a show-biz ritual, addressing the care and feeding of nostalgia. It's as if they respond to the moment the performer acknowledges, "You're a fabulous audience. Your life histories truly matter, so I honour you by playing the soundtrack of your lives!" It's as if the audience also applauds for them-selves — partly self-congratulatory, partly relief ("Phew. Good. This is what I paid to hear!").

It made my job and my life easier that I could strike a few notes of a song, or say the title of a tune I was about to play, and get some immedi-ate applause of recognition and acceptance. I was grateful for that good fortune. But there are complexities in audience-performer dynamics that extend beyond the surface transactions.

I'd often use a little comedic bit about the showbiz tradition of encores: how I was duty-bound to say good night — thank you very much! — take a bow, then (in a roll-the-eyes, nudge-nudge-wink-wink kind of way) go and hide backstage for a short period of time, only to re-emerge for an obligatory encore that was never spontaneous. Sometimes I wanted to find a way past the conventional, to come consistently from a place that was totally real and meet the audience in that place with the dynamics of our interaction free from artifice. But I don't want to blow this out of proportion either. Experience tempered my understanding: keep the conventions simple and routine. The best way to deal with the depth of Pandora's box is: don't open the lid.

Making music is always about reaching a person and making a meaningful connection there. That kind of connection can last a lifetime, which gives the music a vitality beyond commercial success or showbiz hype. As an entertainer, I always felt like I owed people something. They were my audience — many my fans — and I had to try to fulfill certain expectations, even try to exceed them, so that they would be loyal, perceive me as a real trouper, et cetera. But in the last decade of touring and performing live, I gradually stopped putting so much pressure on myself to meet all external expectations. I realized I might — probably could — get along just fine without a spotlight.

Integrity

I'm the guy who used to be the guy playing in that arena band who blew things up and had an outrageous light and laser show. Hey, I wouldn't have written this memoir if that weren't the case, so it even informs this.

But classic rock was not the main ingredient on my menu after '94. While it was hard to extract the ham from all the meals on the bill of fare, much of my music became less in your face. It was singer-songwriter material, often acoustic-based — not electric; much more fingerstyle; not overdriven. I reclaimed my "humble minstrel."

It's always a tricky proposition to balance integrity with courting public acceptance, approval, and support (three varying progressive shades of public life), whilst pursuing personal artistic agendas, private matters, and affairs of the spirit. I was from the classic rock community with life-of-the-partiers requesting "Free Bird" at the top of their lungs. My best paydays always came from the occasional gigs where I played the evergreen greatest hits set, so there was a bigger, bolder image at work there, more inaccessible. That was inescapable. In duo acoustic shows, I tended to blur lines. And the older I got, the more it became a question of achieving balance by blurring, then erasing, lines that had become meaningless anyway. I was shifting the idea of integrity; I was interested in the honesty of accessibility, as opposed to the remote grandstanding of rock star projection.

I do have an affection for people — and a curiosity about strangers. Still I don't suffer fools gladly, so I quickly run out of patience for wilful ignorance. I don't like crowds, but I enjoy making human connections and communicating. There's no question that my avocation required a certain amount of promo; like a politician or a minister, there were lots of complicated reasons to shake hands and kiss babies. It was part of my business and my nature, if it remained within reason and within the bounds of mutual respect. My upbringing and family influences forged in me the hope that others would see me as a charming, courteous, humorous host. But I remained a private family man who did not necessarily need public limelight or adoration, but wanted respect. I never hoped to use celebrity positioning to chase what seemed superficial and desperate (an irony being that the rock and roll machine generated that exact image). I never personally had any interest in empty partying behaviour, which some people mistake for something intimate and special. I've always felt that the value in my humble gifts lay in the giving — which seemed somewhat sacred.

Some might call it naive, but my predominant thought was usually, What's in here that money can't buy?

In my music biz course, I used to teach that a fundamental analysis of corporate behaviour aligns behind fiduciary duty — the obligation and priority of executives and boards of directors to return a profit to shareholders. At any stage of a business's own development, that's a bedrock focus. But a prevailing question still must be ethical — at what cost? By what means? And what kinds of qualities and values do we deliver to people that go beyond commercial transactions and enter the realm of humane, social health and welfare?

I like to keep my ears open, listening for the ring of truth over the din of the marketplace. But with all the cha-ching of the cash register, and the clinking rattle of the bling, no question — it ain't easy.

Business Practice and Tolerance for Risk

Whether or not one is starting out or has been at it for a while, everything in life has an element of risk in it. Go ahead, step off the curb. Fall in love. Put your money in the bank — or bet it on a pony. Bite into that apple. Good business practice begins when the dumb luck of random chance becomes modified by risk, by taking a calculated gamble after you've done whatever you can to make the odds play in your favour. How much of a gambler are you? How risk-averse? The music biz certainly brought this home repeatedly. I'm not very big on taking a chance and hoping it works out. I don't enjoy playing cards or games of chance. I prefer crosswords or a game like chess, where my own strategy and experience can affect the outcome.

I felt that my dealings with promoters, agents, managers, business clients, and partners had to be governed by the application of strategy and measured, disciplined thinking, along with articulate communication and documentation. I wasn't big on flying by the seat of my pants from one mysterious adventure to the next. It's counterproductive to making good music, especially for a guy with my sensibilities.

The handling of my business practice changed a lot over the years, as the business itself changed rapidly. My feeling had always been to establish protocols and policies, then paperwork and documentation, then follow that script as consistently as humanly possible. That forms the essence of professionalism. Invariably human mistakes were made, and outrageous fortune required us to adjust, ad lib, or compromise and modify protocols and policies because deals might go south unless accommodations could be found.

But there were points where I decided, no, enough is enough. I'm not a riverboat gambler, and my reality isn't Mickey Rooney and Judy Garland in a corny old movie. I had certain ethics I tried to live by, certain standards to maintain — plus a shred or two of dignity which I was loath to sacrifice as I aged. Making music for a living, when you're self-employed and relying on your own market value, was already a risky enough business. Dealing with promoters and middlemen added yet another layer to the risk, because theirs is an even more hazardous business world. Without risk, you're not even alive and kickin', so I continued to take 'em — but I was never wired for it. Eventually the constant stress became more than I cared to endure.

The dynamics of diminishing returns and a more elusive A game hastened my decision to retire. My vocal power was never going to be what it once was. Crafty wisdom and artfulness glossed over the realities, and I'd pulled all the known tricks: changed the keys of songs, detuned guitars a half-step, hydrated, often took medication. Near the end, there were two different therapists every week.

Two sixty-minute sets a night was only the tip of an iceberg. It was the grind of so much else. Business administration. Tiresome interviews and meet-and-greets. Accountants and tax returns in two countries. Commitments on the calendar fourteen to eighteen months away. The requirements of annual visa applications. I decided that the right time to retire from the road was when I could still manage to bring a modified version of my game, such as it was.

I spent my life performing. All along, the modest resource of my gifts also brought pressure: stress, anxiety, tension. Those repetitive stress injuries and nervous system issues compounded over the decades. So, gifts, yes; burdens too. A pro can't escape the tyrannies of consumption waiting at the end, market judgment, economic and political validation — so much career machinery getting in the way of the creative work.

I knew what I was getting into and what I was up against. Creating, writing, losing myself in process — that always remained the work focus. Creative process follows the adage of 1 percent inspiration and 99 percent perspiration, closer than most want it to be, or care to admit, but I've never been afraid of that. (Old Zen adage: chop wood, carry water.) It grew more difficult to find the time, because the hours spent doing the PR, marketing, and administration of the job became more omnivorous. Eventually I sacrificed career and job for the creative work.

The game of publicity and promotion is not the same as the challenge of creative work: artists provide entertainment for people, but those performers don't belong to the public, even though the work goes to live there. Art and commerce can put an artist at odds with one's self. Working out your own sense of balance is an ongoing private, critical matter.

An artist owes an audience their best attempt at an optimum performance. Beyond that, they don't owe them a squiggly thing. It's a certainty that one can't please everyone all the time. You come to terms with yourself, and those terms are in a constant state of flux. That balance between public and private is crucial to the maintenance of personal health. Maybe we all need saving from ourselves at different points in our lives. It's necessary and valuable for an artist to have some trusted business relationships, as well as friends and family who are committed to helping the artist achieve their sense of balance in life. It takes a village.

Life is full of conundrums, enigmas, and contradictions. Inside we carry the war between left and right, yes and no, good and evil, seeking that sometimes incredibly hard-to-find area — the middle ground, the balance point, the land of maybe, the grey between black and white, the tones in between the colours in the rainbow. Some folks hate the middle ground and try to avoid it, because they feel more comfortable when they don't have to feel the pendulum swinging, the vertigo of a sense of change. They prefer the status quo. This is very human. Change is inevitable, yet few are keen about too much, too fast.

Artists grapple with this as they try to come to terms with it in their work. If this expression leads to some level of commercial acceptance, a pattern is established of a gift that gets exploited for public consumption. But even though an artist might carry around exceptional gifts, and sometimes the public offerings of these gifts appear larger than life, we're just talking about a person in the end, full of very human traits.

A sensational success establishes a beachhead on the commercial front. Then the business exploitation pattern (often) says, Duplicate it. Triplicate it. Turn it into a quadruple axle. C'mon, you can do it, kid. What do you mean egos are a problem? What do you mean your mental health doesn't seem to be up to the task?

I'd transitioned out of larger commercial pressures by the age of forty-three. The other side of fifty delivered more downhill than uphill on the pathway. As an artist, I kept my own best counsel, searching for my middle ground.

My extended career as an artist (as opposed to a rock star) tended to be fuelled by a blend of ambition, ego, humility, and curiosity in the face of the infinite challenge. The combination of my humble gifts led me further away from the commercial mainstream. The intense focus of a younger person's career lends itself to legend-building and myth-making aimed at fresh, susceptible demographics. A lifetime of morphing, adapting, and changing style, image, and content invariably dulls the lustre of a shooting star.

Image

I never saw myself as some kind of leading man, womanizing star, a front man in the mould of a Mick Jagger, Robert Plant, or Steven Tyler. I was five-foot-eight for cryin' out loud; a skinny, high school jock type, jumping around stages in running shoes, not lizard-skin boots. The strutting and prancing in old videos is cringeworthy now. What was a standard part of the culture at the time now looks so uncool to me. A local newspaper writer once described me as "a mane-waving, sex-appealing punk" — a phrase the other guys in the band often recycled to tease me. Inside it all felt like silly, boyish, class-clown charm — as if no one was ever going to take me too seriously, especially because I never did. Did the ironic sense of humour come through for folks?

I could sing, make music, play wiseass, perform instead of having to be myself — because I was too shy and insecure. A guitar in front of me was like Linus's security blanket, a part of a showbiz game, doing stuff that some might find charismatic. But some of it felt like foolishness to me, and now I look back on it and can confirm — lots of it was. Maybe what fans found attractive was the heat of an uninhibited transparency. At least I was always willing to physically commit myself into a vocal or a guitar solo, 100 percent — jock attitude, really.

Process: The Studio, the Cloister

My best studio recording process is (still) a decidedly private thing that happens between me and an engineer-producer. For me, studio work is an exercise in focus, concentration, and discipline — a far cry from anything exciting. It's intense but boring, if you're not the one actually doing the work. My studio recording sessions are not like concert performances, where I'm trying to tap into energy from people watching. Studio sessions are like scientific research, exercises in internalizing the energy. Sessions are always about take after take after take. Then break for discussion, adjust headphone mixes, scratch out new little cues on the chart — and then more takes. Many are false starts, breaking down at tricky places. Often the artist must rehearse the tricky part in order to get comfortable enough with it for punch-in points — short sections of keepable takes but likely not full songs.

My life, to a great extent, was about writing, practising, lesson planning, sitting at a computer. A life spent mostly in cloistered isolation or in a very small select group of friends and co-workers. No complaints. It's the life I chose, and the studio was a part of the life that happily chose me. But the reality rarely matches up to the romantic notion that the general public has of an artist's life. Moments of performance perhaps give people the impression of a life lived large. For touring concert artists, the drudgery of travelling turns living large into an illusion, mostly. It's more a story of hours spent alone in a hotel room, sitting in an airplane or vehicle, rolling along with one's own thoughts for company. Off the road, my family orbit was an even more private, personal routine.

Every five years or so, a recording artist upgrades their gear, leaving some obsolescence in the wake — a trail of outmoded hardware. That process is ongoing internally in an artist too. As a realist, I remained practical and kept looking forward, evolving my approach, because I still wanted to have a meaningful career. I adapted as the music biz kept changing at the speed of light. That meant the creative content had to become liquid, fluid, ephemeral. Freshness, currency, and vitality needed to service the present moment, because the digital experience guarantees that there are infinite options for the very next moment coming along — and the next and the next. This was the cultural paradigm shift that occurred. Catalogued permanence and universal values had been reduced to that of archiving. The entire catalogue of my life's work could be a subfile of a subfile on someone's cellphone — instantly accessible, instantly disposable.

My energies shifted toward making digital performances and album projects that were of the moment; my creative projects became one-offs. (It strikes me that the idea of a memoir is very much a one-off.)

User Friendly Engineering

I loved being independent and DIY, but I hated engineering my own music. The time-consuming learning curve of new programs, platforms, and technology seemed like a giant mountainous roadblock in the way of being creative, productive, prolific. I guess I was spoiled by all the years of having highly skilled engineers push my buttons for me, so to speak. I'm not much for mouse-clicking in a Pro Tools program. I like writing, singing, and playing music. I preferred a guitar in my hands and a tune in my head, singing my heart out. I think best when notating with an old-fashioned pencil on a piece of paper.

I would have liked to become more fluid with digital technology, more comfortable with the software and hardware, but when faced with a choice of spending the next eight hours reading a manual to experiment with a computer program, or writing a song and practising guitar — no contest. Making music feels organic and intuitive to me. Learning and using technology feels like doing high school math homework. (And I sucked at that.) Digital technology baffles me, which doesn't make me hungrier for it; it makes me resent it and trust it less, because it reminds me of how stupid and powerless I am. It's hard to get in the creative flow of good music-making when you're feeling stupid and powerless.

User friendly is a misnomer — all users are not created equal.

Take a Bow

Performing artists take a bow because it's traditionally the very best way to consummate and conclude the deal between artist and audience, drawing the line in a civilized way. The artist has prepared the performance, presented it to the best of their ability under the circumstances, and tried their best to control what they can. An audience has consumed what was on offer and wants to show its appreciation. The fourth wall dissolves, and the performer — no longer in character, no mask of a song to hide behind — faces the warm embrace of the validation and acceptance, accepts the love, and humbles himself, becoming smaller in the face of this impossible, wonderful communion that, for now, must come to an end.

Just before I took my bow, I usually gave a symbolic quick kiss to my guitar, because she's always been my best friend, my companion on the journey.

I can't fully explain the dynamics of humbling myself in the presence of something greater. It induces awe — "leaves me humble at the beauty of it all." Music does that. Miraculously it works. If I could explain it, maybe it would lose some of its mystical, magical, ineffable, unquantifiable mystery. And I think I like it to have that; it makes me want to keep chasing it.

The bow acknowledges that the mystery has been addressed, left me humble, and the unspoken contract has been fulfilled. Then it's time to go back to the well, to start carrying water and chopping wood again.

———————

At Troubs duo gigs, at the end of the encore, Dave Dunlop would take his final bows, then leave the stage to me so that I could thank the crowd, bask in its applause, and have a few more bows to myself. Through 2018, in that moment I often consciously thought, Soak this up, kid. It ain't gonna last forever.

At the Sunday night gig in Hugh's Room on January 28, 2019, when Dave left the stage to me for the final time, I stood there consciously thinking, Well, now — this is really it.

This had always been such a huge part of me, what I did, who I was — me and an audience. A moving communion is such a sweet feeling — as it always had been in its very best moments. I didn't let it overwhelm me, though it easily could have. There were no tears. I wanted to go out with professional dignity and a smile on my face.

———————

I took my avocation as an artist seriously, making sacrifices in order to honour my humble gifts and to pursue my musicianship, my singing, my writing, my creativity. Sometimes it was a lonely, private, difficult life. Sometimes it's yielded the greatest rewards imaginable. All in all, I tried to bring a certain level of self-discipline to it, to keep myself and my work in balance. Compromised all the time by circumstances, limits, and budgets, I remained determined to find ways to work within those strictures.

Being happy with work also had its weird dynamics; sometimes it was more a question of being happy enough to let it go and move on. On rare occasions, something happens that's spontaneous and miraculous, and that beautiful moment deserves to be respected, left undisturbed. Other times (and more often), I'd work away at the music with the feeling that nothing's sacred. This is all ephemeral, ineffable stuff. Recordings can get remixed with nothing holy lost. A song can be revisited, an idea can get reworked, and if it doesn't improve, it's not like I'm tearing down the ceiling of the Sistine Chapel.

Time gives you distance, and distance offers perspective. Perspective offers the kind of wisdom that told me that I might be wrong, I might be ignorant of a truer nature of life. It gave me a forgiving spirit and a universal humanity. But time also runs out on everyone, so it is a sweet, precious gift. When one is young, it's unusual to truly know that. Having children got me half the way there. Recovering from terrible loss, deep grief, completed the life lesson. Retiring from a career of performance gave me back some of the time and perspective that the road was grinding out of me. It brought me to this: taking stock, reassessing, accounting for all the things that got laid out on the line.

Creativity was always my trump card, my most valuable resource. I was an idea guy, a conceptualist. That gave me value to others, which reinforced my self-worth.

I was lucky to be the right thing in the right place at the right time often enough to cover over my sketchy qualifications. The balance came out in my favour, with my creativity as the thumb on the scale.

That creative life also delivered therapeutic value. It helped me deal with grief and offered me perspective as a humanist. I believe that at the end of life we return to the stardust from whence we came. It will be the end of ego. Creative moments of work offered me this insight, because the work has a transcendent scope. It offered joy and positive satisfaction, but it also carried me through sorrow, pain, and loss, sharpened my focus and awareness and helped me interpret my emotions to give them expression and bring them to life.

The gifts I've enjoyed in this life were modest and humble enough, but they were mine, and I'd been raised to understand that it was my responsibility to respect and care for them, and my duty to use them to offer recreation, joy, and love to others — to celebrate the circle of life.

As the caretaker and temporary conduit for these gifts, I was aware that they were a part of a much greater package — this one life that we're all sharing. I won't pretend that I understand it fully, and undoubtedly I'll still be working this out until I draw my final breath — but for the express purpose of closing out this chapter of my creative life, I think it boils down to this: the gifts of this life are in the giving.

It's often hard to reduce life to simplicity, because it can get so complicated and messy. But the simple transaction of love is always there, always available to us. Gifts pay back — the making, the taking, the giving and getting. The dynamic balance is about love. I loved the creativity, the music, and I loved being able to play, to offer it, give it, share it.

Folks would say thank you, and I would say you're welcome, it's my pleasure. Because the music, the work, the creativity truly was (mostly) my very great pleasure. Love resonated out, then came echoing back with such amplification that I could sense its infinite power. That was always humbling, always made me feel so grateful.

I still can't be sure that I've found the right words to say it, and maybe that's why music is often the best choice for me, because it can work without words. Or with a few select, poetic words combined with the prosody of a melody and the coloured landscape of some chord changes. Music in its emergence creates the circle that is unbroken, the gifts that keep on giving. It's a beautiful thing — such a beautiful, lovely thing.

Life still feels like it's too damn short with its infinite number of ideas out there, waiting to be discovered and learned. Back in '94, my lyrics for "The Longing" spoke of always feeling like I was running out of time, physical skills, vocal range, memory, chops of all manner. As time wore on, I had to be more selective, but was never obliged to be less imaginative or less creative.

Could I do more, say more with less? Could I distill better than I ever had? On good days, I'd look in the mirror and say, Yes, you can.

Get to work.

ACKNOWLEDGEMENTS

Michael Holmes, misFit Editor Supremo, helped to shepherd this project from its scattered origins through to its final form, and I am grateful for the random chaos of the universe that put us on a collision course. The team at ECW proved invaluable all along the way, led by Shannon Parr and Victoria Cozza, with copy-editing by Crissy Calhoun, proofreading by Rachel Ironstone, art direction by Jessica Albert, and layout by Jennifer Gallinger.

My top beta reader, who deserves the largest kudos, is my oldest and dearest old buddy, old pal o' mine, Terence Hart Young, who had the unenviable task of trying to save me from myself (as it has been, ever since grade eleven). Next in line is the incomparable Ross Munro, who always managed to have my back, even when my back was entirely unmanageable. Rounding out the triumvirate of readers is Jeannette, who makes all things possible in my life.

My gratitude goes out to the photographers whose work graces these pages, first and foremost Jeanine Leech: and then, in order of appearance — John Rowlands (front cover), Richard Sibbald, Ed Thompson, Thelma Emmett, Terence Hart Young, Jeannette Emmett, Nick Misetic, Matthew Wiley, John Rowlands, Jim Prue, Sally Wright, Henry Fornier, Rick Wharton, Andrew MacNaughtan, Stuart Hendrie, John Beaulieu.

In my life and career outside of the production of this book, I need to acknowledge the tremendous support I get from Kathy Wagner at Panzyler Group, who coordinates my social media; Adrienne Duncan, who does such a fine job overseeing www.rikemmett.com through SDOC Publishing; and my dear old brother-in-arms, Rick "Spud" Wharton at Eventure Entertainment, who has been there for decades in the marketing and promotion game.

Finally, a thank you to the guys who always went thankless — the roadies who slugged my gear and the road managers who looked out for my sorry backside. In particular, brotherly love to Mike Sponarski, who stood by me, always, and in front of me when necessary — but was always 100 percent behind me in the times when I needed it most of all.

JEANINE LEECH

This book is also available as a Global Certified Accessible™ (GCA) ebook. ECW Press's ebooks are screen reader friendly and are built to meet the needs of those who are unable to read standard print due to blindness, low vision, dyslexia, or a physical disability.

At ECW Press, we want you to enjoy our books in whatever format you like. If you've bought a print copy just send an email to ebook@ecwpress.com and include:

Get the ebook free!*
*proof of purchase required

- the book title
- the name of the store where you purchased it
- a screenshot or picture of your order/receipt number and your name
- your preference of file type: PDF (for desktop reading), ePub (for a phone/tablet, Kobo, or Nook), mobi (for Kindle)

A real person will respond to your email with your ebook attached. Please note this offer is only for copies bought for personal use and does not apply to school or library copies.

Thank you for supporting an independently owned Canadian publisher with your purchase!

My seventeen-year-old grandfather Gordon Neve Emmett, headed off to WW1.

Mom, Dad, and Russ with me at the CNE Grandstand track meet in the summer of 1964.

First band, first photo shoot. From the top left, clockwise: Murray Bone, Jim Todd (centre), Stan Pus, John Todd, and me.

The high school yearbook football helmet picture (from November of 1967) that got my future wife thinking I was cute.

The Sunshine Incident play a Runnymede United Church basement dance, 1968. From left to right: Lou Muccilli, me, Charlie Kresnick, Bohdan Hluszko on drums (obscured), and Peter Mantas.

Playing in Justin Paige's band at the Matador nightclub in Dartmouth, Nova Scotia, during the summer of 1974. The shirtless drummer behind us is the inimitable Dave Breckels.

In a hotel room at the Wallaceburg Inn, spring 1975. From left to right: Denton Young, Chris Brockway, and me.

During a performance on my first doubleneck guitar, with Act III; quite a face, in that first attempt at a beard, but I've now seen this "guitar face" in photos of me hundreds of times.

I'm arriving home and headed off to bed as my dad leaves for work in the spring of 1975.

February 1977: A teenaged Lita Ford (from The Runaways), acting a wee bit scandalous — Joan Jett remains entirely unimpressed. From left to right: Lita Ford, me, Sandy West, Lou Roney (PD at KMAC-KISS), Mike Levine, Joan Jett, and Joe Anthony (DJ at KMAC-KISS). Lou and Joe gave Triumph its first break at radio in the U.S.

1978: A hair and makeup money shot of Triumph in its heyday, by Matthew Wiley.

1979: On the *Just a Game* tour, with my favourite guitar, the Framus Akkerman.

Here I am chatting with the legend Chet Atkins on a couch in his office in the RCA building in Nashville in 1979. He autographed a Nashville Guitar Quartet album for me and wrote, "Thanks for wanting this." Humility, from the man rumoured to be the landlord of that RCA building, who had been the A&R architect of the Elvis signing, which made that label. And — oh yeah — one of the greatest guitarists ever in history.

Maybe I got some rock star stuff right — John Rowlands ended up using this image on the cover of his own book, when he had photos of Jagger and Bowie inside.

Leaping from a drum riser at Oakland Alameda County Coliseum's Day on the Green on July 4, 1980.

1982: A photo of my guitar collection — *Allied Forces* LP era — taken by Nick Misetic.

A few moments from a significant day in the life: May 29, 1983 — U.S. Festival, "Rock & Roll Machine" solo, San Bernardino, California.

June 18, 1983: Jamming "Whole Lotta Love" at the Cotton Bowl in Dallas, with Sammy Hagar and Ted Nugent.

At the Diamond Club on the evening of June 15, 1987. Ed Bickert doing a Jack Benny thing, as the crowd of guitar aficionados would not stop cheering for him. One of my favourite career moments on stage.

Playing with Steve Morse, bearing down but mostly smiling, on June 15, 1987. That was a very big night.

One of my favourite photos of my beautiful wife, from around 1991 — it's the wallpaper on my iPhone.

Autumn 1993: The season we won the Mississauga Men's League Slo-Pitch softball championship. Dad was the third base coach (largely an honorific). Corny posing was (always) Russell's idea.

June 14, 2001 — Jamming "On Broadway" with George Benson at the Tralf nightclub in Buffalo. I was over the moon. George was *on fire*.

In excellent company with the Mississauga North Tigers baseball coaches in the summer of 2003. From left to right: Lino Condotta, Jack Carrajola, me, and Don Moroney.

From the fall of 2009, a studio photo session for the "Trifecta" project: I'm hamming it up here in the PRO Guitar Trio, with Pavlo and Oscar Lopez.

Rocky Mountain Way — *bases are loaded and Rikky's at bat . . .*
Burlington Sound of Music Festival, June 19, 2015.

November 26, 2016: RES 9 on stage at the Living Arts Centre in Mississauga, the band that was an out-of-the-blue gift project from Ed Van Zijl of Mascot/Provogue Records. Getting the joy of great rock music back in one's sixty-second year of life was awesome. I also love this band "bow" photo because (legendary) drummer Paul DeLong looks like he's doing a John Cleese funny walk impersonation, and I wouldn't put that past him.

Dave Dunlop and Rik — The Troubs — performing in Niagara Falls, Ontario, on November 11, 2017.